MAKING TRACKS
With My Horses and Mules

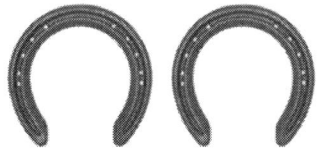
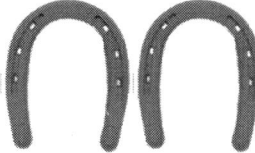

JANE LAMBERT
Author of
CHARLIE RUSSELL: The Cowboy Years

Edited by Nancy L. Morrison

Copyright 2017.

All rights reserved, including the right to reproduce
this book or parts thereof in any form.
Printed & Published in the United States of America
by Word Wright Publishing, LP.
First printing.

This book is a biography.
Names, characters, and incidents are recollections from the author.
Please accept my apologies if there are inaccuracies
and send me corrections.

Cover photograph by Barb Garten. Summer 2016.

ISBN-13: 978-1548150808
ISBN-10: 1548150800
Library of Congress Control Number: 2017909853
CreateSpace Independent Publishing Platform, North Charleston, SC

Edited and typeset by:
Nancy L. Morrison
Editor, Writer, Artist
PO Box 81633
Billings, MT 59108

Proofed by Linda Grosskopf, Editor
Western Ag Reporter

For additional copies of this book,
MAKIN' TRACKS
or
CHARLIE RUSSELL: THE COWBOY YEARS
contact:
Jane Lambert
677 Pine Hollow Road
Stevensville, MT 59870

$20 plus $4 S/H

Dedication

To all my horses and mules.
With all my love.
Thank you.

Acknowledgements

I wrote this book by request. My daughter Lisa Bauer asked me to "write about my horses and mules." I said I would since the winter was a good one to "hole up," not realizing I had just been handed a job! I didn't know until I listed them all that I had stories to tell about 50 head and would have to reach back 73 years for the telling! As I started to write about the early ones, it was apparent that I needed my sister's good memory, so I asked for her assistance.

My sister Judy Hendricks generously offered her time and memory for the project. Her memory for details far outshines mine, and the stories of my early horses and Hemi would not have been as complete without her help. She earned the label, "California Consultant and Co-Author" of the first half of this book. Thanks a lot, Judy!

Patty Patten, age 98 at this writing, is an inspiration. She reared five boys in Scotts Valley and, at times, mothered the whole contingency of Scotts Valley Junior Horsemen in her area. Patty helped me with Pepper's story.

Roy Smith and his dad Blair helped fill in some gaps in Big Enough's story, along with Terry Tallis, Siskiyou County historian.

Frank and Barbara Dimauro kindly provided pictures of Chico, and Sharon Kirkpatrick provided pictures of Arctic Witch and Sissy.

Sharon and Tom Kirkpatrick both provided information about our trip to Bishop Mule Days.

My brother Jerry provided pictures and information about Farmer.

Connie Thomas Wright provided information about and pictures of Colonel L'Abbe. We share many memories there.

A big thank you to Vickie Crawford, Valley Drug, Stevensville, Montana, for her help in getting my pictures scanned onto discs for my editor. Vickie knows how to talk to the machine!

Traveling partner Maria Danforth Freeman provided stories and pictures from our move to Montana.

Here in Montana, my husband Eric and our children—Dan, Dawn, and Lisa—all provided stories and memories about the animals of the last 35 years.

And, again, a special thank you to Eric for being patient and helpful during this book writing project. Living with a totally preoccupied person is not easy—and that is what writers become!

More thanks to Linda Habeck for her "back-up" and chauffeur services.

And, of course, a big debt of gratitude goes to my special and talented editor Nancy Morrison. She always makes my best better!

So here you go, Lisa—the stories of the horses and mules from my life and, in some cases, yours, too. I hope the telling does them justice and gives them all the honor they deserve.

We have been blessed by their presence and lucky to have their stories to tell. When you read this book to your grandchildren, they'll *be makin' tracks* with their ancestors.

California Consultant Judy Hendricks

When my sister Jane called a few months ago and said her daughter Lisa had asked her to write down names and information about horses we have had in the family, I had no idea it would turn into such a major project. Jane sent me a list of horses she could remember. She asked for my input, because I remember all sorts of odd things from the past. I began recalling our childhood, our family and friends, and of course, our horses. We lived and breathed horses!

Maybe riding my rocking horse down cement steps and landing on my head at three; falling down the feed chute in Grampa's big barn and splitting my head open at four; and being dragged under a galloping horse and getting repeatedly kicked in the head at five, had something to do with it. What's another concussion?

It has been really enjoyable remembering the special people who helped us, as well as all the different and unique horses. Horses are every bit as individual as people. The main difference between people and horses is that horses are generally predictable and honest. Some people—not so much.

Jane is a successful author. I am not, but this has been fun. We have had a very special time remembering our horses and lives, growing up. Now that we are getting "long in the tooth," it is really uplifting to think of the great memories surrounding our horses. It makes one forget about the old, worn out bodies we now occupy, and is a reminder of how we got worn out—on a horse—not sitting on a couch!

I hope you enjoy reading our horses' stories!

Judy Hendricks
California Consultant

Table of Contents

The California Years

Hendricks Family History 1
Pal 11
Maude and Nell 16
Becky aka Blue Snort 18
Buck 20
Butch 23
Pepper 28
Big Enough 33
Duke 42
Mary aka Mary Lightning 44
June 51
Chico 54
Honeycomb 56
Colonel Norris M. L'Abbe 59
Kenny and Pete 63
Kenny aka Two Rivers 66
Pete aka Pecos Pete 79
Nugget aka Misfit 88
Princess Dee 90
Farmer aka Farmers Duzzit 93
Sundown aka Poco Sundown 97
Sugar and Baby 103
Patchy 106
Skip aka Skip Past 112
Sissy aka Famed Miss Fancy in CA 113
Hemi aka Ms. Hemorrhoid in CA 121
Torepast aka Miss Torepast 131
Drifty aka Drift Past in CA 133
Chug aka Chug Past in CA 135
The Witch aka Arctic Witch 136
Moving to Montana 141
Sissy aka Famed Miss Fancy in MT 152

Hemi aka Ms. Hemorrhoid in MT 159
Drifty aka Drift Past in MT 171
Baron 177
Buddy 188
Chestnut Brood Mare 190
Joker 192
Fantabar 195
Zeke 197
Jazz aka Jazzie Genie 200
Zack 202
Zipper 211
Hot Flash 219
Brandy 223
Gypsy 229
White Mules 233
Spice Girl 234
Idaho Adventure 2002 241
Zeke #2 247
Cowboy 251
Fooler 254
Freya aka Brandy aka Sweetie 263
Princess aka Baron's Fancy Princess 265
Skinny 269
Sam aka Sam I Am 271
Reba 275
About the Author 287
About the Editor 289

Timeline

1854	Joseph Jones "J.J." Hendricks settled in Scotts Valley. Many place names came from him: Hendricks Road, Hendricks Canyon, Hendricks Creek. He registered the "JH Connected" brand used by the family and passed down to John Hendricks. It is set in stone in front of John's old house and was on our horse trailer. Jane's brother Jerry has the iron.
1884	E.P. Wray family settled in Scotts Valley. Jane's 6-month-old grandmother Alice arrived in a padded wash boiler in a wagon driven by her mother Artemesia.
1861	Green Berry and Mary Ann Hendricks settled on ranch with J.J.
1870	Scotts Valley School built two miles from Hendricks place.
1901	Clear Lake Union HS in Lakeport created.
1904	Alice Wray graduates in *first* class from Clear Lake Union HS.
1906	John B. Hendricks married Alice Wray.
1909	John B. Hendricks bought ranch at head of Hendricks Canyon.
1910-11	First walnuts planted by John and Alice Hendricks at mouth of Hendricks Canyon.
1919	Deacon family bought the old Scudamore ranch of 160 acres.
1921	Scotts Valley School abandoned; all children went to Lakeport for schooling. School became the Scotts Valley Social & Improvement Club.
1927	Clyde & Shelden Deacon split the Scudamore place, each taking 80 acres.
1929	John B. Hendricks died.
1931	Shelden T. Deacon and Alice W. Hendricks marry.
1934	Jared H. Hendricks graduates from Clear Lake Union HS.
1937	Edwyna G. Johnson graduates from Clear Lake Union HS.
1940	Jared H. Hendricks graduates from college.
1941	The Scotts Valley School building torn down, and a new one built known as the Community Clubhouse.
1941	Jared H. Hendricks marries Edwyna G. Johnson and joins U.S. Cavalry.
1944	M. Jane Hendricks born.
1947	Judith A. Hendricks born.
1948	Alice Wray Hendricks Deacon wrote *Scottslandia*.
1950	First horse, Butch.
1951	Jared E. "Little Jerry" Hendricks born.
1952	Pepper.
1956	Parents, Jerry and Edwyna Hendricks, buy Clyde and Rhea Deacon's 80 acres adjacent to Shelden and Alice Deacon.
1956	Mary Lightning, June, and Big Enough.
1958	Honeycomb.
1959	Kenny and Pete.
1962	Jane graduated from Clear Lake Union HS.

1965	Judy graduated in *last* class from Clear Lake Union HS.
1965	Farmer.
1967	Jane graduated from Fresno State College.
	Lisa born.
1968	Jane started teaching high school at Kelseyville, California.
1970	Marta born.
1972	Patchy.
1975	Jane married Ray Neher.
1976	Sissy.
1977	Ray Neher died.
	Hemi.
	Miss Torepast.
	Drift Past.
1981	California fire.
	Jane and Lisa moved to Montana.
1982	Meet Eric Lambert.
1983	Broodmare, Joker, and Buddy.
1986	Eric and Jane get married.
	Zack.
1989	Zipper, Hot Flash, and Brandy.
1995	Gypsy.
1998	Spice Girl and Fooler.
2000	Bitterroot Valley "Fires of 2000."
2004	Reba.
2006	Princess.
2008	Sam.
2011	Jane wrote book, *CHARLIE RUSSELL, the Cowboy Years*.
2014	Russell book wins bronze medal in the Will Rogers Medallion Award book contest.
2015	Jane and Reba star in PBS Special #104, *Backroads of Montana*, find on www.pbs.org under Montana PBS
2017	Jane wrote book, *Makin' Tracks on my Horses and Mules*.
2017	Jane appears in PBS Documentary Special, *C.M. Russell and the American West*

The California Years

 THE CALIFORNIA YEARS

Hendricks Family History

My grandmother Alice Wray Hendricks Deacon wrote a little book titled, *Scottslandia*, in August of 1948. I have used her book as a reference to tell about my early family history.

Edwin Perry Wray Family.
L to R: Clara in buggy, Florence, Edwin Perry "E.P." Wray, Alice (Jane's grandmother), Artemesia Waller Wray, Harold, Horace, Norman, and Kate Waller, Artemesia's mother. Scotts Valley, California. May 1899.

In 1854, Joseph Jones Hendricks arrived in Scotts Valley and settled up a west side canyon, about five miles from what is now Lakeport. The creek, which comes down this canyon, was then named Hendricks Creek. Joseph Jones Hendricks was sometimes called J.J., but more commonly was known as Governor—a title of respect, not of office. Governor Hendricks was a single man and stayed that way.

He bought some land at the north end of Scotts Valley near Blue Lakes and built a toll road, which connected Lakeport to Ukiah. His heirs sold the rights to the county in 1896. I wish we still owned it!

 MAKIN' TRACKS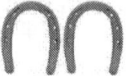

In December of 1861, Green Berry Hendricks, wife Mary Ann, and children Lafayette and Ellen arrived and joined Joseph at Hendricks Creek Canyon. The next year, the family built a new home on the ranch. Added to their family were Lydia, William, Joseph, John, and Edward, making seven children in all.

Green Berry Hendricks' family.
Back L to R: Edward, Jane's grandfather John, Lafayette, and Joseph.
Front L to R: Ellen, Jane's great-grandmother Mary Stephenson
Hendricks Morrison, Lydia, and William.
Mary is the daughter of Lydia Flagg, mentioned in Sundown's story.

They all walked three miles to school until a Scotts Valley school was built—only two miles away.

The Hendricks boys had a treasured pet for many years and hunted rabbits and squirrels to feed it. It hung around the barnyard and was tamer than the chickens. It cracks me up to disclose that my family's favorite pet was a tame buzzard. Imagine THAT, on a leash, on Main Street!

THE CALIFORNIA YEARS

The Hendricks girls all married and stayed in the valley. Green Berry and William died young. Joe remained on the Hendricks Creek Canyon Ranch. Ed, Lafe, and John (my grandfather) all owned property on the west side of Scotts Valley and ran cattle. John owned land at the head of Hendricks Canyon. In December of 1906, he and my grandmother Alice Wray got married. He was 36, and she was 23. In 1910-'11, they planted 45 acres of walnuts on their valley land. This was the first commercial walnut orchard in the valley.

The Hendricks boys owned land from the edges of the west side of the valley, up into the foothills. The land behind it was never claimed and is now the Cow Mountain Recreation area—BLM ground—and open for public use. Hendricks Road runs along the whole west side of Scotts Valley.

Grandfather John Hendricks and his favorite horse Clipper. 1904.

One smart thing John did was to get deeded rights-of-way through his brothers' lands, so that he and his heirs could access the back country. John and his brothers ran cattle back there and helped each other with roundups. John sold most of his cattle when he and Alice planted the walnuts. John was very active with helping others plant walnuts, and he grafted many walnut trees in the county. Commercial walnuts have a black walnut root system and a varietal walnut shoot, so they all need grafts to unite them.

Grandpa John died of a stroke in 1929 when he was 59 years old. Grandma Alice and their three children—Jack, Jerry, and Clydia—lived in Lakeport, but Alice still managed the ranch.

In the spring of 1919, the Deacon family moved to the valley from Hawaii. They bought the 160-acre Scudamore place. Their family consisted of Catherine W. Deacon and her two sons, Clyde and Shelden. Clyde and Rhea had two sons, and Shelden was single. In 1927, the brothers split the ranch, Shelden keeping the 80 acres to the north, which happened to border Alice Hendricks' place.

After John Hendricks' death, Shelden courted Alice, and they married and built a very nice farmstead on Shelden's land.

During his teenage years, my father Jerry Hendricks helped with the ranch chores and learned how to put up hay with horses. He was a basketball player and played during his high school and college years. He was very smart, skipped a couple of grades, and graduated high school at age 16.

> Note: Grandma Alice was in the first graduating class at Clear Lake Union High School; my father graduated from there, as did I. My sister Judy was in the last graduating class from the same high school.

Dad started courting my mother Edwyna Johnson in high school, and they got married after he finished college. World War II was on the horizon, and Dad was in the Cavalry, stationed for a while in Fort Riley, Kansas. Boy, my mother hated Kansas!

Dad traded the Cavalry for Officer Candidate School in the Air Force, trained to be a navigator on a B-29 and graduated, a Lieutenant, in 1944. When you read Pal's story, you'll learn more about that.

After the military, my parents moved to Lakeport, and Dad took a high school teaching job at his Alma Mater. Mom had trained as a cosmetologist and worked during the war, but quit when she became a mother.

THE CALIFORNIA YEARS

My parents had three children—me in 1944, Judy in 1947, and Jerry in 1951. We lived in Lakeport, but spent quite a bit of time at our grandparents' place in Scotts Valley. Grampa Shelden bought my first pony Butch in 1950 and my second horse Pepper in 1952. We kids clamored to go to the ranch. Dad helped out in the summers, especially during haying season. He really wanted to buy a place of his own in the country.

I don't think Mom was as excited about country living. She had a social life in town and hosted Bridge parties, and she and Dad belonged to a dance club. She had lovely hands, kept her fingernails nicely manicured, and enjoyed the finer things in life. She was an excellent cook and enjoyed hosting dinner parties.

In 1956, my parents had an opportunity to buy Clyde and Rhea Deacon's 80 acres. It was the adjoining property to my grandparents' ranch, and had all the original buildings on it from the Scudamores. Dad was gung-ho, as were Judy and I—Jerry was too young to have much input. Mom, to be supportive, agreed to become a ranch wife.

This began a whole new chapter for our family. On these 80 acres were probably four acres of walnuts and seven acres of pear trees. Thirty acres were range land with three barns, and the rest was permanent pasture/hay ground. Scudamore Creek ran along the west side of the property and joined with Hendricks Creek to the north. Buying this ranch stretched the family budget to the max, as we were a one-income family—and a school teacher's income was not large.

We all had to work to help pay for it, and we all did. Through the years, we planted most of the ranch to pears. We laid out where the trees would go, planted all the trees, hauled water to irrigate the small trees, and then moved irrigation pipes, as that system went in. Every October, we picked walnuts, both on our place and in Grandma's orchard. We also worked on the walnut grader belt when we got older. My sister and brother and I took turns driving tractor when Dad sprayed the trees and when cultivating was needed.

MAKIN' TRACKS

In the spring, pears need frost protection, so we put out smudge pots, helped light them when the temperature dropped, and helped refill them after they were lit. Then we picked them up and brought them in after frost season. Growing fruit is a lot of work.

And then, in August, we got to pick pears and haul them to the packing plant. When Judy and I each got to age 16, we worked in the pear packing plant to earn cash for school clothes.

We all worked hard to put up hay. All we had for equipment was old, horse-drawn stuff, which had been modified for use with our McCormick tractor.

The first couple of years, Mom and I took turns riding the old horse-drawn mower, pulled by Dad on the tractor. The mower operator had to run the controls for the mower, as now the "horse" was the tractor. Mom got launched off it one time when Dad hit a hidden fence post.

We also put up our hay "loose." We used a pull-behind hay elevator that picked up the windrowed hay and spilled it into the back of a truck, where it was "arranged" by people with pitchforks. All the hay barns had Jackson Forks, run on a rail, in the top of the barns. By driving back and forth, you ran this "pickup fork" along the rail, as it had a lead-line attached to it. You brought the fork out of the front of the barn, had your hay truck positioned there, dropped the forks into the hay, grabbed a big bite of it, and pulled the fork back up to the rail. Someone would drive the tractor forward, so the fork was lined up with where you wanted the hay in the barn, and someone else would trip it. It was quite an art to build an even stack in the barn. This was a whole-family endeavor.

Later, Grampa bought a hay chopper/blower, and hay was blown into the tops of the barns. It all involved a lot of labor. I think I was in high school before we dealt with baled hay.

We were very aware that snakes liked to hide in that loose hay, as did alligator lizards. We were ready to stab anything when we went to feed!

Grampa also had a good-sized herd of purebred Hereford cattle; his home place was kept in pasture/hay ground. He also had

THE CALIFORNIA YEARS

a big piece of range land to the north of the home place and a couple hundred acres of ground in Big Valley, which was pasture/hay ground. We often helped with working the cattle, and moving them horseback was a very enjoyable "job."

Every spring after calving, we would drive the cattle to the spring range land. It was several miles away, and we always looked forward to it. The spring after Grampa sold that land, no one told the old cows, and they broke out during the night and took themselves there. That was a challenge to get those cows to come back home. They knew where they were SUPPOSED to be—and it wasn't on the home place!

Jane's paternal "step" grandfather and grandmother. Shelden Deacon and Alice Wray Hendricks Deacon. Christmas 1958.

From the time I was eight, Judy five, and Jerry four, we all were involved in Clear Lake Junior Horsemen activities. There were riding lessons during Easter week, once-a-month trail rides, two horse shows, a Three-Day Ride, and participation in the drill during the Lake County Fair every Labor Day weekend.

 MAKIN' TRACKS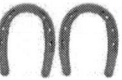

After we moved to the ranch, I joined the Scotts Valley 4-H and was in the horse program, as well as having beef and sheep projects through the years. When Judy turned 10, she joined, too.

Dad taught high school and coached basketball. He was civic minded and belonged to the Lions Club, Konocti Rod and Gun Club, and other clubs. Mom supported us in all our activities, did the domestic chores, and pitched in on ranch work, too.

One funny conversation involved baking cookies for the Three-Day Ride event. Mom always made lots of cookies for it, but she expected us to help crack walnuts for them. Our walnuts came off the tree not shelled, like in the grocery store. It was Judy's turn to crack the walnuts, and she didn't want to, so she made the announcement, "Junior Horsemen do not like walnuts in their cookies!" Good try, but she cracked nuts, anyway.

When I read through the rough draft of my stories, it seems like my dad is catching hell in a number of them. I don't want anyone to get the wrong idea about that. Mom wasn't involved with the horses—she was afraid of them. Dad was in the forefront with us and our horses, and he was also extremely busy and working hard in many areas. We did not have a horse trailer until I was a junior in high school. We either rode to the activity, or Dad hauled us in Grampa's stock truck, which would hold four head—just the right number after Jerry started riding. Everything my dad did, he did with one arm—his left arm—including hauling the horses in a stick-shift stock truck with no power steering. How he lost his arm is in Pal's story.

My parents both supported us to the hilt in all our activities. Looking back, I can't help but think they were both overextended with everything they were trying to do. They were stretched really thin, in both time and money, but they both encouraged all of us to do our best in everything.

Dad's personal experience with horses was limited to driving work horses and going buck hunting. He had never been exposed to the finer points of horsemanship, breeding horses, or showing horses. As Judy and I went in those directions, he became a serious student of what we were doing, took an active interest, and wanted

THE CALIFORNIA YEARS

us to excel. My dad was an achiever, and he sometimes maybe got a little too zealous in making his horse "deals" for us, but he always had our best interests at heart, and he wanted us to succeed.

We learned to work, and we learned to respect the value of money, as we worked hard to earn it. We learned to appreciate our accomplishments with our horses, because the ribbons we won came with a lot of effort and dedication.

I'm not going to give a blow-by-blow life story. This book is written to honor and recognize the horses and mules in my life, and in some cases, you will just have to read between the lines for personal information. I will switch here, from my family history, to my own.

I graduated from high school in 1962 and attended University of California at Davis for two years. I then transferred to Fresno State College and graduated with a major in Social Science and a minor in Animal Husbandry.

I had a brief, unhappy marriage. The old saying is, if you can't say something nice, don't say anything at all... So, I won't.

My beautiful daughter Lisa Ann was born in 1967 and literally grew up on horseback. In order to support us, I took a job at Kelseyville High School teaching U.S. History and Home Economics. Desperation breeds courage, which I needed because I had never taken a Home-Ec class in my life when I took that job. The school was desperate, too, as I got hired in August. It all worked out—I taught cooking while I learned how to sew, and in a few years, I went back to school and got a Home-Ec minor.

Eventually, another teacher took over the U.S. History classes, and I started a Vo-Ag program and became an FFA advisor. I taught at Kelseyville for 12 years, then resigned, and moved to western Montana in 1981. I tell about this in Sissy's chapter.

Hemi's story contains the story of my second marriage.

Since 1981, I have lived in western Montana's Bitterroot Valley. I married my next-door neighbor, Eric Lambert, and the second half of this book details the good times and good animals we have shared together in the last 35 years.

I hope you enjoy the stories, as you *make tracks* with me.

Note: Eric's first wife was Paula Yerian, so their children Dawn and Dan are half Yerian. Here in Ravalli County, the Yerians are very well known for their horsemanship skills. The first year I was at the Ravalli County Fair in 1981, I was at the horse races and watched with fascination as an older gentleman set and re-set the starting gate with a large team of strawberry roan horses. He and his horses worked flawlessly in maneuvering the long gate into exact position across the track. I asked an old cowboy, sitting next to me, who that was. He said, "Charlie Yerian. Them Yerians is half horse!"

When Eric divorced Paula, he kept all her relatives, so we have been "shirt-tail" relatives to the Yerians for the last 35 years. You will notice references to both Charlie and to his brother Asa in this book. Asa hunted in the same area as we did, and we were close friends.

Both Asa and Charlie were talented teamsters and grew up driving horses. Charlie cowboyed until he was 89. He was inducted into the Montana Cowboy Hall of Fame in 2016.

 THE CALIFORNIA YEARS

Pal

According to Grampa Shelden Deacon's daily log, he bought Pal from a horse trader in 1928, who told him the horse was seven years old.

Pal was a rangy, dark chestnut horse and not particularly refined. He had two white hind pasterns, a large star on his forehead, and a brand on his left shoulder, which we can't recall. We were always told he was a Morgan, but we think he had American Saddlebred in him, as he had an upright stance about him and erect, close-placed ears. He tended to be high headed and, in later years when I rode him, needed a tie-down. He was rather hard mouthed, which is not surprising, since he was a work horse, as well as a saddle horse.

Family lore has him wearing out his teammate on the mowing machine by noon and working with another horse all afternoon. Then Dad would saddle him up and ride him five miles to town to court my mother Edwyna Johnson. He was probably among the toughest horses ever created, as you will see.

He was my father's saddle horse of choice, and Dad rode him in the hills for years on buck hunting trips with his cousins. Northern California in the summer is hot, and deer season there is always in August. Although the Coast Range Mountains don't seem as impressive as the Rockies, there is some rugged, steep, brush-covered country there, and it takes a good horse to ride where they hunted.

When my dad finished Air Force Officer Candidate School and became a Navigator, he had a break before he was to direct a B-29 in WW II. The break came in August, so naturally he came home to hunt. He and his cousins Bill and Dean Hendricks rode up the Glen Eden Trail in Northwest Scotts Valley. It is an old, old, well-used trail and, through use and erosion, is a very deep trail. By the time I rode it, the banks grazed your stirrups in places.

Dad and his cousins split up on top and rode to separate ridges. Dad, on Pal, saw a buck, swung off, and reached in the

scabbard for his .30-.30 rifle. Unwisely, he had left a bullet in the chamber, and as he pulled the rifle out, it discharged, hitting him in his right upper arm, about a foot below his shoulder. The bullet severed his brachial artery, and blood was spurting out with every heartbeat. He knew enough to find the arterial pressure point under his collarbone, compress it with his left fingers, and stem a lot of the bleeding. Through all of this, Pal stayed with him, standing sentinel on the ridge, while Dad was on the ground applying pressure.

Jerry Hendricks and Pal. Circa 1942.

 # THE CALIFORNIA YEARS

Cousin Dean glanced over there, saw Pal but not Dad, felt something was wrong, and rode over and found him. He fired shots in the air to attract Bill, and while Bill helped stem the bleeding, Dean got on Pal and galloped him back down out the hills and several miles up the valley to the nearest phone. After two hours of holding the pressure point, Bill said the blood clotted, and the bleeding subsided.

Doctor Craig was alerted and made preparations to come to Dad's rescue. He brought plasma to administer—which was a relatively new invention—and rounded up some men and a litter. Jesse Jones took his old white mule to the Glen Eden trailhead for the doctor to ride. Dr. Craig and a contingency of volunteers drove the eight or so miles to the trailhead, where Dr. Craig mounted up. I don't know if Dean led them up the mountain, or whether he and Pal had already rushed back up to Dad.

It is said that Dr. Craig—on the mule, wearing a derby hat, and with a cigar clamped in his teeth, kept muttering, "Why did the dumb bastard have to come clear up here to shoot himself?"

It took five hours to get to Dad, give him the life-saving plasma, and get him off the hill. Back in Lakeport, Dr. Craig operated on the arm, came out, and said, "I saved the arm, but I don't think he'll have use of it. He will live."

Dad was rushed by ambulance to Hamilton Field Military Hospital in Novato, California. The arm was so damaged that it never regained circulation. It developed gangrene and had to be amputated about six inches down from his shoulder. I have pictures with my dad holding me as a baby with both arms (I was born April 1, 1944). Later pictures the same year show him holding me with just his left arm. To lose an arm—particularly a right arm when you are right-handed—is a big loss. Not as big a loss, however, as losing your life. While he was still home recovering, Dad's B-29 was shot down while sent on a suicide mission, and nearly all on board were killed, so perhaps the hunting accident had a silver lining.

I'm going to divert this story to Dad for a bit. Pal saved his life—in a couple of ways—but the loss of his arm did not keep my

father from recovering and retraining himself, so that we never, ever, thought of him as "handicapped." He trained himself to write, tie his shoes, and button his pants with his left hand and dress himself while still in the hospital. He had been an athlete in college and continued to play softball and basketball in town leagues. He still rode and hunted; taught chemistry, physics, and Vo-Ag; coached basketball; pruned pear trees; put up hay—you name it. He drove all of us in Grampa's old stock truck, which had a Brownie over-and-under transmission. We usually had three or four horses in the back, and Dad, holding the steering wheel with his knee, reached through the steering wheel to shift!

L to R: Judy Hendricks on Butch, Jerry Hendricks on Pal, with Little Jerry Hendricks in front of saddle, and Janie Hendricks on Pepper. Grandmother Alice Deacon in background. 1952.

 # THE CALIFORNIA YEARS

Back to Pal. In running to save Dad's life, Pal nearly lost his. Dean ran him probably four or five miles through rough country to get to a phone; then he was ridden back up the hill and back down again—with no thought of his comfort or safety. He was not offered water or rested the whole time. Wayne Dunnebeck says these trips would have killed a lesser horse, but family members commented that he was never quite the same after this day. He developed ringbones in both front feet from the concussion of the run, yet he remained a faithful saddle horse for many years.

Pal continued to be Dad's saddle horse, and he put each of us kids on the front of his saddle and rode with us there, until we rode on our own. I got Butch when I was six, Judy started riding at five, and Jerry, at four. Pal was NOT a kid's horse. I think I rode him when I was 11 or 12, and he was still a lot of horse. He was on the bit, rarin' to go, and hard mouthed about it. I rode him with a tie-down, because he was a major head tosser, and when he was fresh, he jigged, even at that age. Pal would have been about 33 or 34 years old at that time and was hardly ridden. He started showing his age at 38 and was totally retired. He died on the ranch at the extraordinary age of 42. He was 42, at least—maybe more—because you can rarely believe the age of a horse provided by a professional horse trader. What makes his age even more remarkable is that he had none of the fringe benefits horses enjoy today—like shots, worming, or vitamins.

 MAKIN' TRACKS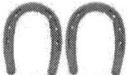

Maude and Nell

Maude and Nell were Grampa Shelden Deacon's last big team. They were both large, black Percherons. Maude was the gentlest, and Grampa threw me up on her back when I was five or six, and I "rode" her in from the field. They were the last team in Scotts Valley, as Grampa loved horses and was the last one in the Valley to buy a tractor.

Being so young, I only have vague memories of them as far as markings go, but I remember them as being evenly matched and pretty big. They were gentle and well broke. Grampa was in the habit of always taking naps after lunch in his later years, and I guess he was prone to naps before that, because Judy remembers Dad telling that Grampa would go to sleep while working the fields with the team. When they got to the end of the row, they would just stop, stand, and wait for him to wake up.

Charlie Yerian, at a Bitterroot Plow Day in 1996.
Horses L to R: Sy & Billie.
Kids L to R: Jane's grandchildren — Kayla, Korri, and Kyle Schoening.

 **THE CALIFORNIA YEARS**

After Grampa bought a John Deere, Maude and Nell weren't used much, and Grampa's brother-in-law talked Grampa into giving/selling them to him. He promised them a good home and said he would use them. This would have been in 1951 or '52.

He lied. He took them to the sale, and they were sold as canners—which was his intent—as he took them to Santa Rosa, where horses were slaughtered. (It was commonly called "the chicken feed plant.") Grampa was horrified and never had any use for that relative after that.

Grampa's John Deere—known as the Johnny Popper—was not as well trained as Maude and Nell, and when he went to sleep in the seat, it just kept going, going, going... Grandma would say, "Poor Shelden, he's had another accident with that tractor..."

 MAKIN' TRACKS

Becky aka Blue Snort

The "Blue Snort" was a large, dappled grey Percheron mare out of either Maude or Nell, Grampa's team. She was full grown when I remember her, but she must not have been very old, as she was pretty dark and well dappled. Becky was her real name, but she came by her nickname with good reason. She was pretty spooky and would whistle through her nose at the slightest provocation. She also could pull back with the best of them. After she tore up a number of work halters, she got tied up with a ¾-inch line and was tied only to inanimate large objects like oak trees. You never knew what was going to ignite her, and she tried lots of trees through the years.

Dad rode her a lot after Pal retired. You've got to give Dad credit, as she wasn't the easiest horse to get along with, and he had to saddle her with his left hand, get the scabbard on her, then the gun, and finally get on top of her. I'd say she was close to 16 hands tall and wasn't very cooperative. She had feet like meat platters and wasn't very graceful, either.

One of my best memories happened on an early camping trip, maybe in 1954. Dad rode Becky and took me and Judy up to John's Cabin, a glen area named for our grandfather, John Hendricks. It was Dad, me, Judy, and Morrie Clifton, and we were going to camp out overnight.

It was dark. We were all asleep, and the horses started raising hell, probably instigated by Becky, although we had quite a line up tied there—Butch, Pepper, Buck, plus Becky. Dad got out of his sleeping bag to go see what was going on. Unfortunately, Dad was barefoot. He only had his boxer shorts on, and he was tip-toeing through the stickers going, "Ooh, ooh, ow, ow, eeh, eeh." Judy piped up with, "See, Daddy, that's why cowboys ALWAYS sleep with their boots on!"

The laughter coming out of Morrie's sleeping bag was muffled, but apparent, and Dad never lived that line down—it was a campfire story told for years.

 ## THE CALIFORNIA YEARS

Foxtail was a major weed problem in dry areas of our hay fields, and it has caused problems for years. We were always cleaning them out of our horses' gum lines. Poor Becky got a large number of them accumulated in her throat and had to be put down.

 MAKIN' TRACKS

Buck

Most horses named Buck are buckskin or dun, but Grampa's Buck was a big, half-draft sorrel. I have pictures of Grampa on him, with me petting his face, when four or five years old. He was a long-time resident of the ranch. When Mom and Dad were dating, Mom wanted to impress Dad by riding a horse. Buck was selected to be her mount, and he ran off with her, back to the barn at a high rate of speed, and came to a big, screeching halt at the gate. It scared her so bad that she never wanted to ride again. I guess she impressed Dad in other ways after that...

L to R: Shelden Deacon on Buck, with Janie Hendricks on front of saddle. Jerry Hendricks on Pal. 1948.

THE CALIFORNIA YEARS

By the time Judy and I were riding, Buck was one of the saddle horses, and one of the smartest and laziest horses I have ever known. He was used a lot in hunting season, as he was big enough to pack Dad's cronies, lots of groceries, and a buck deer all at once.

He did not like to go, and he could walk so slow going away from home that you had to hold a stick up to see if he was moving. This necessitated his rider wearing spurs or carrying a stick to "persuade" him or be left in the dust.

*Shelden Deacon on Buck,
with Janie Hendricks on ground, petting him. 1948.*

Eventually Buck figured out a better trick—faking lameness. When leaving home, he would be so lame he could hardly go— and this got him excused a time or two, but he didn't play out his hand, as he was miraculously cured as soon as he was put away. So, there he would go, leaving home looking like he had a nail in his foot, giving his rider a herky-jerky ride. And always, a miracle

MAKIN' TRACKS

happened when you turned around for home—he would walk right out and take the lead. He was an Oscar winning faker!

Later on, when us kids started riding him, he decided to not only not be caught, but to run us out of his pen. He started charging at us, with his mouth open, and we would run for it! A couple of times of this, and we told Dad about it. He came with us into Buck's pen, where Buck was emboldened by this time and came at Dad, with us kids hiding behind him. Bad mistake, Buck!

As Buck approached, teeth drawn, Dad got him right on the end of the nose with the snap end of the rope. He slid and whirled, and Buck got it again, with the snap, right above his tail. As I noted—Buck was smart, and he got the message, and he quit that behavior.

The fall of 1957, we had discovered a watermelon patch in the middle of the valley. Judy invited her best friend Paula Hallberg to come out to ride, and we were talking about the watermelons. Paula thought we should "procure" some. That sounded like a plan. Paula, a greenhorn, drew Buck to ride, and she was having trouble keeping up, as he was pulling his lame routine on her. Judy told her, "If we get separated, just give Buck his head, and he'll take you home."

On the getaway, we lost Paula. Judy was really worried about her—until we got home, and heard Paula's cheery voice pipe up, "Where have you guys been?"

Buck was FAST going back to the barn!

As we got better horses and became better riders, Buck did not hold much appeal—you had to work too hard to get anything out him. He was retired with Pal on the hill pasture behind Walt Schade's house. Walt's daughter Louise Schade told Judy years later that she hated Buck. She said he was crazy and had bit her in the stomach.

Judy's response to that was, "Yeah, crazy—crazy as a fox!"

After Pal's death, Grampa gave Buck to a girl about Judy's age to ride in the drill, and she got along fine with him in his old age.

 THE CALIFORNIA YEARS

Butch

Butch was a squatty, white Welsh pony with a mind of his own—and my first horse. I was six years old when Grampa Shelden bought him (for $65, if I remember right). He also bought my first saddle—a Keyston pony saddle—which we still have.

It was a good thing that the Hendricks kids were stubborn and hard headed, or they couldn't have dealt with Butch, as Butch had those same traits. I don't remember that Butch had much of a handle on him, but I do remember he was a piggy pony and really liked to eat. If he got on the lawn and got his head down, you were stuck there for a while.

Janie Hendricks on Butch. 1950.

 MAKIN' TRACKS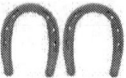

When I was seven, I rode Butch out to Grampa's pear orchard to see the pear picker's kids. I stupidly rode him out there bareback and with only a halter on his head. At the first row of trees, Butch put his head down and waded right into the tree, going after the fallen pears. As the branches started to scratch me, I slid off his back, caught my toe on a dirt clod in the ground, and fell down. It was the least impressive horse wreck of my life, but caused nearly the worst hurt I ever got.

When I fell, my left arm hit wrong on another dirt clod, which snapped both bones of my arm. I remember my arm folding in half—right in the middle—like it was a joint. One of the ladies picking pears came to my aid, supported my arm, and sent one of her kids to the house to get my Aunt Clydia, Dad's sister. Clydia came with a pillow, put it under my arm, walked me to the house, and then drove me to the hospital. I had traction on the arm for a while, as the doctors were trying to pull it apart so they could set the bones. That didn't work, so they operated and wired it back together. Altogether, this minor wreck caused me to have three surgeries and a rather deformed arm. I don't blame Butch, as I knew him and had let him have the advantage over me, just because I was in a hurry to go play.

Mostly I remember riding Butch with other adults, so I was pretty well supervised. After I graduated to Pepper, Judy had the "pleasure" of riding Butch. Judy and I were involved with Clear Lake Junior Horsemen activities by then—taking riding lessons, going on trail rides, and attending local horse shows.

Judy's most embarrassing moment on Butch came when she was five or six years old and was lead flag bearer for the drill team at the Lake County Fair. She had the reins in one hand, the flag in the other, and was in the lead of 35 dressed up and ready to go Clear Lake Junior Horsemen, who were opening the show. She had her red and white drill team outfit on, her hair in pigtails, and had just reached the center of the totally filled grandstand, when nature called Butch. Now Butch always put the brakes on when this happened and would not move until the whole pile was completed. Judy kicked until she was red in the face, and as she

THE CALIFORNIA YEARS

kicked, her pigtails stood straight out. Meanwhile, all the drill team members were stacked up behind her. The sight of her kicking as hard as she could, with her pigtails sticking out with every kick, sent the crowd into hysterics. She was livid and crying, but Butch didn't care. He would not move until he was done. The crowd enjoyed that moment much more than Judy.

Worse, even, was that he pulled this stunt on her two years in a row!

Janie Hendricks on Buck, Judy Hendricks on Butch, Clydia Hendricks Tram on Pepper. 1952.

Note: Retired Cavalry Colonel Norris L'Abbe was generous with his time and gave free riding lessons to all members of the Junior Horsemen the week of Easter vacation. He was a harsh task master and drilled us just like troops—fours to the left flank, NOW!—fours to the right flank, NOW!—serpentine, NOW! He taught us leg

aids, good riding manners, how to handle our reins, and the importance of keeping a horse length between us—all good foundation riding techniques.

He was also really intimidating if you didn't follow directions, and he wasn't above calling you out for errors in front of everyone. We were all a little fearful of him. He also would chastise the mothers sitting on the hill, who were spectators, if they got to chattering too loudly. He ran things just like the cavalry. I'm telling about this for two reasons. One is to acknowledge the Colonel for his years of good instruction, and two is to underscore Judy's problems with Butch...

During the riding lessons, no matter what, Butch would stop, lift his tail, and refuse to move until he was "done." The Colonel secretly thought it was very funny and conveyed this to Bernice Thomas—but Judy didn't know it, at the time. She always told the Colonel, in the middle of one of Butch's episodes, "Butch won't go when he has to go!"

Judy took the brunt of Butch's rude behavior, because I was not involved in the Junior Horsemen at the beginning of my riding career, so most of my troubles with Butch happened on the ranch and not in public view. Also, I had to have two surgeries on my arm, which slowed up my riding him. When she got Butch, I had moved up to Pepper for my public performances. It is no wonder that she holds no love for him, even now, and says he was a *little bastard* to ride.

I would never pick a half-broke, unruly pony for my child's first horse, but that's what we had. Dad put Little Jerry on Butch when he was about four—with no lead line—and took us up in the hills. Butch ran away with Jerry hanging on the side, bouncing like a rag doll. He hung on to the horn for all he was worth, before coming loose. Then he hit the ground, ending up with broken glasses, two black eyes, and a beat-up face. As Judy says, "Butch was a piss poor kids' horse!"

 # THE CALIFORNIA YEARS

One episode I had with Butch was when I was older—maybe 5th grade. I caught him over by the old dairy barn, and I had a bridle on him but no saddle, as I was planning to ride him bareback. I jumped across his back, intending to throw my leg over his butt and be aboard. "Butch the Brat" started jogging through the gate and towards the road, while I was trying to do this. I jiggled too far over his right side and landed on the blacktop road on the top of my head. It laid me out in the middle of the road—stunned. Butch never looked back, just jogged on to eat on Grandma's lawn. When I got my wits, I had to walk the half mile to get him, with a knot the size of an egg on my head. Good thing for a hard head... No one ever thought of concussion back then.

One thing I remember from this era is that getting Butch shod cost four dollars—a dollar a foot. Wayne Dunnebeck was our family's farrier and remained so until he retired at around age 70. He worked for Grampa in his youth, and his memories, which he related to Judy, have helped fill in some of our horse stories.

Dad finally decided Butch had to go. In the try-out period of one sales session, Dad had a man get on him bareback with just a halter. Butch, being Butch, ran off with the guy, not responding to any signals to turn or stop. Dad, trying to push the sale, told him, "Well, I guess Butch isn't a hackamore horse."

Anyway, eventually Butch went down the road. The only reason we didn't lose interest in horses after dealing with him was that we were all as hard headed as he was—not all kids would have reacted the same. Parents, choose your child's first horse wisely!

 MAKIN' TRACKS

Pepper

Floyd Norton of Kelseyville was the first known owner of Pepper, and he sold her to Tom and Patty Patten in the late 1940s. In 1948, she had a filly "Pepita," a wildly colored foal by a palomino stallion, name unknown. Pepita had a tragic accident and died young.

Tom and Patty rode in the Clear Lake Horsemen Association Quadrille—a drill team unit that performed square dances on horseback. They had a gelding, "Patches," who matched up very well with Pepper, color-wise. They both had brown around their ears, one blue eye and one brown eye, and small, brown patches around on their bodies. Pepper had a slender body type, and Patches had a heavier body, but they were about the same height and matched up well. The Quadrille, at that time, competed against other drill teams around the state and performed in Calistoga, Santa Rosa, Sacramento, and Healdsburg. Their focus was performing every Labor Day weekend at the Lake County Fair. Grampa Shelden Deacon was on the fair board as Livestock Superintendent, and he was a strong supporter of both the Senior and Junior Horsemen's drill teams.

In the early days, Teresa Holdenreid was drillmaster for the Junior Horsemen, and she also performed in the Quadrille. Patty and sons Danny and Petie rode Pepper while they owned her, and they drilled on her and showed her in local horse shows.

One hairy ride Pepper and Patches had in a horse trailer occurred on a trip to Calistoga. Patty couldn't ride, because she was pregnant with her fourth boy Douglas, so she and Tom followed Nick Stanley and his daughter as they drove over Mount St. Helena. On the downhill side, the Stanleys lost their brakes and literally went screeching down the mountain, with the horse trailer pushing them. In those days, you didn't have good trailers or brakes. Patten's trailer was an old, wooden-sided, open-topped, double-trailer, with no springs at all that I remember. Patty says the trip was a "nail-biter," but they made it, and the horses performed.

 THE CALIFORNIA YEARS

Grampa Shelden was impressed with Pepper when the Patten's helped drive his cattle, and he offered to buy her in 1952. After he did, she became my second horse to ride, and Judy took over Butch. Lucky me, Grampa also bought me another new Keyston saddle for her. It was a junior form-fitter, which my brother Jerry later inherited.

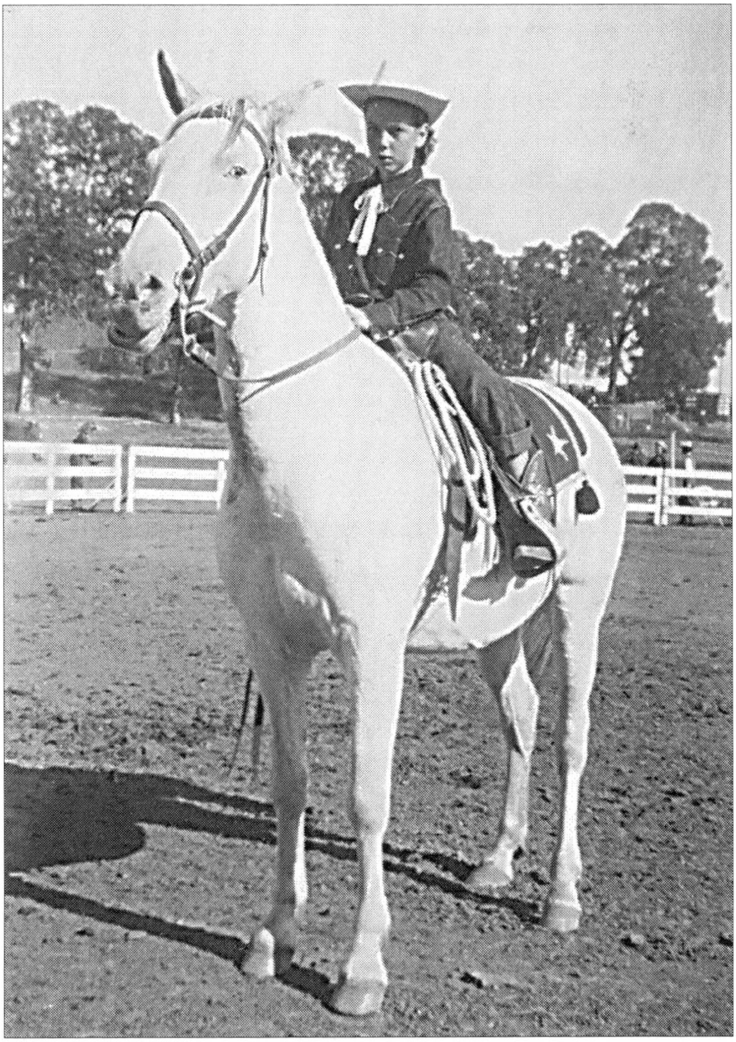

*Janie Hendricks on Pepper.
Looks SO serious — and cowboy hat on backwards!
It was probably bobby pinned there by her mother. 1953.*

MAKIN' TRACKS

Pepper loved kids and would do anything for them. I'm sure she liked Patty, too, but she did not like to have men ride her. Dad and his cronies tried to take her deer hunting, and she would only go so far before she would quit them, lay down in the trail, and refuse to get up. She was also hard to catch, so the combination of not volunteering, and then quitting, got her out of many buck hunting trips.

Another quirk of Pepper's was loving water. She would stick her head way down in the water trough and blow bubbles out her nose and splash. If you crossed a creek and did not want to get wet, you'd better keep her head up, because she would paw and splash and then lay down. Patty says Pepper laid down and filled her boots with water in Scotts Creek.

I rode Pepper until 1956, when I got Big Enough, and then Judy became her rider. In 1958, when Judy got Honeycomb, Jerry took Pepper over. Later, first our cousins Debbie and Betsy Tram became her riders. We all rode on trail rides, in horse shows and parades, and as drill team members. Pepper was always hard to catch, but once you had her, she was a great babysitter. She would stand patiently while kids clambered on her, and she would put her head way down to the ground, so you could put her bridle reins over her head. We always rode with split reins in the early years and had a knot tied in them so we wouldn't lose them. Pepper would follow all directions from little kids and not try to take advantage. I would describe her as a priceless kids' horse.

But even priceless kids' horses can hurt you, if you are not paying attention or using good sense. We were always barefooted in the summer, even around our horses. One time, before the Lake County Fair, Dad had dropped Mom and all three of us kids off at the fairgrounds to wash our horses prior to performing. I was wearing shorts and was barefooted while washing Pepper with a soapy brush. She stepped forward, right on top of one of my feet—on pavement. I yelled, which scared her, and she stepped down on my OTHER foot, and I was pinned down. I had hold of her mane, so I wouldn't fall backwards. And the only way I could think to get her off me was to bite her—which I did. When she jumped

 # THE CALIFORNIA YEARS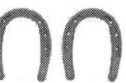

backwards, she drug the toenails off my big toes, and the blood flew! My mother, not having any bandages, tore up my brother's tee shirt and wrapped the pieces around my big toes. My dad was working as a field man for a pear packing house, and he had dropped us off, because we only had one car. This meant that we had to walk home. We still lived in town, and our house was a mile or so away. My mother said we looked like a bunch of Okies walking down the street with buckets, hoses, and me—with bloody rags on my feet. I don't remember trying to put on cowboy boots for the drill team, so I don't know what I had on!

After Pepper became Judy's horse, she led her up to Grandma Alice Deacon's back door. Judy hollered for a while to try and get someone to come and give her a leg on Pepper, but got no response, so she decided to just take Pepper in the house. She led her up the cement steps, into the back porch, past the chicken scrap bucket, through the hall, and into Grandma's kitchen. Fortunately, it was a large kitchen, and Grandma was present—and not too happy about having a horse in her house. I had followed and thought Grandma Alice maintained a fairly calm demeanor as she said, "Get that horse out of my kitchen!"

Pepper bumped her butt on Grandma's stove when she turned around, and Judy led her out, with Pepper leaving permanent hoofprints on the kitchen's linoleum floor.

Judy had a bad wreck with Pepper—caused by me—at the Bull Ring at the Lake County Fairgrounds. We were waiting for Mom to come pick us up, after some kids' event. I talked Judy into riding Pepper, so I could play around on Butch. All of us older kids took off, away from Pepper, and she followed us. Judy fell off, got caught up in the knotted split reins and drug under Pepper's feet, and kicked in the head. Mom took her to the hospital for X-rays. When they untied her pigtails, they discovered that Pepper's shoes had cut big bunches of hair off her head, and it fell in piles on the floor. She had knots all over head, but no broken bones. Again, no thoughts of concussion...

In those days, we RODE, and it was nothing for us to completely wear out a set of shoes on our horses in six weeks.

 MAKIN' TRACKS

Pepper had a habit of slightly dragging her feet, and I have seen her shoes come off in two pieces—they were worn thin as a dime and had been worn in two at the toe. We did not have a horse trailer for many, many years, and it was common for a whole contingency of Scotts Valley kids to gang up and ride the five miles to town, when there was a function there. Of course, it was also five miles to get back home.

Pepper's blue eye caused her eventual demise. In old age, she developed a cancerous tumor in it, and she had to be put down.

Her pink nose was always getting sunburned, causing it to peel, and she squinted a lot in the sun, due to the stark white around her eyes. A learned lesson in this is that we could have better protected her with sun screen and a mask—but that was in the 1950s, and such things were not available or thought of.

The last impression I have of Pepper is that she was probably the best kids' horse I have ever been around—she tutored and carried two Patten boys, three Hendricks kids, and two Tram girls—and was a valued baby sitter to three families, for a good 25 years. Thanks, Pepper!

 THE CALIFORNIA YEARS

Big Enough

In 1956 when I was 12 years old, I wanted a new horse. Dad's friend and hunting partner Bob Sylar had friends—Blair Smith and family, who owned the historic SS Bar Ranch at Hilt in Siskiyou County. They knew of a little bay, half-Quarter Horse, half-mustang gelding which was for sale for $100. He was owned by an interesting Portuguese man named Joe Gasten. Joe had some well-bred QH mares, but he was too tight to pay a stud fee, so he just turned them out on the range to get bred by the wild studs, which is why Big Enough had the lineage he did.

Joe liked to drink beer, and Joe liked to bet on horses. Every Saturday afternoon, he'd belly up to the bar, drink beer, and bet all comers that Big Enough could beat their horses in a run down Main Street. Hilt at that time was open range. The main street was a dirt road, and all the houses had their yards fenced in to keep the cattle off the lawns. So, Big Enough had a small career as a Saturday afternoon race horse. He WAS fast and later won gymkhana ribbons to prove it.

Sy, Dad, and I went up to the SS Bar, and I rode Big Enough all one day helping move cattle. It was kind of tough country, with lots of rocks and rimrocks. Big Enough had really hard, black, flinty hooves which held up well without shoes. In fact, he was shod only once in his life, when I rode in a 64-mile endurance race in Calistoga, California. Big Enough also showed another couple of traits on that first ride—he was tough as a boot, and he was a jigger.

I liked him well enough to buy him and bring him home. I was a Will James fan and knew about his book, *Big Enough*. Santa Claus brought me one for Christmas that year. The illustrations of the horse in the book look remarkably like the horse from Hilt, and the book was a treasured gift. Big Enough had a little white on his back feet and was a pretty red bay. He had an M Bar on his left shoulder. I roached his mane and shortened his tail, as that was the popular look then. As he aged, he got grey eyebrows. He

 MAKIN' TRACKS

had a nice QH hip and rump, but a kind of ewe-neck and unrefined head. He was the closest thing to a Quarter Horse I had had so far, and I loved him.

Big Enough, in front of old ranch house. 1958.

Big Enough's race career was enough to make him competitive, on the bit, and rather high-headed to ride. He could jig all day long and did. The only time he relaxed and traveled on a loose rein was when we participated in the Clear Lake Junior Horsemen's Drill. He learned the routine, knew exactly where his spacing should be, and performed in a perfectly relaxed way. On the trail, in the arena, or in parades, he could jig your liver loose.

Old Joe had him pretty well trained, though. He was on the bit, but was still responsive, and he neck reined and had a "whoa."

His world changed when he came to our house, and he soon learned to be a world class beggar. I would ride up to the back porch at the old farm house, drop the reins, and go inside. He

 # THE CALIFORNIA YEARS

would wait outside, nickering softly in expectation, as he knew some kind of treat was forthcoming. As time went on, we discovered that he was up for eating almost anything, but he really liked the slices of Wonder bread we offered. One time he was getting some bread, when my little brother Jerry, who was sitting on the steps cross-legged, stretched out his foot. Big Enough saw this as more Wonder Bread, grabbed his foot, and pulled him right down the steps. It was hard to tell who was most surprised, the horse or the boy, as the look on both their faces was pure astonishment!

Our mother expected us to take our little brother along much of the time. And even though he had a rough early experience with Butch, he liked to ride. He learned how to stay on pretty well, although for a while he had the posture of a monkey on a limb. When your older sisters throw you on, say, "Hang on!" and lead you off at a trot, it is "do or die!"

Anyway, one day I had to take Jerry, and I put him on the back of my saddle on Big Enough. I was probably 13, and Jerry was about six. I didn't want him clinging to me, and I didn't want to hold onto him, so I took the back saddle strings and tied them around both of us, so we were tied to each other and tied to the saddle. Brilliant! Unfortunately, I was going through a phase of riding with a loose cinch. I had read somewhere that good horsemen should be able to give their horses a break with a loose cinch, as they should have good enough balance to keep their saddles in place. I did well enough with that until I had a tied-on passenger.

I rode over to Schade's house. Walt Schade was Grampa's hired hand, and I was good friends with his three daughters. There was a trail off the road, up a hill, and around a turn into their yard. Big Enough jumped up the hill into a lope, Jerry hanging on tight. We were upright until the turn—Big Enough turned, we turned, the saddle turned, and we arrived behind Walt's house hanging upside down under Big Enough like bats. Good thing we were on a good horse. He stopped, stood, and looked around like "What the...?"

MAKIN' TRACKS

Then came Walt... Walt was a great guy and the most talented swearing man I have ever known. He could run a line of swear words out like a musical and never repeat himself for minutes on end. He had a cadence and a good vocabulary, and he used up a lot of it while he untied us, telling me what a really stupid stunt that was, and what the **** was I thinking, and I could have got my **** head kicked off, and why the **** didn't I tighten my cinch? He made some very good points in that conversation, and I'm glad he was there to get us out of a mess.

Big Enough was prone to get summer sores on his belly, and the little gnats would hound him. He found a cedar fence post, which was a gate-stopper, that was just the right height to scratch on. He would straddle it and rub himself on the belly and butt. Through years of use, that post had a highly polished, shiny top on it.

When I was about 7th grade, around 1957, we had a chance to buy a two-seated Studebaker spring wagon, a two-wheeled breaking cart, and a bunch of driving harness from Paul Kiel in Upper Lake. I think it all cost $200. My good friend Pam Ussery had a little half-Arab sorrel mare named Misty, who matched up height-wise with Big Enough. Being that age, Pam and I thought we knew much more than we did, and we harnessed up our horses to drive as a team and hooked them to the wagon. God looks after damned fools, because we got away with it. Our horses were good natured, had been ridden for miles, and were pretty much bomb proof, but what we did was plumb foolish. Grampa looked us all over and tried to tell us how to properly tie the horses together and drive them with one set of lines. Being bull headed and independent, we were each driving our horses separately, and we each had a set of lines. Neither one of us wanted to let the other one do all the driving, so that is the way we kept it during our driving careers. We even drove in a couple of parades. We would even drive at a high lope down through rows of pear trees! Re-reading this brings back to mind what my father said quite often during that time, "When you and Pam get together, you don't have half a brain between you!"

 # THE CALIFORNIA YEARS

*L to R: Back of wagon, Judy Hendricks and Doug Patten.
Front of wagon, Janie Hendricks and Pam Ussery,
using four lines to drive two horses.
Horses are Big Enough and Misty.
Photo by Patty Patten, at the Patten place. 1960.*

    I could hook up Big Enough to the two-wheeled cart and drive him solo. Misty was more high strung and didn't seem to want to be part of that, but Pam was determined that "anything my horse could do, hers could, too," and we hitched up Misty alone at our house. The last we saw of her, the cart was hitting the ground about every 20 feet, and she was gaining speed as she went out of sight through the neighbor's pear orchard, heading for home. She almost ran over Pam's grandmother Mimi in the driveway, made a sharp turn between a tree and the tack shed, and broke one of the shafts and the harness. That pretty much ended Misty's career as a driving horse.

MAKIN' TRACKS

Big Enough continued to pull the wagon. We made a surrey top with fringe and painted the wagon dark blue with red wheels. He never turned a hair over the whole deal.

Janie Hendricks on Big Enough, wearing the drill outfit for the Clear Lake Junior Horsemen. Big Enough, wearing my first silver-mounted bit—a Crockett. 1959.

Another stunt that proves what heavy thinkers Pam and I were involves having a horse race down Scotts Creek. I don't know what triggered it, but we were bareback, barefooted, and running our horses for all they were worth. Misty was a little to the outside, on the gravel, and Big Enough was taking the water. All of a sudden, a big, deep, dark blue hole in the creek loomed up in front of me. When Big Enough hit it, he went down into the water head first, and I got launched past the hole and piled up in the ripples. I got sat up and looked back at my poor horse, as he was rising up out of the water looking like a drowned rat, blowing his nose, and shaking the water out of his ears. Of course, when no major injuries were discovered, we laughed ourselves silly, thinking it a great adventure. It pays to have good guardian angels…

THE CALIFORNIA YEARS

L to R: Pam Ussery on Misty and Janie Hendricks on Big Enough, swimming in Scotts Creek, below the Scotts Valley Bridge. 1960.

One thing Big Enough would do, after he had been run in gymkhanas for a while, was get overly wound-up, balk, back up, and sometimes rear up a little—like most horses do when they are over-run in those things. Mom thought if she baked Big Enough an angel food cake and laced it with some of her little purple nerve pills, maybe it would calm him down. So she did—and put blue frosting on it! It was a real treat for Big Enough, and he drooled blue frosting for half an hour. It worked! That calmed him down and solved his behavior problems. So, I'm maybe a little ashamed to admit that I drugged my horse, but the result was that he was a safer horse for me and the rest of the kids around him.

I want to regress back to Colonel L'Abbe for a minute here. While I had a lot of fun riding Big Enough, he wasn't what you would call a well-trained horse. He really had no "feel." I didn't know it... I had no yardstick to judge him AGAINST. The Colonel was a real stickler for the proper use of our hands on the reins, saying your rein hands needed to be separate entities from your "seat." He always told us, "You should be able to balance a full glass of water on your rein hand—it should be that still!"

 MAKIN' TRACKS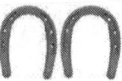

And, of course, he stressed the use of leg aids and how they should coordinate with your hands. I did not get it, until one day, when I was 13 or 14, the Colonel let me ride his beautiful, well-trained, Polish Arabian Witalis—a son of Witez II. What a revelation that was! The slightest cues were Witalis' command! Lay a leg on him, he moved away. Lay a leg and a rein, and get a smooth turn. I will be forever grateful to have ridden Witalis, because he exposed me to the possibilities of horsemanship and showed me what I should be striving for in riding Big Enough and my future horses. If you have never ridden a well-trained horse, you just don't know what you are missing—and what you should be TRYING for. Thank you, Witalis, and thank you, Colonel L'Abbe!

After I graduated to Kenny, Jerry took over Big Enough, probably to his great relief, and Jerry rode him for several years.

One time, Mom thought she would ride him. Big Enough seemed nice and calm to her, standing at the back porch, eating Wonder Bread. Mom was afraid of horses after Buck ran off with her, but for some reason she wanted to ride Big Enough on a Moonlight Ride with the Senior Horsemen. She loaded herself up on beer and purple pills to gather courage. Dad rode Kenny, so this must have been about 1962. Anyway, we were all asleep when the riders returned. They were all three sheets to the wind. Floyd Baldwin got on Kenny and rode him up and down the old rotten, back porch and then down off the steps. (A porch that, Judy says they recently discovered, had an old, hand dug well underneath—imagine THAT wreck if the porch had given way.) Floyd rode Kenny over to put him and Big Enough away, and Dad got in the '57 Buick and knocked the garage off the foundation while backing out. Mom looked like she'd been run through a meat grinder, as the brandy chasers she had on the trail caused her to fall off and roll down the hill. They had a WONDERFUL time…

When Big Enough was older, he contracted pneumonia and was seriously sick. Our veterinarian, Dr. Don Wasson, saved his life. Dr. Wasson was also a personal friend, and he knew what a deeply beloved family member that Big Enough was. Dr. Wasson

THE CALIFORNIA YEARS

made daily ranch calls for two weeks, gave shots, administered fluids, etc., in an all-out fight to save him. He later said that the only reason Big Enough lived was that he did not lay down. That horse backed himself into the corner of the barn, supported himself there, and remained upright until he got his strength back.

Later, we got a bill for $150. Can you imagine that in today's world? Granted, $150 was not chicken feed then, but it probably did not even cover Don's expenses. We were SO grateful to Dr. Wasson!

Big Enough was retired on the ranch, and when he started doing poorly, he was put down. That was in 1968 or so, and he would have been about 24 years old.

MAKIN' TRACKS

Duke

The spring after we moved to the ranch in Scotts Valley in 1956, Dad volunteered Judy to ride a tall, high-headed sorrel and white pinto gelding named Duke. He was from Kelseyville and was too much horse for the girl who owned him—Kristy Morrison.

I can't imagine why Dad did that, as Judy was only nine years old, and Duke was half broke, kind of goofy, and was the highest headed horse we had ever seen. You had to ride him with a tie-down, or he'd hit you between the eyes with his poll and stun you. I speak from personal experience. Riding him bareback was out of the question. His tie-down strap was always as tight as a bow string, and you'd better be sure it was made of strong material. Dad always said you could "play a tune" on it. He was half American Saddlebred and looked it.

Our farrier Wayne Dunnebeck knew every saddle horse in the county, and he told Judy years later that, when he saw her on that horse, he was absolutely flabbergasted. Dad had entered Judy and Duke in the trail class at the big Open Horse Show at the fairgrounds. The Clearlake Junior Horsemen Association sponsored two shows every year, a Closed Show just for members and the large, well-attended Open Show.

Duke didn't place, but Judy got him through all the obstacles—her only deducts being a step out of the back-up, and taking too long on the gate. Duke wasn't wearing his tie-down, either, as AHSA rules wouldn't allow it. Pretty good for a nine-year-old!

One episode I remember involving Duke and Judy happened on the ranch. We had a big dairy barn up on the hill. The area where they milked the cows had a cement floor, with a shallow trough running the full length of it, and wooden head-catch stanchions to hold the cows in place for milking. We kept the head-catches open and sometimes threw hay into the feeders for the horses. Well, one day Duke had his head through a stanchion, and

 **THE CALIFORNIA YEARS**

Judy thought it would be a good way to catch him, so she latched the head-catch shut and trapped his head.

THAT created some excitement in a hurry! Duke started to back out, felt his head trapped, and went berserk. He was pulling back for all he was worth, but couldn't get much purchase on the cement floor, so his hoofs were slipping and sliding, and the metal shoes he had on weren't helping him. He didn't quit until he squeezed his head out of the wooden two-by-fours. He left some major hide and hair behind and was a scabby mess for a couple of weeks. That was a big lesson for Judy and I both, because I think he would have killed himself if he hadn't had a narrow head and was able to pull free. That is a BAD way to catch a horse!

Judy did a good job in riding that horse, and then Kristy rode him for years in the Junior Horsemen activities and got along fine with him. You could always pick him out in the drill, though. With his high, high head, he stuck out like a spotted giraffe!

 MAKIN' TRACKS

Mary aka Mary Lightning

Interesting name, isn't it? Mary was a registered Tennessee Walking Horse (TWH) that kind of came with the ranch, when my parents bought it in 1956.

Our place, called the old Scudamore place, had been Clyde and Rhea Deacon's and was 80 acres in size. It abutted Grampa Shelden Deacon's, which was also 80 acres. Grampa Shelden was not our biological grandfather—actually our step-grandfather—but he was the best grandfather we could have had.

I'm diverging a little from Mary here, so that the lay of the land and the family connections get clear. I'll try and not repeat too much from the family history.

Our real grandfather, John B. Hendricks, had died of a stroke in 1929. He had deeded rights-of-way through his brothers' lands, so our family had a number of ways to get to our range and to BLM ground. John's and his brothers' lands took up most all of west Scotts Valley and extended up into the foothills above it.

Our grandmother, Alice Wray Hendricks Deacon, came from another early Scotts Valley family. Her father was a nurseryman and was very influential in providing trees for some early pear and walnut orchards. When John B. and Alice got married, he had the land, and her father had the trees, so they planted a walnut orchard on their flat, valley land.

The Deacons bought land bordering the Hendricks' property, to the south. Grampa Deacon came a-courtin' and he and Alice Hendricks got married. Shelden and Alice kept a separate accounting of their properties. They would speak of "Grampa's tractor" and "Grandma's cultivator," etc. He ran Hereford cattle on the home place, the spring range, and the lake pasture in Big Valley. Grandma ran the house, yard, and walnut orchard. Grampa's cattle utilized both her range land and his. She was a modern woman for her time. She was a civic-minded businesswoman, artist, gardener, writer—and a lousy cook—but that's another story…

 THE CALIFORNIA YEARS

The point of including all of this is to explain that, from the time I was 12 years old and lived in Scotts Valley, I had access to acres of family land next to BLM land, and could ride on all of it at will.

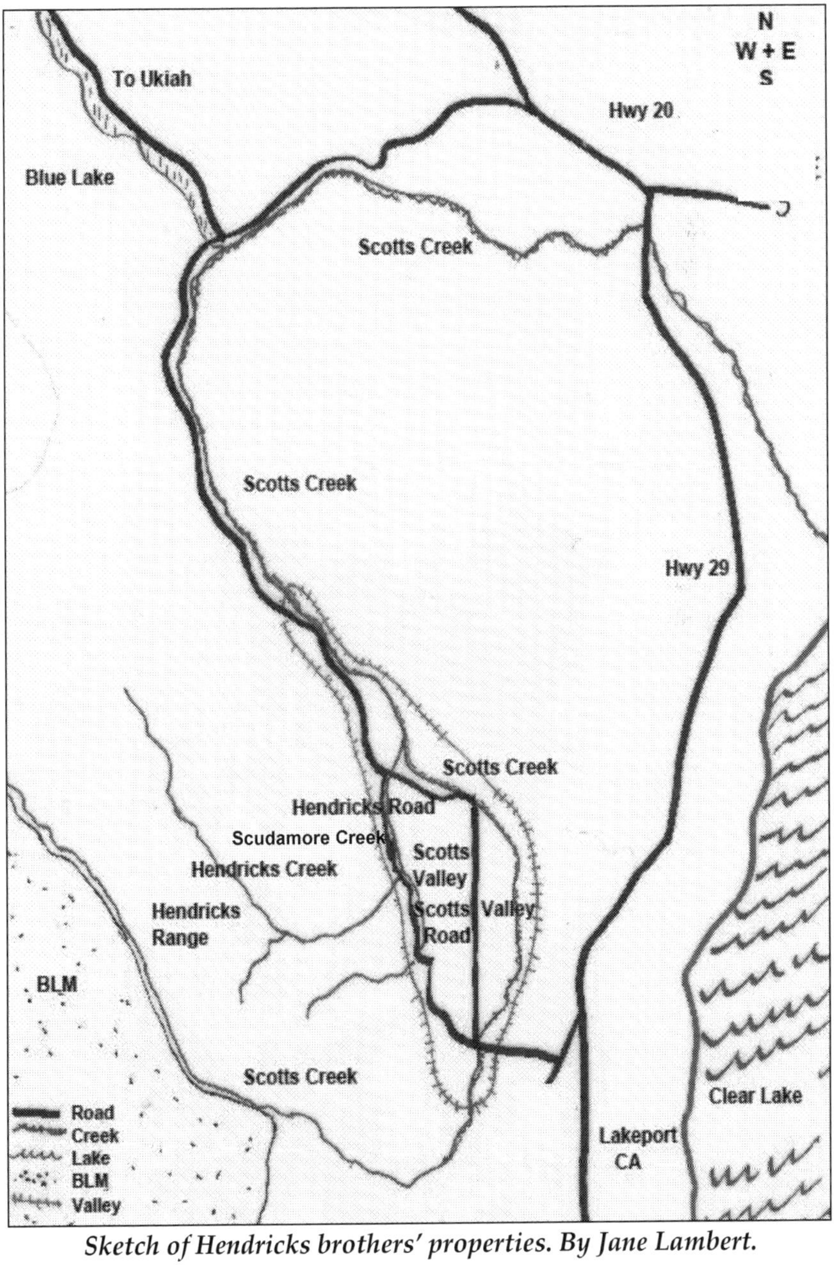

Sketch of Hendricks brothers' properties. By Jane Lambert.

MAKIN' TRACKS

So, back to Mary Lightning. She had been Clyde Deacon's, and he sold her and her filly at side to brother Shelden in 1956 for $200. We don't know what the background story was on her, but her papers showed she had Foundation TWH breeding.

Have you heard the expression, "Homely as homemade soap?" That fit Mary. She was black, about 15 hands, and had a blaze face. I think she had some white on her legs, and her tail kind of curled over to one side. She was fine boned, had a pot belly, a hind end about like a buck deer, and a long, typical TWH head. When you rode her, though, she was beautiful. She had wonderful gaits, and could really cover the ground. She could hold an eight-mph running walk, all day. She was smooth, and she was tough.

She had been shown somewhere along the line, and we figured her tail's posture was caused by being forced into a crupper for the show ring. The other result of her show career, was her training to STAY ON THE BIT. I could make these letters even bigger on that account. She was the hardest-mouthed horse we have ever ridden! Her trainers had totally numbed her, and the more you pulled, the more it seemed she bore down on the bit. We all had a heck of a time controlling her when we first started riding her. She was totally trained differently from any other horse we'd had.

Boy, though, was she fun to ride! You could run her through the gears and feel her leg strides change, as she picked up another gait. It was a whole new experience. One of us put a mechanical hackamore bit on her, and voila—a whole new horse! She was as responsive as she could be, as the hackamore bit was putting pressure on undamaged nerves, and she could feel what you wanted her to do. No one in our immediate family ever rode Mary with anything else. Grampa, though, could not fathom how a bit, which was not IN her mouth could possibly control her. One day, we were moving cattle up on the range, and he was riding Mary— with a bit, and out of control—and she took him down through a gully and up under a big oak tree. This scratched him all up, knocked off his grey Stetson, and almost unseated him.

We still could not convince him to try another way. In his mind, you put a spade bit in hard-mouth horses, and he had

THE CALIFORNIA YEARS

several old spades hanging in his tack shed. Anyone, who knows anything about bits, knows what hogwash that idea is. Spades are for highly-trained horses, not hard-mouthed ones. Spade bits used roughly will pry a horse's mouth open, confuse him, and not cure the problem. Grampa found out the hard way.

Mary became Judy's favorite horse to ride. I was busy with Big Enough and June.

One time, we were all ready to go to Lakeport to a function and were taking four horses—all in the stock truck. Across the front we had Big Enough, Duke, and Pepper, and Mary was loaded sideways across the back end. As I remember, we were in a hurry, and Dad didn't want to mess with wrestling the back panel into place on the stock racks. That left an opening with just a chain strung across it, and Mary on the other side.

Everything seemed good until we were crossing the Scotts Valley Bridge. Duke decided to two-barrel poor Mary and kicked her right out of the back of the truck, onto the pavement in the middle of the bridge! We were yelling at Dad to stop! Mary had hit on her side and was either stunned, had the wind knocked out of her—or both—as she was laying pretty still. We ran back to her. She was slow to get up, but when she did, she seemed okay—at least nothing was broken—on her. Judy's new one-ear-headstall was not so lucky. In the big hurry, Mary was tied up by the bridle reins... Sometimes I think we all took dumb pills...

Dad, still being in a hurry, found another hole on the headstall, boosted Judy into the saddle, told her to ride to town, and then he roared off with Jerry and I and the other three horses. I told you Mary was TOUGH—and thankfully she never had any issues from the fall.

Mary was saddled with Judy's brand-new "Monkey Ward," fully-carved saddle, with a "Little Wonder" tree. When Mary hit, one thing that kind of protected her was the swells on the saddle. Judy, besides being upset over her new headstall, was also dismayed to see one of the swells flattened somewhat and covered in road rash. She thinks it may have cushioned Mary, though, as the saddle took the hit and saved Mary's head. Usually I try to find

MAKIN' TRACKS

some humor in dire situations, but in this case, none becomes apparent. Poor Mary was just damned lucky!

When Judy got Mary to ride, she joined up with me and Pam—kind of like the Three Musketeers. Unfortunately, this just added more antics to the mix. (Maybe we were more like the Three Stooges?) We discovered that our horses would jump off the stock truck loading ramp out behind our ranch house. It was probably three feet high. We would go 'round and 'round in single file, jumping down. Then somebody asked their horse to jump UP. So we reversed and went 'round and 'round, jumping up. This led to a flying maneuver where we would pass in the air, one horse and rider jumping off, while another set jumped up, with both horses passing airborne. We were bareback, as usual. We were also out of sight behind the wood shed, while all this was going on.

Then someone had the bright idea to jump off the ramp, continue straight ahead, and grab a knot in the tree swing rope, which was hanging from a large walnut tree. Then holding the knot in the rope, let your horse keep galloping, and swing off, setting your horse free. We took turns doing this, with the two not swinging off being outriders to catch the loose horse. We were having a lot of fun, until Mom looked out the kitchen window, discovered what was going on, and got so agitated about our break-your-neck game, that she came out onto the porch and started yelling, "J...J...J...J...," and then, "Stop that IMMEDIATELY!"

Because our names were Janie, Judy, and Jerry, the stuttering Js were a common occurrence in high-stress situations for our mother. She always said that our family had too many Js, and that, if she had a chance to rename us kids, she would!

Judy's wonderful, brand-new saddle didn't look new for very long as, after Mary fell out of the truck in it, the three "ramp jumpers" were on another adventure down in Hendricks Creek. We had a neighbor we were kind of feuding with. He had married a Hendricks cousin, finagled the ranch out of her when she thought she was dying and wouldn't give it back after she

THE CALIFORNIA YEARS

recovered. Anyway, we figured his property was Hendricks land, so we could ride on it—even if he didn't want us to.

There is a very beautiful creek canyon just up Hendricks Creek from our property—waterfalls, rocks, moss, and ferns and we wanted to have a picnic there, so we were sneaking our horses through a barbed wire fence, between the two places.

> Note: We figured out how to get through old barbed wire fences quite a lot in those days—in search of stealing watermelons in the fall and getting in and out of this disliked neighbor's place. Usually we would loosen the wires of a few posts in a row, have two people stand on the strands so they were ground level, and lead our horses over. Sometimes we would put an article of clothing down, over the wire. Slick!

Since this fence was across the creek, it had a high wire along with two low ones. Pam and I were standing on the low ones and holding up the high one. Big Enough and Misty were shorties, so they fit under the wire really well, saddles and all. Judy and Mary were last, and we didn't have the wire up high enough to clear Mary's saddle horn, and it snagged right in front of the horn and across the swells. Big problem, as this was before Mary was wearing a mechanical hackamore. Pam and I were on barbed wire duty and had to stand on the low wires. Mary wouldn't stop, and she was snagged on the top wire—which was now really tight and lodged under the saddle horn. We were all yelling instructions at each other, Judy was fighting Mary for all she was worth, and the barbed wire was trying to saw the horn off the new saddle. We got out of the mess, but the "Little Wonder" bears the scars to this day.

Another story Judy remembers is that of Dad riding Mary and taking Little Jerry on the front of his saddle. This was an all-day ride with the Junior Horsemen, and the plan was for Mom and the other parents to meet us at the lunch stop, and then Jerry would go home with Mom. Well, Dad's passenger would not go home! He wanted to keep riding, and did—all day—with no complaints.

 MAKIN' TRACKS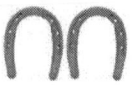

Dad rode an old turn-of-the-century, deep-seated saddle with a high front and back. As Judy points out—not only was Jerry only three years old, but also Mary wasn't the easiest horse to control, and Dad only had one arm. We all just took for granted what Dad did, but I don't think this would rate well, in the safety section of a parenting manual!

After Judy got Honeycomb and then Pete, Mary went back to Grampa's and became Aunt Clydia's daughters' horse to ride.

Mary Lightning, with a load of kids.
L to R: Jerry Hendricks, Greg Eickhoff, Judy Hendricks, Cindy Eickhoff, and Melissa Eickhoff. Taken at a picnic at Scotts Creek. Circa 1958.

Judy remembers Grampa's last ride on Mary, when he was 80 years old. He took her to gather some cattle over by the big barn, again, with a regular bridle on her. He couldn't control her, and she ran him through a tree, skinned him up, knocked him off, and he came leading her home. You can't teach an old dog new tricks, sometimes...

 THE CALIFORNIA YEARS

June

In 1956 when we bought the ranch, June was a two-year-old filly and still nursing her mother, Mary Lightning. June was taller than her mother, and it was a funny sight to see. June was soon weaned.

June was owned by Grampa Shelden Deacon and was a pretty thing. She was by a Standardbred stallion, and her mother was a registered Tennessee Walking Horse. She was a light bay with two white hind pasterns and roan patch on one hip. We figured the roan patch came from her mother's ancestor, Roan Allen, and the TWH in her gave her a natural pace in her gaits.

That summer when I was 12, Grampa asked me if I would like the project of training June. Of course, I jumped at the chance—it was my first training opportunity, and I was really excited about it. I had horse training books for reference, and I bought more. I had *Hackamore Reinsman,* by Ed Connell, and *Breaking and Training the Stock Horse,* by Charles O. Williamson, plus others. I was pumped!

It was fortunate for me that June had a willing personality and a laid-back demeanor, because I'm sure I was a trial to her. They say that there is no substitute for wet saddle blankets on the way to a good horse, and that must be true, because her blankets were plenty wet! June turned out well, and she served our family for many years. One thing I regret was trying to eliminate her little racking gait. I wanted to show her, and I wanted her to jog, not pace. I fought her natural instincts for a long time, before wising up and leaving her alone to follow her genetics.

As stated before, an advantage I had to create wet saddle blankets on my horses was that our range land backed up to thousands of acres of BLM ground. You could pick your terrain from country that was fairly flat to REALLY steep, and you could take as much time as you wanted or your horse needed.

When we were growing up, no horses were specialists—they were asked and expected to do everything we were involved in—

MAKIN' TRACKS

all the Junior Horsemen activities, helping with Grampa's cattle, and our various escapades. After we did our chores—moving irrigation pipe, driving tractor, putting up hay, whatever the season required—our time was our own, and we were horseback.

Our parents knew that everyone in our neighborhood acted as surrogate parents, and if we got into trouble, my mother would know it before we got home. We usually were pretty good, because our parents did not believe in sparing the rod, and even worse, our horses would be put off limits.

Getting back to June, one vivid memory sticks in my mind. I entered her in a local gymkhana in the Quadrangle Stake Race. I won't explain it, but it involves four poles set in a square, and you go around them, and it is a timed event. We made it in good shape around the first two, and on the third, I was leaning into the turn, when something outside the arena spooked June, and she abruptly turned the other way. I was flung out horizontal to the ground, when my spur caught under the Cheyenne roll on my saddle, and I had a state of suspended animation. Being young and agile, somehow I got the saddle horn and pulled myself back on. Aaah, sweet youth!

A story Judy remembers involves both Big Enough and June. We had gone up on the range to cut a Christmas tree, found one, and loaded it up on Big Enough. I wish we had a picture of that, because the tree completely enveloped that little bay horse. He looked like a tree with hoofs. Anyway, he was loaded and standing in the trail.

Dad, riding June that day, spotted some "California Holly" berries (Toyon) on the hillside and wanted them for Christmas, as they were loaded with bright red berries. He rode off a little ways, got off, and had someone hold his horse while he gathered a big handful. When he came back to get on, this presented a problem, because he had to get back on June, who was about 15.2 hands. With his one arm, whose hand was clutching a berry bush, he got a foot in the stirrup and a hold on the horn. June did not like this and took off. Dad was running with his one available foot, holding on with his one available arm, and the bright red berries were

 THE CALIFORNIA YEARS

raining down. Fortunately, June was on the main trail, and that trail was blocked by Big Enough and the Christmas tree. Dad was saved, but his "arrangement" was the worse for wear, and had mostly just sticker leaves left on it. Dad was still pretty athletic with it all, though, but he could have asked for help…

In her life June produced two foals: a colt by Kenny (Kenny's story is later) and the second by this same colt. Grampa did not get him cut, so he bred back his own mother. Getting veterinary services early in a colt's life solves this problem.

I was there when June's first foal was born. It was at Grampa's, and he was also there. There were no problems, and all was well. June had stood up and was licking him off, and the colt was starting to try his legs, so less than an hour had passed. Grampa decided that she was late in delivering her afterbirth (NOT), walked up behind her, and started pulling on the umbilical cord. I didn't know much about foaling at that time, so didn't say anything. He proceeded to keep pulling until the placenta came, and he yarded it all out and pronounced it "done."

Many foals later, I know what risky behavior that was. He could have ruptured a vessel, causing her to bleed to death, or he could have pulled her uterus out, since equine placentas have a diffuse attachment to the uterine wall. Remembering him doing that makes me shudder. Poor June!

June carried me, my dad, my Grampa, my Aunt Clydia, and her two girls, Debbie and Betsy. I give credit for the success in starting my first horse to good luck, good books, a good horse, and the opportunity provided by my grandfather!

 MAKIN' TRACKS

Chico

In 1958, I was offered my first paying horse trainer job. I was in 8th grade. Frank Dimauro had bought a dappled grey, half-Arab half-Shetland pony for his daughter, Barbara, and he wanted to hire me to train him for her. I told him I would do it for the princely sum of $25. Well, when he brought Chico over, it was apparent that he had not yet seen a vet's scalpel, and he was very full of himself.

Another life lesson—get ALL the details in a transaction. Being 14, I wasn't too concerned about those not so tiny details, and I started working the pony every day. He was a handful, but a small handful, and my feet were about six inches from the ground on both sides when I rode him.

I saddled and unsaddled him and drove him with a pony saddle, but never rode him with a saddle. After a couple of weeks, I thought he was going pretty good. I rode him up on the road in front of Grampa's big barn, a large, two-story Pennsylvania Dutch-style barn, with a full loft in the top story for storing hay and mixing feed. All of a sudden, Chico saw some horses in the corral and had a sudden surge of hormones. He began whinnying for all he was worth and really showing his "stuff," and I got after him. He stood straight up on his hind legs, so I stepped off, and as I stood up, he pirouetted and struck me right in the mouth with one front foot. It numbed my front teeth, and I wasn't even sure they were still there.

I tried to wear out the snap end of a rope on his nasty little butt and had him longeing about 25 mph in the middle of Hendricks Road. My arm gave out before the snap, and I could feel my lip swelling out like a cream puff, so I led him home, put him away, and put ice on my fat lip. Then I called Frank and told him I was done with Chico as he was, but if he had him gelded, I'd try him again.

A month or two later, a new Chico arrived. The wind was out of his sails, and I made great progress with him. He ended up

THE CALIFORNIA YEARS

being a nice little horse for Barbara, and they had him a long time. Barbara drove him to a cart when she got too big to ride him anymore.

The best part of this venture for me—in addition to still having my teeth—was that I took the $25 down to Mahnke's Saddle Shop, and Rick Mahnke made me my first pair of chaps. They were shotguns made from a rust-colored buckskin and had a hand-carved belt. We still have a smaller version, because later on, I cut them down for my daughter Lisa, and then her kids wore them. Thanks, Chico, for providing us with a family heirloom.

Barbara Dimauro on Chico. Circa 1960.

 MAKIN' TRACKS

Honeycomb

Honeycomb was Judy's horse after Pepper. She got her around 1958 from Herb Robertson, a neighbor who lived at the north end of Scotts Valley. She was a good-looking, red dun Quarter Horse mare, with a MAJOR problem—she was a pull-back artist.

Judy hadn't had her too long when she tied her up to one of the posts that supported the back porch on to the house. We lived in an old, Victorian, two-story house, and the posts were of the "turned" variety. Honeycomb was wearing a halter, and her lead rope was used to tie her up to the porch post.

Well, surprise! All of a sudden, Honeycomb laid back against the post, jerked the whole thing loose from the house, and disappeared into the pear orchard with it. Everyone was pointing the finger at everyone else, "Who spooked Honeycomb?"

Turned out, Honeycomb didn't need ANY reason to pull back—it was on her own time schedule, and her time schedule was very erratic. One of her worst episodes happened on a Three-Day Ride (a major, annual event, where the Junior Horsemen rode for three days and camped out for two nights. In the middle of the night, she pulled back and threw herself down, and her rope somehow got under the front bumper of the old 1948 Chevy pickup we had. There was a lot of noise, thrashing around, and confusion. People ran over with flashlights, which didn't calm the mare down! She was just about to breathe her last, when someone cut her free. She seemed to recover, but she straightened out the bumper on the '48 Chevy, so it had a kind of "longhorn" look after that.

She was a good horse to ride, *when* you could catch her, but chancy to tie up.

This is probably a good time to talk a little about the bad habit of horses pulling back. It is dangerous to be around, and it is a very hard habit to break horses from, once they get started doing it. Beginning with Becky, and up to the present, I've been around a

THE CALIFORNIA YEARS

number of pull-back horses. They have a psychological problem, which can start from many different circumstances, and I have never had good luck in eliminating this habit.

Any time you tie to a solid object at a horse's head level and they pull back, the war is on. In the ensuing panic attack, anything can happen. The newer idea of tying to an elevated, moveable object on a high post seems to alleviate this struggle. It may prevent the bad habit from forming in the first place, but I have never had this set up.

I have also seen people tie to a breakable string, so that it pops under pressure, releasing the horse, and eliminating the struggle. If they release themselves, in the middle of the night, though...

Judy got very tired of this behavior in Honeycomb, and when the opportunity arose to trade her off for Pete, she took it.

L to R: Honeycomb with Judy, Big Enough with Janie,
our dad, Jerry Hendricks, and Pepper with Little Jerry.
We are all wearing our Clearlake Junior Horsemen Drill outfits.
Dad is wearing his opposite colored, drillmaster shirt. 1959.

 MAKIN' TRACKS

Note: Dad took over Teresa Holdenreid's position and became the Drillmaster for the Clear Lake Junior Horsemen's Drill Team. The number of riders had greatly mushroomed, and the drill had become unwieldy in its performance. He totally redesigned the drill, divided us into Flag Bearers, an "A" Team and a "B" Team, and greatly improved the drill's efficiency. Dad's coaching made us into one of the state's best Junior Drill Teams, and we began to travel outside Lake County to perform.

 THE CALIFORNIA YEARS

Colonel Norris M. L'Abbe

As noted in several chapters in this book, we were very lucky to have had a generous and thorough horsemanship instructor in Colonel L'Abbe. Judy and I have always been grateful for his teachings, but in researching his background for this book, I am now aware of just how REALLY lucky we were!

The Colonel began his army career in 1914 as an enlisted man and worked his way up in rank to Colonel by the end of his career in 1949. He was stationed in many areas during this time—Fort Riley in Kansas, Fort Clark in Texas, the New Hebrides, Honolulu, Fort Eustis in Virginia, and Fort Reno in Oklahoma. He earned a number of medals and awards for his service. He was a horseman and was in the U.S. Cavalry for his entire career. He was a riding instructor early on and a Tactical Commander in the Pacific Theater during WW II.

His last assignment was a heart-breaker for an old Cavalry man. He was in charge of liquidating the last of the U.S. Army's horses and mules, including the Lipizzaners, Hungarian Warm Bloods, and Polish Arabians liberated by General Patton at the War's end.

In May of 1949, these horses were all sold at public auction. It's interesting that some of the Hungarian horses were purchased by the Hungarian Countess Bessenyey and sent here to her Bitterroot Stock Farm in Hamilton, Montana. She was a granddaughter of Marcus Daly, who had established the ranch.

The Colonel bought 18 of the Polish-bred Arabians, many by Witez II, and brought them to Lake County, California, when he retired later in 1949. He kept six and re-homed the rest.

One of these horses, Witalis, became his favorite mount to offer instruction from. He was a bright sorrel with a blaze face and some white on three feet. He was beautifully trained, and when the Colonel let me ride him one day, he opened my spirit to the real possibilities of horsemanship. He was a revelation, and I have never forgotten him.

MAKIN' TRACKS

Colonel Norris M. L'Abbe.
Photo courtesy of Connie Thomas Wright. Circa 1945.

The Colonel volunteered his time to give free horsemanship instructions to the Clear Lake Junior Horsemen every Easter week, and he also gave lessons to kids in the Colusa area. He later teamed up with Mose Lusk, the Lake County 4-H Extension Agent, and the two of them created a pilot program for the 4-H Light Horse

 THE CALIFORNIA YEARS

Program. It was in its infancy, and the work they did, and the program presented to us, are the basis for today's national program. We met once a month and got a complete horse education—riding, feeding, stable management, grooming, disease control, parts of the horse, and equipment... We were in on the ground floor, but didn't know it at the time. The Colonel volunteered his time to us from about 1953 until 1959.

Colonel Norris M. L'Abbe on Witalis and his wife Jessie on Ralla. Photo courtesy of Connie Thomas Wright. Circa 1955.

While devoting his time to kids, he also was judging major, nationally-recognized horse shows all over the country.

 MAKIN' TRACKS

Clear Lake Junior Horsemen Drill Team after a practice.
Judy Hendricks on Butch 7th from left.
Janie Hendricks on Pepper 7th from right.
Lake County Fairgrounds.
Photo courtesy of Connie Thomas Wright. 1953.

When he left Lake County in 1960, he and his wife Jessie moved to Sonoma County, California, and he remained active in the horse community. He continued judging horse shows—like the one in Santa Rosa, which is still a special memory for me.

I'm sure the other "old" Junior Horsemen members in Lake County are equally grateful for the Colonel's time and expertise, as he gave us a foundation in horsemanship beyond compare. Thank you, Colonel L'Abbe!

THE CALIFORNIA YEARS

Kenny and Pete

In 1959, when I was 15, I had outgrown Big Enough, both size-wise and challenge-wise. I wanted a real Quarter Horse, one of those old fashioned, heavy muscled ones, like those Orren Mixer was painting on the covers of *Western Horseman* magazine!

Dad was on board with this idea, and he was researching the want ads all over northern California looking for a good, affordable horse for me, and we were going to go horse shopping. When the time came to go, however, I couldn't go, as I was selected to go to pear packing school at the local pear shed. It was an opportunity to make more money. Since school clothes rode on "pear money," I couldn't turn it down.

So, Judy went with Dad, and she was going to be my "agent" and try out the horses advertised. She says there was a lot of false advertising on those culls she rode, and she rode quite a few. They finally landed at a horse trader's place in Martinez, California. This horse trader, "G," was a real pro—if you know what I mean—and had 15 or 20 horses for sale. Judy did not see any horses there which she thought I'd like, but she did spot a big, bay, Thoroughbred gelding, who called to HER.

Dad, in the throes of the horse deal, had been shown a three-year-old, 1/2 TB 1/2 QH bay stud, and he decided that was THE horse for me. Judy tried to point out that this horse was far, far from what I actually wanted, but Dad was enamored with the colt. "G" was a real salesman. He said the horse's name was "Kenny S," and he showed Dad his sire and his papers, which Judy tried to point out did *not* match the colt in question. "G" said it was a minor mix-up, and they would get it straightened out. "G" had become Dad's new best friend, and they were making a deal and talking money, so Judy gave up on Dad and started dealing for herself.

Judy told "G" about the dynamite dun QH mare she had to trade in on the TB gelding. One of her bargaining chips was that she was willing to give up the mare ONLY because she wanted to ride English, and Honeycomb wasn't suited to that. She built up the mare pretty high, got to ride the TB, and convinced the trader to give her $250 worth of equity against the TB's $325 asking price. Thus, she got a new horse for $75. She was a match for "G" — Dad wasn't.

A deal was struck. "G" would deliver the horses to Lake County in October. Dad was to give $775 for Kenny and $75 for the TB, if Honeycomb met with approval, and the trade went through. He came, got the money, took the mare, and left a Bill of Sale for "Kenny S," saying he would get the papers fixed and transferred. Yeah, we found out later why he was in such a hurry to take the mare and leave!

Judy came out good on the deal. As "G" was unloading her new horse, he called him "Pete." When asked if that was the gelding's name, he said, "Naw, I call all of them that." But it stuck, and "Pecos Pete" was a star in Judy's world for many years.

I didn't know what to think. Kenny was far from what I had visualized and a stud to boot. Dad just thought he was the greatest looking horse ever. He was half TB and looked it! He was no Orren Mixer horse! Dad had big plans to breed him, before gelding him, so he could get his money back. Mom was madder than a wet hen over the whole deal, as we couldn't afford the horse and Dad went to the bank for a loan. Since I thought an awful lot of Dad, I guess I got wrapped up in the idea, as well.

Big obstacle — a stud horse without legitimate paperwork, and no paperwork seemed to be forthcoming. "G" was full of excuses, the AQHA had record of a Kenny S, who was a sorrel and registered to an unknown person... "G" really played Dad for a sucker — which he was! Finally, some truths began to be known. My "Kenny" was actually a registered horse named "Two Rivers" (what kind of a name is that?), and he was a full brother to "Kenny S." The owner of Two Rivers was owed money by "G" and wouldn't release the papers until he was paid — one of THOSE deals! It took all winter, but we did get AQHA papers to match my horse. Horse traders don't have the reputations they do without good reasons!

 # THE CALIFORNIA YEARS

We are going to split the stories of these two horses now, writing first about Kenny and then about Pete. Kenny got his name through usage, since his registered name wasn't user friendly and was only used for shows.

 MAKIN' TRACKS

Kenny aka Two Rivers

The first order of business for Kenny—even before he arrived—was building a stud pen, so he would have safe quarters. Right below the big dairy barn was a smaller one we called the calf barn, because it was where Clyde Deacon had kept the dairy calves. It was a good little barn, with hand-hewn rafters, a nice hay storage area, and an attached lean-to. Off the back side of it, we built a sturdy board fence, about six feet high, and painted it white.

Kenny, when he was still a stallion. Terry Wright is holding him. 1960.

Of course, the second order of business was tracking down his papers. That spring, the third thing was to get him broke to ride. Dad hired Terry Wright, from Kelseyville, to get him started. Terry rode him for a couple of months, and then I rode him.

 # THE CALIFORNIA YEARS

Dad put out the word that he was standing a QH stud and generated some interest. We knew nothing about handling a stallion or breeding mares, but a friend Tobe Butler did. He said he would handle the breeding operation, if he could breed his mare for free.

It turned out that Kenny bred 10 mares and produced nine foals. Dad collected stud fees on seven mares. We bred June at no charge and Tobe's mare at no charge and refunded money to the open mare, so we got $350 back on Kenny's purchase price, making him more affordable, and making the bank and Mom happy!

Let's say here that I got by riding a young stud, but I would not recommend it to other teenage girls. He was a handful, and I enjoyed riding him much more after he was gelded, which happened right after the mares were bred, in 1960, when I was a junior in high school.

Janie, holding Kenny out on Hendricks Road, wearing the shotgun chaps bought with the money from training Chico. That double Navajo blanket cost $27. 1961.

MAKIN' TRACKS

I really wanted to train and show a performance horse. Big Enough won a lot of ribbons in gymkhana events, but now I wanted a pleasure/trail/equitation horse, and that was my focus with Kenny. I started him in a hackamore, went to a snaffle, and then a bit. We grew up surrounded by good vaquero riding habits and had the opportunity to watch the best bridle horse men and women in the country.

Our family's BIG EVENT every October was to go to the Grand National Horse Show and Rodeo at the Cow Palace in San Francisco. They held the Pacific Coast Stock Horse Championships every year. We were there in 1961, when Sheila Varian won that Championship riding her good Arabian mare Ronteza. She had such an amazing performance and beat all the good-ol'-boys on their Quarter Horses so BADLY that Judy and I still talk about it today! She has definitely been one of my role models since that time.

Sheila Varian and Jane Lambert.
Paws Up Ranch, Greenough, Montana. 2008.

THE CALIFORNIA YEARS

Note: Sheila and I talked about when my sister Judy and I watched Sheila and Ronteza "Win the World" at the Cow Palace in San Francisco in 1961. She was as gracious as she was talented, and I was so thrilled to be able to meet and visit with her all those many years later. Another note of interest here is that Ronteza had the same father that Colonel L'Abbe's Witalis had—Witez II. He was one of the premier Arabians saved by General Patten's troops at the end of WW II, and he has had a profound influence on the Arabian breed.

Christmas 1961, I really wanted a silver-mounted Garcia bit, and I studied the catalog for hours before deciding which one I wanted. It retailed for $50, which was more than Santa Claus could afford. Mom said Santa had $25, but if I sprung for the difference, my bit could be under the tree. Because my 4-H project was profitable enough, it was! I still have it, and its value has steadily risen.

Kenny required a lot of riding. Being half TB, he had a lot of energy and a lot of stamina. His natural temperament was to get up and go. That first year of showing him, I would spend the whole day before the show putting hard miles on him in hilly, brushy country. He would sometimes yawn, yawn, and yawn, while standing in the final line-up for judging. If he wasn't pooped out, he was no "pleasure." Good thing I had stamina, too.

Kenny was registered as *Appendix* and had no number in the early days. At that time, a half TB half QH could move up to *Tentative* and get a number if, when inspected by an official of the AQHA, their conformation met criteria. The QH inspector called the house and said he was on his way to inspect my horse. Judy was home—again, I was working at the pear shed. She caught him and groomed him—and did some smart thinking. Kenny had a really nice QH head, but he also had a droopy lower lip, and he let it hang down when he was relaxed. Judy gave him a quick "cure" for the inspector, by putting some ice pieces in his lip and holding them there before the guy came. Kenny passed, got his number, and kept his lip puckered through it all! Thanks, Judy!

Through many miles and my hours of pure determination, he made a "horse," and we won a number of trophies and a box full of ribbons. By 1962, Jerry was showing him with success, too. He was the only boy in his age group (11 & Under) showing at the time, and he liked gathering up blue ribbons from the girls.

From 1960 through 1962, we were going to horse shows almost every weekend all over northern California. One memorable trip was to the Colusa County Fair in Colusa, California. On the way over to the show, we made a stop, and someone noticed a crack forming in the horse trailer tongue. We had Kenny and Pete in the trailer, and Judy and I wanted to immediately abort the trip and unload our horses. Dad was determined to forge on to the show, saying, "Aw, hell! It'll be all right until we get there!"

That was a TENSE drive, let me tell you. Judy and I were both mad and scared—our prize horses were at stake! The silence in the back seat was deafening. Mom, usually a non-stop smoker, had a Camel in her fingers and was twirling it like a baton and also not speaking. Highway 20, from Lake County to Williams, is both hilly and curvy, before it flattens out in the Sacramento Valley to Colusa. It seemed to take FOREVER to get there.

We made it there all in one piece, and Dad took off to find a welding shop to fix the trailer. We were waiting to be called for a class, when we heard over the loudspeaker, "Jerry Hendricks, report to the fair office. Jerry Hendricks, report IMMEDIATELY to the fair office!"

We knew Dad was gone, so Mom went to see what was going on. She came back flabbergasted and embarrassed. It seems, when Dad went out through the main gate, he had failed to notice that the horse trailer was taller than the opening. He tore down the main entrance gateway to the Colusa County Fairgrounds—and KEPT GOING.

A witness wrote down his license plate number, so they had him, dead to rights. How embarrassing! And since I had painted

 **THE CALIFORNIA YEARS**

our family brand on the front of our horse trailer in bright red—a JH connected—this deemed most of us guilty, as four out of five had JH initials.

Not only was the top of the trailer dented in, but Dad also got a big repair bill. I guess the trailer tongue wasn't too weakened, as it stayed on the car while Dad tore the entrance down…

Jane Lambert holding the trophy at Santa Rosa, when Colonel L'Abbe was the judge. 1962.

There were two shows in 1962 that stand out for me these many years later in terms of being gratifying. The first one was in Santa Rosa, California. Colonel Norris L'Abbe was the judge. He had moved to Sonoma some years before and had not seen me since I had grown up. He did not recognize me, although he had been my early riding instructor.

 MAKIN' TRACKS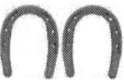

I had entered in both the Western Equitation and Western Pleasure classes and don't remember which one came first that day. Colonel L'Abbe as a judge was just as thorough as he was a riding instructor, and he put us through the paces. The Beck Arena in Santa Rosa is large, and it was a big class with many horses. We did every kind of gait transition there was, even from an extended gallop down to a trot. At one point, he asked for an extended gallop down to a stop and said, "Drop your reins and hold out your arms." Kenny worked flawlessly that day.

When they announced the winner of the class, I don't know who was the most surprised—the Colonel or me, as we both had astonishment written all over us—him, when he heard my name, or me, at the award. I won the second class, too. I was always very proud of those ribbons, because I came out on top of some tough competition and at the judgment of my strictest mentor, a man I greatly respected!

My other favorite memory was winning the Western Riding class at the Petaluma Quarter Horse Show against some of the best known and most respected showmen of the day. To win a blue over "the best" really put a feather in my hat and got my horse some ROM points (Register of Merit points awarded by the AQHA at their recognized shows, which can add up and get horses national recognition). I might also say that Western Riding really showcases a horse's training, as it requires many gait transitions, flying lead changes, and working through obstacles. I was very proud of my horse that day—and still am.

When Judy and I were showing, there was a lot of stiff competition, and we were up against kids with trainers for themselves and for their horses. We couldn't afford that so, any time we won, we really earned it, and our awards had value to us.

Another Dad-generated adventure happened in 1962. My best friend Karen Hernandez and I wanted to run for Queen of the Junior Grand National at the Cow Palace in San Francisco. It was always held during Easter week. We had the old '57 Buick and the dent-top horse trailer for transportation. I had Kenny, and Karen had Charm's Pride, a line-backed buckskin.

 THE CALIFORNIA YEARS

We had all our stuff loaded, horses loaded, and Judy, Karen, and I loaded. Looking back on all this, I sometimes wonder about my father's thought process. He decided to go the fastest route — over Hopland Mountain. This is California Highway 175 and is a narrow, winding, steep mountain road. If you are interested in experiencing it yourself, go on YouTube and take that drive via video from Lakeport to Hopland. You will also get an idea of the brush country we used to ride in.

Janie and Kenny posing before entering the Cow Palace Queen Contest. 1962.

 MAKIN' TRACKS

About halfway down the other side, our brakes went out. Imagine that! The automatic transmission on the car couldn't hold the trailer back on that grade. We finally got stopped and unloaded the horses. Judy, Karen, and I had all bought new, beaded moccasins to wear—we thought they looked jazzy. Karen's foot didn't look that way after her horse stepped on it and ground down on it, coming out of the trailer. Judy took Karen's horse for her, and we all trailed down the mountain, with Karen limping behind. We ended up walking a good three miles before re-loading and wore the bottoms right out of our brand-new moccasins.

We gave the queen contest a good try and had fun—except for Karen trying to get her cowboy boot on. We got no crowns, just worn out moccasins, a black and blue foot, and one more adventure to remember.

Karen Hernandez and Charm's Pride. 1962.

THE CALIFORNIA YEARS

By the time I was done with Kenny, he was as bomb-proof as they come, and I could work him with just a string around his neck. However, horses will be horses, as I found out. Judy and I took four head down to Scotts Creek. We had Kenny, Pete, Princess, and Darling, a friend's horse. We were going to play around and then "wash them" before the fair. We tied up Darling. Judy had Princess and was going to tie her, and I was on Kenny, bareback with a halter, leading Pete. I decided to swim them through a deep hole, which I did, and Kenny lunged up out of it and gave a big crow-hop, which launched me in front of Pete into water that was about two feet deep. I had Kenny's halter rope in one hand and Pete's in the other and was getting drug underwater between Pete's legs. Poor Pete was doing everything he could to not step on me, but I stayed underneath him until I was about to drown, before letting go of the ropes in my hands. I had some rock rash and bruises, but good old Pete did not step on me. Kenny and Pete ran off, Princess ran off, and Darling was unhappy at getting left behind.

Our mother was also unhappy when three wet, loose horses came home without us and ran free in the yard. Fortunately, we did have one horse left to get back home on.

In the spring of 1962, I wanted a new saddle. The one I had was a '50s style roping saddle and very low in the cantle. I had saved about $250 towards a new one, and I talked Dad into taking me "shopping." (I should say here that my high school graduation was looming, and my mother wanted to buy me Samsonite luggage for a present.) Anyway, we went to Petaluma first to Palm's Saddle Shop. Jim Palm was the proprietor and a very good saddle maker. At that time, I could have had a Palm custom saddle built, fully carved in either an acorn or wild rose pattern, for $325. If I wanted it buck-stitched, the cost was $100 more. I think he was six months out on orders. I would have loved to order one, but didn't have enough money.

We went several more places and didn't find anything. Then we went to Olsen Nolte Saddle Shop in the San Francisco Bay area. There was MY saddle! It was basically brand new—the cinch on it wasn't even dirty. It had been custom made for somebody by Don Bentley, Oakland, California. It was completely tooled in an upgraded floral pattern, was fully buck-stitched, and was an equitation saddle with a nice, deep seat—exactly what I wanted. It also had sterling silver conchos, cantle plate, rivet heads, and maker's plate. It was top of the line, and I was in love! The price tag said $350. I needed $100, and I needed it BAD!

Boy, did I get to work on Dad... I made every kind of promise I could think of, offering ways I could work off a loan. Then I remembered Mom's budgeted amount for luggage. I pulled the graduation card! Please, please, PLEASE, Dad! He caved, and we came home with the saddle. My mother had a conniption fit, finally telling me, "Well, then, when you go off to college, just tie your clothes on the back of your SADDLE!"

Luggage would have gone to the dump by now. That saddle has been one of the best buys I ever made. We did not know it at the time, but Don Bentley was the premier show saddle maker of his time. He "invented" the buck-stitched show saddle, and he had a year and a half waiting list to get one. His prices started at $1,500 THEN. It is a pleasure to ride, and I used it hard for a good 30 years. The silver on it is worth more today than I paid for the whole saddle. It is in my daughter's tack room and is *her* treasure now.

Getting back to Kenny, Dad got to ride his "dream horse" after he was trained, and he rode him quite a bit after I left for college. He was riding him one time with the Senior Horsemen, when he got to demonstrate his bronc riding skills. Cardinal rule number one when riding a double rigged saddle—always tie your back cinch to your front one! Dad did not do this, and when he started up a steep grade, his back cinch fell back into a flank strap position, and Dad was no Casey Tibbs! He was "the entertainment." Fortunately, he wasn't injured—just his pride...

I graduated from high school in 1962 and went to college at University of California-Davis for two years. Dad had gone to school there, so I thought that was the place for me, too. When he went, it was an Ag school—they are called the Aggies—and that sounded good. Well, I hated it! I hated the flat, foggy Sacramento

THE CALIFORNIA YEARS

Valley, and I hated riding a bicycle a mile to school every day while wearing a skirt—in all kinds of weather. And it was NOT an Ag school, except for having a veterinary school. I rode the Greyhound home as often as I could, which wasn't often enough, because the bus took me only as far as Williams, and it was another 120-mile round-trip from Lake County for my parents to come and pick me there. It was a major inconvenience for them to come and pick me up, especially knowing that the trip would have to be repeated in a short time.

I only enjoyed two things there—visiting the barns at the vet school and taking a Horse Husbandry class. That class and P.E. were the only As I got.

I really enjoyed visiting a TB race horse named Candy Spots, who came to UCD for treatment. He was a noted race horse in 1963, as he ran third in the Kentucky Derby, second in the Belmont Stakes, and won the Preakness. He was a big, beautiful sorrel with wild black and white spots on him. I still remember him, and he seemed as unhappy to be there as I was!

I got so desperate to leave that place that I wrote my mother a letter and begged to quit school and just come home and "fix fence."

She and Dad brought Kenny over there, so I would stay. I had a roommate, Stephanie Wagner, who was a hunter/jumper rider of high caliber, and we were both overjoyed that we had a horse to play with! Stephanie gave me some English lessons, and pretty soon, we had Kenny jumping 3'6." I'm sure we spent more time at the barn than in class, but we were happy and even entered a horse show over there in the spring. Stephanie won 4th on Kenny in the Open Jumping Class.

My grades didn't set the world on fire, but I didn't flunk out, and I got credits in all my classes, thanks to Kenny.

I told my parents I was not going back to school there. Older friends had gone to Fresno State College and liked it a lot. They said it was a real Ag school, so I thought, if I was going to make it through college, I would need to transfer down there. The big dilemma was that I had no car, and Fresno was a long ways from

 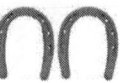

Lake County. It was a VERY hard decision, but I decided to sell Kenny and buy a car with the money. I hadn't ridden him much since high school and knew I could not afford to have him in Fresno. He was going to waste just standing around, and he was used to being ridden and fussed over. He needed a job.

I advertised him, and a teenage girl from Salinas, California, came and looked at him. She wanted a broke show horse—and that's what she got—for $1,500. I got a good, used Falcon.

He went to a very good, well-supervised home. The girl was stabling her other horse with, and was taking lessons from, Marvin Roberts, and that's where Kenny made his new home. It is too bad that Marvin's son Monty disparaged his father in his books, for Marvin had a good reputation in Salinas then and still does. The girl took Kenny to a show down there and won four blue ribbons, right off the bat. I heard they got along well, so I was happy.

Selling Kenny was a hard thing to do, but I never would have earned a college degree if I had not done it. Fresno fit me like a glove, and I still have lifelong friends that I met there.

THE CALIFORNIA YEARS

Pete aka Pecos Pete

You already read about Judy's horse trade to get Pete and how he got his name. I'll describe his appearance when he came to the ranch. He was a lean, 16-hand bay Thoroughbred gelding with no white markings. He had a large 96 brand on his left shoulder and a "rat tail." I describe his tail that way as corral mates had eaten off all the hair for about a foot down from his tailhead. He had a roached mane, which gave him a ewe-necked appearance since his withers were so high. He had a very nice, typical TB head. Both front legs had pin-fire marks on them, so we figured he had been on the racetrack at some point in his career. (He always got higher than a kite, when on a track, too.)

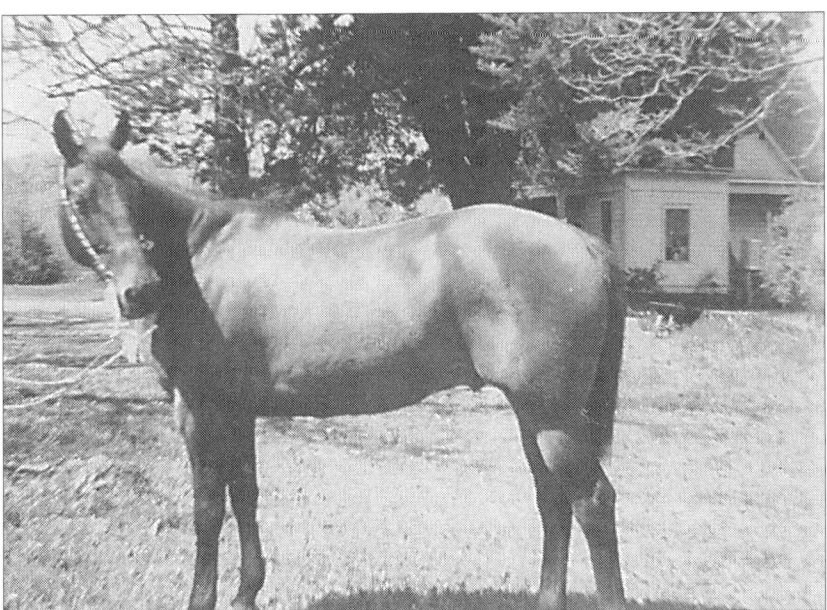

Pete, at the ranch. About 1960.

As Judy rode him and got to know him, she discovered that he had very smooth gaits, had a very good *handle* on him, and was both fast and very catty for such a big horse. One thing he did not know was taking cues to take his leads, so he probably had not been shown. He had been loaded in the back of pickups, though, and would jump right up in one. Since a lot of ranchers used stock racks on their pickups at that time, maybe that's where he learned that.

One day Judy had seen Grampa heading to town, so she decided to see if Pete could work a cow. She took him into the pasture and started moving Grampa's Hereford cows around. These were gentle, placid pets which had names, so they were not spooky or especially horse savvy. They mostly just got moved, as a group, from field to field. They weren't particularly easy to separate and "work," but Pete proved to her that this wasn't his first exposure to cattle. He knew how to shoulder a cow and move it with his own body, and if it didn't heed that, he knew how to give it an "enforcer" with his teeth. That all pointed to a ranch background. Some of Grampa's pets got a real education that day and had Pete's slobber marks to prove it!

L to R: Big Enough, wearing ribbons, and Janie. The '57 Buick. Pete, wearing ribbons, and Judy. Picture taken at a horse show in Redwood Valley, Mendocino County. Circa 1960.

After a year of riding Pete, Judy had learned a lot from him, and he had decided he liked her well enough to work for her. They were a dominating team in the show ring in the years to come. Pete understood his job by the gear she put on him. If he had a mechanical hackamore bit on, he was ready for speed events. If he

THE CALIFORNIA YEARS

had Judy's silver-mounted Garcia bit on, he was ready for performance classes. If he had a big ring snaffle on, he was an English horse. He was wise and talented.

Judy Hendricks on Pecos Pete at Lake County Fair. Lakeport, California. Pete wearing his performance bridle with the Garcia bit he loved to rattle when upset.

No matter how good he worked in the Western performance classes, he rarely placed, as the breed of preference for those classes was the Quarter Horse. In speed events, however, the stop watch picked the winners, and Pete got mostly blues, as his speed and handiness were hard to beat. His strides were long, and he really grabbed ground, so even though he may not have looked as fast as a shorter-legged horse, the watch told a different story. The spectators were often amazed at how fast he *clocked*.

 MAKIN' TRACKS

Pete always placed well in the English classes Judy entered, and her visualization for herself, in trading off Honeycomb, definitely came to pass. In the 1950s-1960s, the northern California horse shows just didn't feature a lot of English classes, but she entered in all she could, and Pete performed and placed well.

Pete was good on his feet and was a tough and handy horse out on the range, but he hated trail horse classes. Having to go through the obstacles made him mad. Judy remembers one of the first ones she entered — at Colusa, California. By the third obstacle, Pete was angry — he always took it out on his bit and would start gnashing his teeth and spinning the roller. His bit had a copper covered, Salinas mouthpiece, and he could make it sound like he had a rattlesnake in his mouth! In Colusa, the fourth obstacle was a sidepass. Judy lined him up and started asking him to move over. No response, just roller noise. She started kicking him and using a spur on him. No response. As she kicked him harder, he grunted, but wouldn't move. Then, still using his roller hard, he kicked back at her foot which was kicking him.

The judge, Lou Fisher, said, in an aside to her, "You might as well forget it!" Then he coughed to cover up his laughter as he turned away, hiding behind his dark glasses with shaking shoulders.

The next time she entered trail at a show in Ukiah, the last obstacle was a two-foot high jump. It had a sudden stop area on the other side. Pete cleared the jump by at least two feet, stopped hard, jabbing his feet into the ground, threw his head up, and whistled through his nose, like a bull elk. That was his last trail class performance.

Pete was never a "push button" horse, and he would not work for, or cooperate with, a person he was not familiar with. Jerry found this out the hard way when he was about 10 years old. Without asking anybody, he decided he would ride Pete. He went into the tack room, got my good bridle out, threw my rawhide reins over Pete's neck, and then tried to bridle him. Pete was tall and had a long neck. He just put his head way up, and Jerry couldn't reach him. After a few minutes of this, Jerry got frustrated

 THE CALIFORNIA YEARS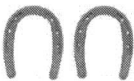

and lost his temper. He picked up a stick and hit Pete on the butt. Big mistake! Pete took off, dragging my bridle, and as a parting shot, he kicked Jerry in the head, giving him a grazing blow and a scuff mark on his scalp! Pete ran down the road, dragging my silver mounted bit, leaving sterling smudges on the pavement.

Judy Hendricks on Pecos Pete, wearing his gymkhana headstall with a hackamore bit. Picking up a win ribbon and trophy. Quadrangle Stake Race. Petaluma, California. 1962.

Big lesson, Jerry! In addition to receiving Pete's *love tap* on the head, he had to foot the bill to get my bit repaired. Fortunately, there was a talented silversmith in Ukiah, who had the interesting name Romi Pomi, and he reapplied the silver overlay. Pete and Jerry NEVER did get along, after that.

One time at a show, a neighbor, who was a pushy, horse show mother, kept after Judy to let her daughter ride Pete in a pleasure class. Judy tried to tell her that was a bad idea, but the mother insisted. Her poor daughter Cindy didn't know what she was in for. As the class went on, we could hear the cricket in Pete's bit. When they called for a lope, the lope very rapidly became an extended gallop, and Cindy was hanging on for dear life and was lapping the class. Judy opened the gate and stepped in front of him, yelling, "Whoa, Pete!" and got him slowed down and out the gate. No push buttons on Pete, pushy Mom!

Pete didn't like me on him, either. I once tried to run him on barrels, and he just ran *off*, instead of *around*. He was pretty much a one-person horse, and Judy was his person.

About once a year, Pete would also give Judy a lesson in "who's in charge" by bucking her off. He was a big, powerful horse and, on the good Scotts Valley feed, had blossomed to his full weight of 1,325 pounds—and that did not include any extra fat, because he didn't carry any.

One time, Judy was practicing for the Cow Palace and was loping Pete around, making circles on a loose rein, and telling Mom how good Pete was feeling, when he suddenly jumped sideways, lit, and spun, sailing Judy off onto the lush, spring grass. She did a body slide for a good 10 feet, which turned her clothes grass green.

Pete, feeling good, but knowing he was in trouble, sped off, and made two laps around the shed where his stall was. He gained speed as he went and then darted inside. Judy had been riding my Bentley saddle, and when she saw how fast he was going and thought about the two 90-degree turns he had to make to get into his stall area, she was worried about my saddle. All was well. Pete was standing at high alert, right in the middle of his stall—head and tail raised, with my saddle, untouched. He WAS catty!

As I mentioned in Honeycomb's story, Dad had taken over the Clear Lake Junior Horsemen's Drill Team and had coached us into a crack unit. The Santa Rosa Fair contracted us to perform for them, which was a high honor for us. It was a huge effort for our parents to get over 50 kids to Sonoma County, with all our gear and horses. And it was going to require some re-arranging of our drill spacing,

THE CALIFORNIA YEARS

because we were to perform on the racetrack in front of the grandstand, instead of in an arena. It was a much narrower space than we were used to. Dad talked to us about how we could make it work, and we ran through it that morning to practice.

At one p.m. for the performance, the grandstand was packed. We were all nervous, but ready—but not ready enough—for the Marine Corps 60-piece brass band stationed in the infield right along the rail, their instruments glinting in the July sun. Dad blew the whistle to start, and the band struck up a tune. On the grandstand side, all was well, but as the lead columns approached the band, all hell broke loose. Horses were bucking, horses were running away, and the flag bearers lost their flags and grabbed their saddle horns! It was complete bedlam! And, Judy points out, the band members seemed to be enjoying the chaos they were creating—especially the cymbal player, who was giving it his all, with flashy flair!

Finally, between us yelling, some crying, Dad requesting, and the announcer reinforcing, the band quit and moved back off the rail. We regrouped, reformed, and started over. Everybody was frazzled, but game, to go again. We were doing pretty darned well, considering how upset the horses were. Of course, Pete was particularly wound up, both by the band and by being on the racetrack. Judy was supposed to lead out, everyone else to follow, and form a wheel for the drill. Pete must have accelerated a little too fast, as he lost his footing and fell down, right in the midst of the other horses. When he stood up, Judy was hanging upside down—her armitas (like chinks, but with a solid belt) had hung up on the saddle horn. Pete's head was up, his eyes bugged out, and his nostrils were huge. Everyone in the drill stayed quiet and did not move. Even the grandstand was hushed. The only sound was Judy, talking quietly to Pete, "Whoa, boy. Easy now, easy now. Whoa, Pete, whoa."

It was a hold-your-breath few moments, because if he had run, no one could have caught him. He held, while Judy gave a super-human effort, using her stomach muscles, to pull herself upright. When she sat up, got in the saddle, and got unhooked, the crowd

MAKIN' TRACKS

gave her a standing ovation. The drill team members started breathing again. Judy says she was so embarrassed she "could have died." At age 15, that was *too much* attention!

Being troopers, we all finished the drill and were greatly relieved to have it over with. That was the first and only time I can ever remember that we all immediately took off our drill outfits. Usually we wore them after a performance because we were a proud group. In this case, everyone was so embarrassed by all our troubles that we didn't want to advertise who we were. At least *only* our egos got hurt...

Pete was a hell of a performance horse, winning well over a hundred ribbons and many, many trophies in his career. With a change of gear, he would change his focus and could come off a barrel race and go win a stock horse class. We never found out anything about his former life, where he came from, or who his trainers had been, but he came to Judy with a lot of experience. She wrote, "I will never forget that big, beautiful, bay horse. He taught me how to ride and to respect a horse."

Pete was used for much more than a show horse, of course; all our horses had many jobs. One very unusual job Dad gave Pete was as a portable ladder. As was mentioned at the beginning of this book, Dad was very busy, as he taught high school and had all the ranch work to do, too. Pruning the pear trees was a big job, and as the young orchard grew and prospered, the job became bigger and bigger.

Dad discovered that he could get around and prune the bottom part of the trees a lot faster from horseback than he could wrestling the pear ladder with one arm. And he could totally prune the young trees from his saddle. At times, with the short daylight, he would climb aboard with his teaching clothes on. He was quite a sight from Hendricks Road—out there, pruning the young pear trees on a big, bay horse, while wearing a suit and tie. He was the best dressed pruner in Lake County!

Pete's last horse show was at the Lake County Fair in 1966. He had been laid off for a year. But he looked so good after being on Grampa's permanent pasture all summer that Judy brought him

 ## THE CALIFORNIA YEARS

out of retirement and entered him in the Open Pleasure Class. He seemed pleased to be back in the show ring and performed flawlessly. He really showed off in the extended trot, lapping everyone else in the class. Judy thinks old Pete was smiling as big *inside* as she was on the *outside* as he collected his last blue ribbon. This was no small victory, as the Lake County Fair attracted the top show people of that time and was a top-flight event, with live music, flower girls in prom dresses, a highly decorated arena, and very large purses. Pete had a great *last hurrah!*

After that, he and Big Enough retired together out on the permanent pasture. Mom called them Mutt and Jeff, because they looked funny, standing head to tail, switching flies for each other; Pete was 16 hands and 1,300 pounds to Big Enough's 14 hands and 850 pounds.

They are both buried on the ranch.

 MAKIN' TRACKS

Nugget aka Misfit

About 1960, Nugget came into our lives. I think she was another one of Dad's "deals." She was owned by Jack Walton, who also owned and ran the Frosty Freeze in Kelseyville. I don't know where Jack got her, but she came with a resume and was a well-broke mare.

Nugget's show name was "Misfit," and the girl who owned her before Jack had shown her in reined stock horse classes—and at a high level. She won second place at the Cow Palace Junior Grand National in San Francisco—no small feat, because kids like Bobby Ingersoll, Pat Hubbard, and Monty Roberts were showing at the time.

I had Kenny going pretty well and was showing him in the slow events, but didn't have a gymkhana horse. Jack wanted to see his horse compete, so he loaned her to me. She was a nice mare to ride. She wasn't a very big horse, maybe 15 hands, and was light bodied. She had a star and stripe on her face and was a copper penny sorrel. She was as honest as the day was long and a real pleasure to ride.

Janie on Nugget, picking up a ribbon at a show. 1962.

 # THE CALIFORNIA YEARS

Unfortunately, when I was competing on her, I was competing against Pete and Judy, who usually always won first. Nugget was good enough to place fairly high and always ran an honest race. I don't remember her ever trying to cut corners.

One time at the Mendocino County Fair in Ukiah, California, Judy and Paula Hallberg were there. It was a big show, with many entries in the barrel race. Nugget was there, but no one had entered her. Paula was riding her good dun horse Daniel Boone, but Judy knew Nugget was faster and told Paula to change her entry and ride the mare. There were 94 entries that year.

Judy writes, "Nugget was a small horse, but extremely catty and quick. You never had to encourage her to run full out. She knew her job. Nugget gave Paula the ride of her life. When Paula got off after her run, she had to hold on to the horse because her legs were shaking so badly she could hardly stand." Nugget and Paula placed third, and Paula still remembers it with joy.

Jack Walton sold his business in Kelseyville, bought a dude ranch in the Fort Bragg area, and took Nugget with him. She was quite a mare, and I'm grateful to have ridden her. Thanks, Jack!

 MAKIN' TRACKS

Princess Dee

Princess Dee belonged to family friend Gene Dorsey, who let us ride her. She was a bald-faced sorrel with four evenly matched stockings. She was really flashy and a nice mare. Gene said she was by an Idaho stud named Sundae and out of a Morgan/Arab mare. When Gene decided he would part with her, somehow Judy ended up being a negotiator in the deal.

You would have to know the two characters involved to fully appreciate the dickering. Gene was an old, hard-bitten cowboy. Louis Rose was an old vaquero, originally from central California. They were both regular consumers of alcoholic beverages, and both were hard bargainers. Gene's price was $850—a substantial sum in those days. Louis didn't want to pay that much, but he really liked the mare. Judy rode Princess to all of Louis' directions—for an hour. Louis kept mentioning a low-ball price.

This is a picture of Louis Rose on Princess Dee. Lakeport, California. Photo courtesy of Gary Rose. 1984.

THE CALIFORNIA YEARS

The next day, Gene came over from Ukiah, and he and Louis went head to head. They negotiated. Gene went through all kinds of acrobatics showing how calm and easy going Princess was. They had both been "nipping." Judy says, when Gene got down on the ground on all fours under Princess and was head butting her in the belly, Judy left. She says, "I was sure Princess was going to run out of patience and kill one of them."

The deal ran on for several days—face to face. Gene held firm, and Louis bought her for $850. Louis was also nice enough to let us ride her when we wanted or needed to.

My first big memory of riding her came at the Colusa Spring show in 1962. It was at the fairgrounds and was a pretty good-sized show, with silver buckles for first and a lot of competition. Boy, I wanted to win a buckle! I had no trophy buckle on my belt...

I was running both barrels and poles on Princess, and I knew I had the best chance of winning in the pole bending, if everything went right. Well, everything DID go right, and I did win! However, no buckle—they decided to give trophy stable sheets that year—and I have to say that I was very disappointed, because I had pictured myself wearing a bright silver trophy buckle. I was happy enough with the win, though, to still have the stable sheet in my tack room today—maybe they can cover my casket with it...

The next memory I have of riding her was embarrassing. I was running the barrels at a big show in Santa Rosa, California. Now, Princess ran hard, and when she turned, she leaned hard and pushed with all four legs going around a barrel. This worked well in good, loose ground, but in Santa Rosa, the second barrel was right in front of the bucking chutes. The ground had not been worked up since the night rodeo, and it was packed hard. We made a good turn around the first barrel, but when we came to the second one, all four legs went out from under Princess, and she went down sideways. I was pretty athletic then, so I got my foot out of the stirrup, sort of did the splits above her, and was able to get away from her.

I got back on and rode out of the arena and was met with some laughter—and my sister telling me I had another split—right

down the back seam of my new, bell-bottomed, emerald green riding pants. My nylon underwear was waving out of the split like a white flag of truce!

The result was that I had to tie a jacket around my waist for the rest of the day, as I had not brought spare pants. Princess wasn't hurt at all—just my pride and pants!

Later on in 1964, Judy had entered in both the Reined Stock Horse class and the Speed and Handiness class in the Lake County Fair. Pete came down with Equine Influenza and was sick, so Judy asked Louis if she could ride Princess in his place. Louis alone had been riding her for a couple of years, but as noted earlier, Louis had talents as a horseman and had brought Princess along in her training. He also brought her along to the fair in his custom trailer made by the local blacksmith, emblazoned with a big red rose on the side!

Princess really surprised Judy with a terrific pattern in the dry work. She brought the crowd to their feet with her sliding stops and spins and then really locked on in the cow work. They placed 5th, which was quite an accomplishment, as the fair horse show offered good purses and attracted tough competitors like Red Randall, Barbara Worth, Harry Rose, and the like. It was prestigious in the old days. Princess also placed 2nd in the Speed and Handiness—a keyhole race. Louis about busted his buttons, wore his ribbons on the pockets of his shirt that night, and paraded around in a "show and tell."

Louie and Gene had bargained long and hard, but I do believe Louis definitely got his money's worth in Princess Dee, and he enjoyed her for many years. After Louis died, Gene Dorsey bought her back. Princess was an important horse to both men.

 THE CALIFORNIA YEARS

Farmer aka Farmers Duzzit

Farmers registered name was Farmers Duzzit. He was owned by the horse herdsman for Fresno State College when I was a student there. This would have been in 1965. I was in the market for a barrel horse, and Farmer was rated Top AA on the track, so he had the speed.

I think the horse was four or five and was a rangy, dark bay gelding, about 15 hands tall. He had a good hip, but kind of a crooked right foreleg, which didn't seem to bother him. I bought him and brought him home to the ranch.

Farmers Duzzit. Circa 1984.

Farmer was a flatland horse. He had been bred and raised in Arizona and then went to the San Joaquin Valley, and I don't think he had ever been off the level. The first time I rode him up on the range, he was very nervous, and at the slightest grade, uphill or downhill, he would lower his head to study the ground. When asked to go uphill, he really labored and didn't use his hind end for power. I figured out the situation, held him in, and drove him hard with my legs, helping him to figure out how to use his hind quarters for power. Learning to go downhill took a lot longer, and for several months, he traveled like an anteater, with his nose close to the ground, studying hard where he was going to put his feet. He was so nervous he made me nervous, but eventually he figured it out and became a strong, sure-footed, mountain horse.

In December, Judy rode Pete and I rode Farmer up on the range to get a Christmas tree. The game plan was to find a tree, cut it down, drag it to the jeep road, and then drive up and get it. All went well until I asked Farmer to drag the tree. I took my dallies and started to move the tree, and it was as though the starting gate flew open! He was in high gear, and the tree went air born! This spooked Pete, so he and Judy stampeded in a different direction.

Farmer was picking up even more speed and jumping the brush as he went. In a flash, I was on the jeep road, but I couldn't get rid of the tree, because my dallies had overlapped—I was "hard and FAST!"

Judy had got turned around, was trying to catch up, and was yelling, "Dump the tree! Dump the tree!" Not an option…

I managed to stay the course until Farmer was winded, and I got him stopped. Judy rode up, and our horses were breathing fog and sounded like freight trains. We got off, and checked the tree. It looked good—until you turned it over to discover it was bare, scrubbed clean of needles and bark. It was half a tree, but after THAT ride, it was going to have to do!

Good things came out of this episode, though. It was an adventure to talk about, no one got hurt or lost any fingers, we didn't have far to drive for the tree, and the tree didn't take up much floor space with its back to the wall. Farmer's footwork on rough ground improved, as did his confidence, and he pulled all kinds of stuff after that with no problem.

I rode him quite a bit, and he ended up with a good headset and handle. I must have given up the barrel racing idea, because now I don't remember doing that on him. I used him as a demonstration horse when I gave riding lessons, because he was well trained and responsive.

THE CALIFORNIA YEARS

I entered him in an amateur race in Grass Valley in a maybe dishonest way. It was for non-pro horses that had never won a race. (I'm almost sure that Farmer hadn't.) It had a lap and tap start and was for 440 yards. The old horse won it, and the wind was hitting me so hard in the face that I was blinded by tears. Pulling a tree or not, he could run!

I did some team penning on him, and he could work a cow as well as run.

Jane's daughter Lisa, holding Farmers Duzzit. 1973.

Farmer ended up being Jerry's horse, and he rode him for many years. He says that Farmer turned into the toughest, most sure-footed mountain horse on the ranch and was bomb proof. Farmer, however, never got over his race track life in that, when Jerry tried roping on him, Farmer saw the roping chute as a

starting gate and turned psycho coming out of the box. I should have mentioned that he was a Joe Reed bred horse, known for their quirky behavior. Farmer also had issues in the horse trailer, stemming from his starting gate phobia, and would sometimes put his head down to the floor like he was trying to hide. He didn't like to be tied in there, either.

Jerry let his friend Bob, who had cowboy aspirations, ride Farmer one time. Bob had just gotten out of the Navy, had hung around some rodeos, and thought he could ride. It took Farmer about 15 minutes to rake him off under a pear tree and come running back to Jerry with a look that said, "Don't put that idiot back on ME!"

Jerry also relates that Dad and Rick Marshall took Farmer on a pack trip into the Yolla Bolly Wilderness area and didn't tie him up—as he usually stayed in camp. Farmer took off towards the Eel River and was gone for three or four days. Dad rode Sundown 30 miles looking for him and finally met two hippies leading him up the trail. They had their backpacks tied on him and were happy to have him. Rick said he thought Farmer was as stoned as the hippies when they got him back, so I guess it was a happy escape.

Farmer lost weight and got crazier than a loon in his old age, so Jerry called Dr. Tim Strong to come look at him. The thought was he had eaten loco weed up on the range somewhere. A physical revealed that he had an abscessed tooth, and when it was removed, Farmer got a new lease on life and lived another three years as his "normal" self before being put down.

 THE CALIFORNIA YEARS

Sundown aka Poco Sundown

Poco Sundown's story is going to be written mostly by Judy, as I graduated from high school in 1962, and was busy making plans to attend college. Sundown's story started with Dad meeting a new friend, Jack Turner, right at this time, and Judy remembers better what went on. Judy tells the story...

I first met Jack Turner when I was 14. I was grooming Pete at the hitching post, when a man drove into the yard. He got out of his car and, without speaking, began examining Pete, slowly walking around him like he was a horse show judge. Never having seen him before, I became irate. The madder I got, the more Jack inspected. He finally asked for my dad.

After getting to know him, I learned that this is the kind of thing he loved to do to entertain himself.

Top Hat. Sundown's grandfather.

 MAKIN' TRACKS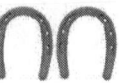

Jack's father, Jack Turner, Senior, was a renowned breeder of Palominos, and his horses had been sold worldwide. Jack Senior, mounted on his head stallion Top Hat, had led the Tournament of Roses Parade in Pasadena, California, with the Long Beach Mounted Police for many years. Top Hat was spectacular. He was a bright golden color, stood 16 hands tall, and weighed 1,350 pounds. His tack was made by Bohlin. It was totally covered with hand-engraved sterling silver and weighed 235 pounds. It took two men to put the saddle on Top Hat and two men to put the chaps and vest on Mr. Turner, after he got mounted. Today's value of Top Hat's parade tack is somewhere around $200,000.

Son Jack was a superb horseman and taught our whole family a lot about feeding and fitting top show horses. He had moved up from Long Beach and had brought two palomino mares with him, Pirate's Darling and Top Hat's Sage, a daughter of Top Hat. Sage was bred to Poco Costalotta, a stallion owned by Curtis Beech, a well-known trainer in Long Beach.

Jack told me that, if I behaved, I could ride and show the foal. Sage foaled in April of 1962, and Jack took us to see the new baby. He was newborn, wobbly, skinny, and cream colored. I thought to myself, "I'll be ancient before that colt will be rideable." Jack said his family believed in early training using careful practices—like leg wraps, rubber-wrapped bits, good nutrition, and light workouts—and that I'd be riding him in two years.

When Sundown was two, Jack sent him to Curtis Beech, who had a lifelong career with horses. He had done a lot of movie stunt work, as well as being an excellent and skilled trainer. His training was based on dressage, with a "Beech Twist." Curtis trained Sundown for 90 days and then returned him to Jack in the fall of 1964. Curtis stayed in Lake County for several days, worked with me, and showed me how to continue his training.

At this time, Pete was unsound, and this was my last year to be able to show at the Junior Grand National at the Cow Palace. Sundown was my hope, now, to do this. I really doubted that he would be ready, as the Cow Palace is a very challenging place, even for seasoned show horses.

THE CALIFORNIA YEARS

I rode him daily, rain or shine. A missed day meant suffering the consequences. He was full of energy, both from his breeding and from the high-powered nutritional supplements he was getting, including large numbers of carrots for his Vitamin A deficiency. He was very athletic, quick, and smart, and he progressed quickly in his training.

Sundown's first horse show was at the Cow Palace in March of 1965, and he wasn't quite three years old. My sister Janie came up to San Francisco from college in Fresno. Our plan was to ride him until he was too tired to misbehave. For the day and a half before showing, Janie and I took turns riding him. It paid off, and he performed like a pro. I won the Junior Grand National 4-H Queen Contest. I had a lot of good people to thank for helping me, but especially Jack Turner.

Back to Jane's memories:

The Junior Grand National 4-H Queen Contest is a coveted title and very hard to win. Unlike a rodeo queen title, these contestants must also have livestock entered in the show—in this case, Judy had a market lamb. To prepare for this, she not only had her horse to ride, but also she needed to feed, fit, and show her market animal. Then, after she won, she had many PR duties, photo shoots, and interviews, as she became the 4-H representative for the whole Junior Grand National. We were all pretty proud of her and the golden gelding she rode!

Back to Judy's memories:

A year or so later, Curtis took Sundown again to finish his training. When he brought him back home to Lakeport, he stayed a few days and gave Janie and me some riding lessons. Sometimes, when you least expected it, Curtis would vault onto your horse from behind and demonstrate the technique he was trying to teach. He made us ride backwards, sideways, no reins, no stirrups. By the time he left, we had balance.

When full grown, Sundown was 16 hands tall and was a bright, golden palomino color. I had the good fortune to ride and

show Sundown for a number of years, thanks to Jack. Our family could never have afforded a horse like that or paid for the professional lessons that Curtis gave us.

Judy Hendricks and Poco Sundown, after winning Junior Grand National Queen, Cow Palace, San Francisco, California. March 1965.

The Lake County Fair, at that time, had an excellent horse show and was on the main circuit of professional trainers. Jack decided to sponsor two palomino classes at the fair, as the owner of the Richfield Oil Distributorship. One was Western Pleasure, and the other was a Parade class. Of course, Dad and Jack entered me in both. I don't remember much about the Western Pleasure

THE CALIFORNIA YEARS

class, but I'll never forget the Fiesta Parade class. For starters, I was riding the old sidesaddle, and Sundown would only go sideways, away from my leg. By using my romal, a type of long quirt attached to the end of closed reins, I finally got him to move forward. Secondly, I never felt comfortable riding sidesaddle, and this sidesaddle was made for a small woman and didn't fit me right.

Kudos to our great-great-grandmother, Lydia Flagg, who crossed the plains, riding sidesaddle. She never in her life rode astride. Lydia lived to be over 99 years old.

So, here I was, decked out in my Spanish costume, riding a confused Sundown. All went well, until the announcer called for a "parade gait." I was thinking, "What the hell is a parade gait?"

I had no clue what to do, so I watched to see what the other contestants were doing.

Meanwhile, up in the grandstand, Jack was really enjoying himself! He said to Dad, "NOW, what is she gonna do?"

I gathered Sundown up, pushed him into the bit, and got a prancy gait out of him, which was as close to a parade gait as I could get. We placed 2nd out of four contestants.

Back to Jane's memories:

When Lisa was about two, I had gotten divorced from her father and was trying to hang onto the Scotts Valley Training Stable, which we had built. I was attempting to get the arena fence painted, and it was hard to do while watching a busy toddler, so I enlisted Sundown as a babysitter. I put Lisa on him in the arena, as I could keep an eye on her and keep painting, too.

Sundown was SO smart; he really took care of her. He walked slow and let her turn him in circles and serpentines. This wasn't enough for Lisa—she wanted to go faster. I caught her lifting the romal to smack him. I immediately told her, "Lisa, do NOT hit Sundown. Put that whip down and just ride slow. Do not hit Sundown!"

Being related to me and being very hard-headed, as soon as she thought I wasn't looking, she smacked Sundown with the romal. He picked up a horse show slow lope. I heard her make a noise as she fell off, looked up in time to see her go and to see

 MAKIN' TRACKS

Sundown immediately stop. She landed in front of him, with the back of her head resting on his front foot. He put his head down, with his nose right on her, like he was apologizing.

She had the wind knocked out of her and was scared, but not hurt. After she got back on, she was happy to just walk around.

Sundown, at that time, could compete in reined cow horse classes with anybody. You'd better have Velcro on your butt to stay with him—and yet, he would also babysit a two-year-old. He was quite a horse!

Janie on Sundown, with daughter Lisa on front of saddle. Taken after Sundown won the Parent Pleasure at the Lake County Fair. 1969.

That same year, 1969, at the fair horse show, I entered in what was called "Parent Pleasure," and I showed Sundown with Lisa on the front of my saddle. He worked perfectly, and we won the class.

Jack's life situation changed after that, and he moved and took Sundown with him. Judy and I were very lucky to have had him in our lives.

 THE CALIFORNIA YEARS

Sugar and Baby

In 1968, Dad met an elderly Italian couple who had an Appaloosa mother-daughter duo they wanted to give away to a good home. Dad was civic-minded, and he belonged to many different organizations where he could have met them.

Sugar was the mom, and she was a big, fat, drafty-looking mare, eight years old and green-broke. I didn't like the looks of her and didn't have any dealings with her. Jerry and Dave Petray rode her some. One time, while Dave was on her, she ran a stick into her foot. They doctored her, but the foot got badly infected, and after much treatment and a large vet bill, they had to put her down.

Baby was a fairly nice-looking filly, kind of a red roan color with spots. She was maybe three or so and about 14:2 hands. She was unbroke, but had possibilities. I owned a business named Scotts Valley Training Stables at the time, so I had all the facilities to train the filly.

I spent quite a lot of time with her. I could saddle her and was ground driving her, and she was getting a pretty good handle on her. BUT she had a temper, and every once in a while, she would balk and then rear up, so I wasn't too keen to get in the saddle.

HOWEVER, my 17-year-old brother and his friends were all 10-feet-tall, bulletproof, and riding bareback horses. Jerry's best friend Rick Marshall was game to try her.

I saddled her, and I saddled Judy's big TB gelding Pete, figuring to "pony" her a little from Pete. I told Rick that she'd been driven, that she turned both ways off the snaffle, and that she knew "whoa," so if she got away, to just double her into the fence. I was mounted on Pete in the round pen and had her halter rope dallied on the horn. As soon as Rick hit her saddle, Baby reared straight up and put both front legs over Pete's neck, so I let my dallies go. She made a big jump, and Rick doubled her. Another big jump, another double, and as she came around, the inside rein broke, and Rick hit the dirt. Damn!

MAKIN' TRACKS

We made repairs and left Pete out of the equation. I held Baby while Rick eased on her, and then she was off! A repeat of the first performance, except the tack held. After about three doubles, her temper kicked in, and she reared up and then did a body slam. Fortunately, Rick was catty enough to get out from under her, and he was clear. Baby was not so good. She had slammed her head into the ground, too, and was bleeding out of both nostrils. Yikes!

I ran to the phone and called Dr. Ralph Lewis, our veterinarian. Ralph had been a Wyoming cowboy before getting hurt riding colts. As he lay in a round pen, looking at his leg—which was pointed in the wrong direction—he decided vet school was a better option. Ralph had a rather direct "bedside manner."

Of course, this was a Sunday afternoon, and I caught him just going out the door to take his family for a picnic. It took 15 minutes for him to get there, and he pulled up in his big boat of a car, along with his wife and two boys, got out, and came over.

Well, in the meantime, Baby had expired. She was dead as a doornail! Doc Lewis came over, prodded her with the toe of his boot, and said, "Kitchie-kitchie Koo, you SOB! Well, she's dead, obviously broke out her sinuses. Better get those shoes off her before she stiffens up—they look new." (They were.)

Then he got back in his car and took his family on their picnic. Later, I got a bill for $25 for the diagnosis.

So Rick's first training operation ended tragically—for him, too—as he felt terrible about the poor, dead "Baby." He'd have felt worse had he known that our intention was to give the mare to him, as he wanted a horse of his own.

I wasn't feeling sad at all, just thinking about where we were going to bury her. I told Rick, "Don't feel badly about this at all. It wasn't your fault. Better HER than you!"

But I sure was thinking, "Better YOU than me for this first wild ride!"

It just shows that, with horses, you get what you pay for, and *free* isn't *necessarily free*.

 **THE CALIFORNIA YEARS**

Judy was working as a hairdresser, and the lady who had given us these two horses was a regular client. Her husband's name was Frank. Every week, when she would come into the salon, her first words were, "How are my Sugar and Baby?"

Every week for over a year, Judy fibbed and said, "They are doing great!"

Then the old folks wanted to come and visit their horses, and Judy had to come up with more alibis and some creative lies as to why they were unavailable. Why not be more forthcoming? Rumor had it that Frank had Mafia ties, had a temper, and was nobody to mess around with.

Don't look gift horses in the mouth, they say…

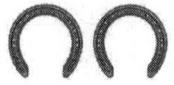 

MAKIN' TRACKS

Patchy

Patchy was my daughter Lisa's first horse. I saw an ad for him in the *Penny Saver*, went to look at him, and bought him for $125. He was a dandy. A pretty sorrel and white pinto, about 13:2 hands high, built like a Welsh, but with a lot better disposition than Butch. This was 1972, and Lisa was five years old. She started riding in front of my saddle at a very young age and was riding Sundown at age two—with supervision—in the arena. She literally grew up horseback, and she and Patchy clicked right away. He was big enough that, if he started to give her trouble, I could ride him and straighten him out.

We bought him in the spring, and that summer we took a 10-day pack trip into the Yolla Bolly Wilderness area in northern California. It was a long trip, with some long days in some rough country, but Lisa and Patchy had a great time. Phil Phelps was our experienced guide and mountaineer, as he had made many trips in there. He had two little mules about Patchy's size, named Pat and Mike, and they packed his stuff. Mary Pat Adams, a fellow teacher and friend, rode one of her horses and packed the other one. I rode Farmer on the trip. As the days went on, Patchy developed some kidney issues, so Lisa rode him bareback. Mary Pat started calling Lisa, "Little Leatherbutt," which didn't please her too much, but the nickname stuck with M.P. for years.

Another trip into the Yolla Bollys provided an interesting twist. A doe had three fawns right outside our camp, and after a day or two, she left with two of them and abandoned the third one. I now know that this was not the best thing to do, but I put the fawn across my saddle and brought it out with us. Farmer didn't care. Anyway, we got down to Covelo, bought a bottle and some goat's milk, and got some nourishment into the fawn—which took right to it and seemed to want to live. We got it home, where we kept it in the house for a while, and it was flourishing. Lisa was feeding it, and it had become a real pet. It was August, and I got a job driving pear truck. The fawn was living in the garden, shading

THE CALIFORNIA YEARS

up in the corn patch. Like many of these things, it had a bad ending. The Lyons family came driving past; their dogs flushed out the fawn; and it met a bad end. There is a lesson in this story. The doe couldn't raise it, which is why she left it. Mother Nature controls these things. All we did was prolong the inevitable and have a heartbreaking experience.

Lisa on Patchy, winning a 4-H class at Lake County Fair. 1976.

Lisa rode and showed Patchy for a good five years, and that little horse was worth his weight in gold. He was a cute little horse with a great disposition and did whatever he was asked to do.

Through horse activities, I had known Ray Neher for years. We started dating and got married in 1975, when Lisa was eight years old. We combined our horses and remained active in all kinds of activities.

MAKIN' TRACKS

Lisa on Patchy at the Lake County Fairgrounds. 1976.

A pack trip, back into the Yolla Bollys, with Ken and Jewel Ware, saw us all get caught in a tremendous thunder storm. We had started out on a beautiful sunny day, only to have a storm move in after lunch. We were right on the top of Mount Linn, at 8,098 feet, one of the highest peaks around and well above timberline. We were traveling single file and hoping no lightning would find us. Lisa was riding in front of me—we took her double Navajo blanket out from under her saddle, and she was wrapped up in it, like a little Indian. As we rode, I couldn't help thinking, "Does lightning strike the front, middle, or end of a line of riders?"

I was well aware of all the metal we and our horses were wearing, and I finally put my hand on top of my silver horn cap, so it wouldn't shine up so obviously... The guardian angels were with us that day, and we made it back to camp.

Lisa gained a lot of confidence riding Patchy, and he did a good job of taking care of her. One time she was riding him at a fast gallop down through the pear orchard towards Aunt Clydia's

THE CALIFORNIA YEARS

house (she lived in Shelden and Alice Deacon's house by then), and it seemed to Lisa like Patchy was going to duck under a big apple tree. Instead of riding it out or fighting him for his head to turn him, she decided to jump off. She jumped, but held onto his lead rope. She landed close to his feet and was drug a ways in the dirt. Patchy stopped, turned, and put his head down to look at her like, "What the heck are you doing down there?" Since she was bareback, her next challenge was to get back on!

A lot of the same adventures Pam and I had as kids were repeated by our children, as the neighborhood remained pretty much unchanged. Lisa, Steph, and Chris all had their pinto ponies, and all spent time in Scotts Creek—just like their mothers. The creek is lined with wild blackberry bushes, and in August the picking is easy—and easily done from horseback. The girls amused themselves by swimming, picking blackberries, and then using the berry juice to draw Indian designs on their horses. The white parts all got purple Indian symbols painted on—and the girls had plenty of purple marks, too.

One time, the three girls went down to the creek. Pam didn't know where they went, but of course knew the creek bottom like the back of her hand. The girls had raided their grandmother's cupboard and had a box of Fruit Loops they were snacking on. They were busted, as Pam rapidly tracked their cereal trail to the latest "fort," and they were all escorted back home.

Lisa says one time they got seven kids on Patchy. She helped boost six Littrell kids on him, then stood on something, and took the last perch on his tailhead. That's a load for a 13:2-hand Welsh Pony.

A story I *just* heard about was evidently an annual event for the valley riders of Lisa's generation. They held an annual rotten pear fight—guerrilla warfare on horseback—in one of the pear orchards in September when there were lots of rotten pears under the trees. It was a pitch-and-run war, with much mounting and remounting for fresh ammunition. Lisa says she, Pam's girls, the Littrell kids, and Carolyn Fullerton were all involved. This is a messy but fun form of country kid entertainment. Wish I had seen

MAKIN' TRACKS

them! (Reminds me of the chicken gut fight we had in Patten's pear orchard when I was a kid!)

Patchy put up with Lisa's costume class adventures. One year, he was a ghost and was decked out in several sheets for Halloween. Another time, he wore a life preserver around his neck and swim goggles on his eyes. Lisa rode in her bathing suit. He was a good first pony. The only difficulty Lisa remembers having with him was getting him to take his left lead—a minor defect, compared to Butch and all his bad habits!

In 1977, I gave Sissy to Lisa, and Judy's daughter Marta got Patchy for Christmas.

Judy remembers Marta giving Patchy a "Make-Over" one time. He was happily eating on the lawn, while getting a "pedicure." (Judy was a licensed cosmetologist for years, you may have noticed her hair color changes in her photographs, and Marta became one, too—maybe this is where Marta found her calling?) Marta was sitting between Patchy's legs, holding up his foot, and using her mother's good manicure scissors to cut the rough edges off Patchy's frogs. A later check on Marta and Patchy revealed his total transformation, as Marta had expanded into Judy's make-up kit. Patchy had lipstick, rouge, eyebrows, and mascara on his eyelashes. Judy says this took a big toll on her professional products, and her scissors were never the same.

Judy also remembers a time at Moranda's arena, when Patchy displayed a new talent—jumping. There was a fake rock wall jump—fairly large being three feet high and three feet wide. Marta and the other kids were goofing around in the arena, when Judy saw a bareback Marta on a roached Patchy, with his mane hand holt already missing from use, heading at a gallop for the rock wall. She was afraid to yell, as they were close enough to be committed. Patchy, with a happy, alert look, sailed over the jump with ease, carrying a laughing Marta. Judy says it was a surprise to see Patchy enjoying the jump, because he had always seemed a little lazy.

Judy says Patchy's eating habits helped save Grampa's big barn in 1981. A huge fire came east, clear from Mendocino County, became a firestorm, and burned my place up—right before I

THE CALIFORNIA YEARS

moved to Montana. Patchy had a tendency to founder, so he was dry docked at the big barn and ate that hillside vegetation down to the bare dirt, giving the CalFire guys enough of a firebreak to save the barn. Anyway, we give Patchy credit with helping the firemen save the barn.

This was the first firestorm any of us had ever seen. There is a decided atmospheric change when a fire becomes a firestorm, and once you experience it, you will never forget it. It had already happened, and my house and all its contents were burning, as we rushed to try and save the barn. Believe it or not, the dry horse manure in the green field across the road from the barn was spontaneously lighting and smoldering in the green grass. It makes no sense—there was no heat or flame to cause it; it was atmospheric electricity, somehow. This is off the subject, but I saw the same phenomena, in 2000, in Montana.

After we moved to Montana in 1981, Patchy began having health issues and was getting progressively worse. Judy had to make the hard decision to put him down. We all get faced with this decision for our horses and pets, and it is never easy, but it is a final gift we can give them when they are suffering. With horses, one can have a veterinarian euthanize them with chemicals, or they can be humanely shot. Because Pete's chemical death had not gone smoothly, Judy chose to end Patchy's life with a bullet.

Patchy got to go out onto the green pasture he had been kept from for years and then had a last supper of apples and oats. He died immediately and, we think, happily. He is buried in the green fields, where he always wanted to be.

> Note: In the hills, if a horse got knocked off the trail and rolled out of sight, we were prepared to shoot it, if need be. I have always been grateful for the article I read somewhere that explained how to do it properly. If you draw an imaginary line from the right ear to the left eye, and from the left ear to the right eye, and place a bullet right where the lines intersect, the horse will die immediately. All horsemen should be prepared to do this, if necessary.

Skip aka Skip Past

Skip Past was Ray's mare, and she was nine years old in 1975. She was a well-bred AQHA mare by Palleo Star by Palleo Pete by Leo. She also had Joe Reed breeding. She was a bright sorrel with some white on her face. She had injured her knees somewhere, and they had large knots on them. She was a good saddle horse and gentle, but we mostly kept her in foal and producing QH babies.

She had a sorrel filly Miss Torepast in 1976, a bay filly Drift Past in 1977, and a bay filly Chug Past in 1978.

One memory I have of her was hooking her up to a buggy to see if she would drive. I was going to be the outrider on Sissy to catch Skip if she didn't like the idea. Ray had the lines. Old Skip drove like a seasoned veteran, but Sissy was scared to death and ran off with me. That wasn't what we expected—and Sissy was always scared of buggies and carts after that.

We gave Skip to a good friend, who continued her life as a broodmare.

THE CALIFORNIA YEARS

Sissy aka Famed Miss Fancy in CA

Sissy was Ray's horse. He got her when he was living in Fall River Mills, California. He bought her as a youngster, with the hopes she would be 16 hands, like her mother. He was a good-sized guy and was doing a lot of roping, and that is what he had in mind for her.

She was a gorgeous liver chestnut mare with a trickle of white down her face, but she did not grow to expectations, being about 15 hands tall. She had beautiful QH conformation and more heart than two horses.

When she was three, Ray tied onto a bull at Tino Luccetti's and asked Sissy to pull him out of a mud hole. She did, but at a cost to her legs. She popped wind puffs on her front pasterns, which she had for the rest of her life. They never bothered her, but they were very unsightly. They were evidence of her *try*.

Ray roped on her for a few years. He and Tom Kirkpatrick were great friends and roping buddies. Tom and Sharon had regular team ropings at their indoor arena in those days.

Ray started riding other horses, and I started riding Sissy. I might say here that Ray was a rough and tumble cowboy. He could ride, but he had no finesse with horsemanship and was hard on both his horses and himself. Sissy and I were both lucky that I got her, I think.

She had a good handle, but was hard mouthed and scared of the bit, as Ray's rein hands were awful, and when he roped, he just hauled on her. One exception to Ray's lack of fine horsemanship was he could put a really fast walk on a colt. Every horse he ever rode could WALK, and Sissy was no exception. He had the gift of giving them a bump with his legs at just the right time to get a little faster, longer stride in their step.

I enjoyed riding Sissy. She could really cover the country and was extremely sure-footed. She was also tough as a boot. One time I got her high-centered in a brush patch, and she had her hind legs entangled in some buck brush. I got off her, slithered through the bushes, and was directly under her stomach. She knew I was there to help her and let me crawl around under her, getting her hind legs free, so she could go. It wasn't easy, but she was calm and patient, and we got out of the jam. Some of that brush in the Coast Range Mountains can be 10 to 12 feet high, and it grows thicker than hair on a dog's back.

My dad knew all the old trails and showed us where they were. They had not been cut out for years. Ray and I spent hours opening them back up, and many horsemen enjoyed the benefit of that.

One trail we opened was on the back side of Scott Mountain; it went down a really steep, brushy side hill into the headwaters of Scotts Creek. We were going in there to camp overnight, but didn't get an early enough start, and it got dark on us. AND the batteries were dead in the flashlight. AND it was in the dark of the moon. AND by the time we were halfway down the steep slide into the creek, it was so dark you couldn't see your hand in front of your face—literally!

I thought I knew more than Sissy and got off to lead her. All at once, she wouldn't lead. She locked up and wouldn't go. Thank goodness, I was smart enough to trust my horse! I got back on her, and she turned, found the trail, and took us down to the creek. The next morning, I found where she had stopped me. A few more steps, and I would have fallen over a sheer rock cliff, about 100 feet to the creek. Always trust your horse's instincts and eyesight over your own!

This is the kind of situation where Charlie Russell's adage, "Never spur your horse in the dark," came from! Through lots of hours and miles, I finally got Sissy to relax her mouth fears. I started riding her in my Fleming bit with Santa Barbara cheeks and a Mona Lisa mouthpiece. She liked it, and the balance of that bit helped put a nice headset on her. I rode both Sissy and Hemi with that bit and had great results.

I grew up in "vaquero country." I like good, well-balanced, silver-mounted bits, rawhide reins with a romal, some silver on my headstalls and saddles, and tightly woven, all wool, double Navajo blankets. I also like real mohair cinches. I have been a

THE CALIFORNIA YEARS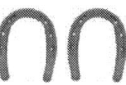

serious student of good horsemanship my whole life and like to look good while riding well. California-style gets the job done and presents a pretty "picture" doing it. (Yes, I am prejudiced.)

> Note about tack: When you ride hard in steep country for hours and in hot weather, your horses need natural fibers next to their skin. I have found out the hard way that, if your tack won't "breathe," it will blister your horse.

One thing I didn't give Sissy credit for was her speed. She could RUN, and she was fearless. I was, too, in those days, so at times, it was a deadly combination. One time, I got in a horse race—up on the range. It was during a Horsemen's trail ride, and adult beverages were being consumed... Anyway, bets were made, and several horses were matched up against Sissy. The start was made at the head of Fee's Opening—a fairly level, grassy open area, with oak trees, and a jeep road—which leads to a trail. She beat everyone to the trail, and when she hit it, she did not feel the need to slow down. She took it like a rabbit, and I was ducking and dodging brushy overhangs and tree limbs at a rapid pace. Everyone else lost their nerve and quit us, so we were the winner! Looking back, I think, "Damn lucky winner," as that ride makes me shudder today... I have had good horses *and* good graces!

And I will state unequivocally that, overall, Sissy was the best horse I have ever had the privilege to ride. She was a pleasure to know and was a BIG horse in a small package. She had pride, a regal carriage, and self-confidence. When you rode her, you were HORSEBACK!

Sissy's first colt was a dandy. He was foaled in 1977. I don't remember the stallion we used, but he was a beautiful, chestnut stud colt. He was a handful, too. We tried right from the first to handle him, but he wasn't really happy about it, and he was a muscular, strong colt. When we finally got a halter on him, after a huge struggle, we foolishly decided to leave it on him. That was a terrible, terrible mistake! He and his mother were in a small pole corral, which also had Grampa's old squeeze chute in it. Sometime in the night, the colt tried to rub his halter off or maybe just scratch his head on the pipe arm of the head catch. In doing so, he ran the pipe through his halter and was caught fast. From the looks of the torn-up ground, he put up a ferocious struggle and eventually got his nylon halter off. But he paid a horrible price. When we found him, he was in excruciating pain, standing with his head down and making ghastly wheezing sounds.

(This makes my stomach turn over as I write this.) In his fight, his ribs had struck a hook that was on the side of the squeeze chute, and he had torn a piece of rib out, and his lung cavity was exposed. He was partly breathing through his side. It was just sickening!

I got hold of Dr. Wasson, and he came out to see what he could do for him. He didn't hold out too much hope for his survival, but he sewed the lung covering tissue back together, then wired the hole in his rib cage shut, sutured what he could of the outside hide, and filled him full of long-lasting antibiotics. It was rather a miracle, but the colt made it. He had a dip in his side right where a cinch would go, so it was questionable if he would ever make it as a saddle horse. It doesn't take a genius to figure out what the lesson is in this story... And I have NEVER left a halter on a colt again. I don't turn ANY of my animals out with halters, for that matter.

That spring was a tough one, as we also found out Ray had terminal lung cancer. That summer, he went downhill fast and passed away in September. (More about this in Hemi's chapter.)

I gave Sissy to Lisa for Christmas that year, and I gave her colt to Tino Luccetti, who was a good friend, and managed a cattle ranch in Hopland, California.

Lisa got along well with Sissy and jumped right into Junior Horsemen and 4-H activities with her. Lisa was 10 years old, had been horseback since before she could walk, and was already a good hand with a horse.

Lisa's stories about her horse:

I remember the first time I rode Sissy. We were in Hopland at Tino Luccetti's place working cattle, and the adults were at the

THE CALIFORNIA YEARS

corrals and working the chute. I remember being told very sternly that I was to be very careful and watch my hands and feet, etc., etc. I was cautious at first and so very excited I almost couldn't contain myself. I went out across the field below the house. I tested the waters. I gave her a leg, and she went one way; then I gave her the other leg, and she moved the other way. I asked her to go faster, then slower, and turn circles. She knew what I wanted before I even asked. I was in love. I remember thinking, "Oh-my-god, this is the most wonderful horse, ever!" She was alert, attentive, and willing to do anything. I went back to the corrals where everyone else was working cattle. I was thrilled. This was the beginning of a long and wonderful friendship.

Lisa on Sissy. 4th of July Parade, Lakeport, California. 1980.

I remember bugging Mom for months to let me have Sissy. I had Patchy at that time and was *so* ready to move up. Finally, she sat me down and said I could have her, but there was one condition—I had to give Patchy to Marta. I remember thinking that I wanted to have both. Then, after much thought, and Mom repeatedly asking me if I was sure, I said, "Yes." After all, Patchy was still in the family; it wasn't like he was leaving forever.

MAKIN' TRACKS

I spent many hours with Sissy. She got her mane and tail braided so many times and in so many different ways that I am surprised it all didn't fall out. She was horrible to catch, but she sure did teach me perseverance, strategy, and patience. I remember spending over an hour to catch her on many occasions.

Sissy loved to swim and loved the water. We would go up to the lake above the house and take the horses swimming. You could point her at the water, and kick her into a trot or lope, and she would head straight to the water. At the edge, she would give a jump and dive in. Her whole head would go under, and she would swim, come up and blow water and air out of her nose, and just keep going. It was awesome! I would just hang on and enjoy the ride. We would take turns holding onto her tail or mane or each other, and she would swim and swim. We would also just go out into a deep hole, "park" her, and use her for a diving board. She would just stand there.

When I got her, I couldn't get on her bareback by myself. She was patient with me as I tried and tried, doing belly flops against her side. Finally, I learned to grab her mane and swing up on her. I pulled out plenty of her mane before I learned.

One day, I was mad or upset, and Sissy was in a corral down at the bottom of the driveway. I went down there and got on her with no halter, no nothing, and laid on her, backwards. This was something I had done many times, but this time, I was feeling sorry for myself, and she must have known it. She let me lay there for a bit, and then moved just enough to dump me on the ground. I got up, mad and betrayed. She didn't move or leave; she just looked at me. So, yes, I figured out I needed to get over myself. I gave her a big hug and changed my attitude... Well, for the moment...

I was good friends with Steph and Chris Sorenson. Their mom Pam was a longtime friend of Mom's. Anyway, I heard Mom tell about her and Pam jumping their horses off the loading chute, so we had to try it. It was fun, but we were so scared we would get caught that we only did it once.

THE CALIFORNIA YEARS

Lisa and Sissy, displaying their ribbons. 1980.

Lisa in 4-H outfit, getting ready to show Sissy. 1981.

I was in the Junior Horsemen Drill. I started with Patchy, who was great, but not nearly as athletic as Sissy, so when I started riding her, I moved up in my position on the team. I got to be the center pivot horse and got to do more intricate positions, which made me a better horseman.

 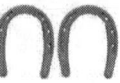

MAKIN' TRACKS

One clear memory is about a time when Chris, Steph, and I rode to the fairgrounds, which is a five-mile ride. We used all the back roads and cut-across trails, so we could go fast. We made an adventure out of it. Anyways, we got to the fairgrounds early and decided to put the horses in stalls, walk to Safeway, and get something to drink. We left our tack on a hay bale in front of the stalls and walked to the store. When we came back, our bridles were gone! Boy, did we freak out! We knew we were in trouble!

We called Mom on the pay phone. We searched everywhere. When Mom got there, we were in trouble... I got grounded for a month, and there was hell to pay!

After about two weeks, I had to get something out of the truck, and I saw my bridle behind the seat! Mom had shown up while we were gone and decided to teach us a lesson about appreciating and taking care of our stuff.

Back to Jane:

These were silver-mounted headstalls and bits. The bit Lisa was using was old and especially valuable. She got it much later, as an adult, for her birthday. I'll bet she doesn't leave it lying around anymore...

Back to Lisa:

Sheri Goss and I had an obstacle course with jumps set up along the creek bottom by her house in Kelseyville. After I got Sissy, boy, did that step up my game. She was fast and agile, and we would race to see who could get through the creek bottom fastest. She would race at crazy speeds, through the trees and brush. I hung on, with pure pleasure!

I wanted to run her in gymkhana events, and Mom made me teach her the right way. This started our journey to learn barrels, poles, etc.

 THE CALIFORNIA YEARS

Hemi aka Ms. Hemorrhoid in CA

In May of 1976, Ray, Lisa, and I loaded up our pickup camper and headed to Bishop Mule Days—the biggest mule and donkey show in California. We were going as spectators, along with a group of Lake County friends. It was an adventure.

We had fun camping out, enjoying the show, visiting with friends, and making new ones. Ray met and befriended a lady named Ann Greer at a gas station on the way down there. We were fueling up, as was Ann, and she had a mule in her trailer, which Ray had to check out. Whoa! Big discovery! The mule in the trailer was an iron-grey mule with a lighter color face; color-wise, a dead ringer for our friend and neighbor Sharon Kirkpatrick's new QH filly, Arctic Witch.

Immediately, Ray wanted that mule so he could show up at home with it and offer to ride "matched pairs" with Sharon. Well, Ann said that "Drifter" was not for sale, but that she had his full sister, a year younger, at home in Woodland, California, and she would sell her. She said the mules were the same color.

Well, nothing would do but we had to go look at "sister" on the way home. It was fairly dark when we got to Ann's house, and we looked at the mule with a flashlight. She was jumpy as a wild deer, but was a color match for Arctic Witch. Ann said that an "old vaquero" had started the mule, but that she was "pretty skittish." That was an understatement! Anyway, Ray had to have the mule, and he bought her for $375. We made a date to come back and get her.

That mule was much more than skittish—she was a scared-to-death psycho case! They put her in a chute, got a halter on her, and scared her into our four-horse trailer. After we got her home, we put her in Grampa's corrals, and she paced like a tiger, looking for a way out. You could not catch her, and if you tried to touch her after she was caught, she would squat and tremble. Touch her ears, and she would have a meltdown. She was terrified of being hurt. It was obvious the "vaquero" hadn't been a "whisperer."

 MAKIN' TRACKS

Ray construed all this as a challenge and began to work with her. He left the halter on her, with a 20-foot rope attached. Now, I'm not kidding when I say you needed a 10-foot pole with a hook to snag the 20-foot rope she was dragging. She was a snake! When you got the rope, if she was going away from you, you couldn't hold her—she would bolt and drag you. She was a lunatic! I thought he was crazy for buying her, and I wanted nothing to do with her!

He got her caught, tied some more rope on her halter, and tied the rope off to the bottom of a 6" x 6" corral post. Then he let her get ahead of him and make a run for it. When she hit the end of the rope, she did a flip and came down right on her nose. I thought she broke her neck. She didn't, but she had a nose like an anteater for a few days. She quit the bolting routine, though, and began to calm down some, with gentle treatment and grooming. She was never mean or vicious, and she never kicked or bit—she was just scared to death. Her father was a Mammoth jack, and her mother was a Polish-bred, grey Arabian mare, so it was no wonder she couldn't put up with abuse and was so flighty.

A few weeks went by, and Ray was riding her. She was afraid of her own shadow, though, and did some pretty good bolting and running away, at the slightest provocation. Ray was riding his Uncle Charlie Booth's saddle, with a good seat and a three-inch cantle. Ray had a breast collar and britching on her, and the saddle fit pretty well. He thought he had her going well enough to take her on a Senior Horsemen trail ride.

She went pretty good for a while, but was really nervous. Then something set her off, and she ran away in a panic. She ran Ray underneath an oak tree, which had a main branch that would just barely clear the cantle of Uncle Charlie's saddle. Ray leaned back, and his body got hung between the tree and the saddle, and she wiped him off the back end and kept going. It was a big hit and a bad wreck. Ray's belt buckle got turned inside out and bore down pretty hard on his body parts below before he came loose. I won't repeat the ensuing conversation, but he ended up in the hospital with "major bruising and contusions."

THE CALIFORNIA YEARS

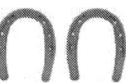

The other guys were then charged with catching the orangutan mule and getting her unsaddled. Both the mule and her reluctant handlers were petrified, but all survived.

Eventually Hemi calmed down and became safer to handle and ride—but not before she earned her full name—Ms. Hemorrhoid, the "pain in the ass" mule! She kept this full name for quite a while, too!

Of course, Ray ribbed Sharon about how well matched his new mule was to her mare. As it turned out, both animals had personality faults and were less than perfect.

Later that fall, Ray and Tom Kirkpatrick were riding up on the range. Their dogs "treed" a baby feral hog in some tree roots. To show how far Ray's mule had come—Ray put the baby pig in his saddlebags and brought it home. The mule's name was beginning to change. Tom and Sharon owned the Scotts Valley Training Stables by then, and the pig grew up there in a paddock. They named her Elvira, and she grew into a terrifically ugly sow.

As the winter drew on, Ray wasn't feeling well and was very irritable. In the spring, when he finally went to the doctor, he was diagnosed with terminal lung cancer. This was a terrible blow and a lot to take in. It had been Ray's goal to haul his mule back to Bishop Mule Days and show her, but his diagnosis shattered that idea. Although I had hardly laid a hand on her, I told him I would start riding her and see what I could get out of her. It was a bad reason to start, but was the start of the best relationship I have ever had with an animal.

For some reason, Hemi and I just "clicked." I started riding her in March and had her ready to show by the end of May, as Bishop Mule Days is always held Memorial Day weekend.

The beginning was rough, though, as that damned mule would grab her tail, take off, and run right through a snaffle bit. I finally put a double-twisted wire snaffle in her mouth and worked her over pretty hard with it when she wouldn't respond. She got a black and blue tongue, but she learned to pay attention to "whoa." My self-preservation demanded it. Hemi was my first experience with mules, and she taught me a lot.

 **MAKIN' TRACKS**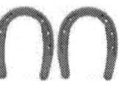

Getting Hemi ready to show in Bishop, California. This is in the Bull Ring at the Lake County Fairgrounds, at a little practice show. April 1977.

Mules are highly intelligent, have a very strong sense of survival, and take good care of themselves in tight spots. If something makes it very inconvenient or painful for them, they heed it. You want to do a lot of thinking around mules, so you don't make mistakes the FIRST time. They will accept discipline, if it is understood and justified, but they will not tolerate abuse — they will get even! Another thing: you cannot "pattern" a mule like a horse. Mules learn fast and know what you are asking them to do — but they will decide, each and every time, if they will follow directions OR NOT. You need a strong sense of humor to deal with mules and exceptional horsemanship skills to excel at it. Once you get a mule to WANT to do for you, you have it made. My good

 # THE CALIFORNIA YEARS

fortune was that Hemi learned to trust me and became my willing partner for 21 years, despite a rough start.

Tom, meanwhile, had borrowed a mule and was riding him. He and Sharon and their daughter Carolyn were planning on going to the mule show, too.

I was riding a lot at Kirkpatricks' arena to train this mule. It is a nice facility. One day, I wanted to take a break and put Hemi into one of the stalls—saddled. These are nice big box stalls with Dutch doors. The top of the bottom door is about four feet high. The next thing I knew, Hemi jumped out. She nicked my saddle horn on the top of the barn on the way out and stood on her nose—again. That mule could, and did, jump like a deer—that day and other ones, too. She could pop over a four-foot pole fence with ease—be tied on one side and pop over to the other. She was athletic!

One thing we did prior to going to Bishop, is get a bunch of t-shirts printed with the logo, "Mule Riders Do It On Their Ass," and I did artwork of a mule and rider coming to a sliding stop. We figured, if we sold them down there, we could help defray our expenses—which we did.

Ray wasn't feeling very well, but he wouldn't have missed this show for anything. Ann Greer was bringing Hemi's brother Drifter back down, and we were going to ride in Matched Pairs. I made us shirts, and we both had grey hats and chaps. I entered in a number of different classes and held my breath that Hemi was ready.

Tom Kirkpatrick did the driving to get us there and remembers having a lot of trouble with flat tires on the trailer. We pulled into one gas station, and a guy ran us off with a shotgun—so Tom had to change the flat out on the roadside. Things sometimes are just not easy...

Our first obstacle at Bishop was the facilities. The barns and stalls were full, so we had to tie up to a cyclone fence along a busy road. Hemi didn't like the traffic, and she didn't enjoy being tied out in the hot sun for four days, so her attitude kind of deteriorated as time went on.

MAKIN' TRACKS

We started out really well. Ann and I won the trophy for Matched Pairs, and the mules worked good and looked good together. We gave Ray the trophy for show and tell. There were 80 entries in the Western Pleasure class, and we made the top ten in the eliminations. Finals were scheduled for Sunday night. She did well in the trail class and went through all the obstacles. Because of some hesitations, she didn't make the finals, but I was proud of her. I got a fifth in something, but don't remember what. Anyway, Ray was happy and proud of his mule, and I was, too.

Tom and Ray got in the team roping, and it wasn't very pretty—neither mule knew what they were doing. Sharon showed in the reining class and got run away with. At a mule show, you just never know…

By Sunday night, Hemi had had it with the whole thing. She drug her feet back to the arena. We started the class, and a breeze was blowing, with trash fluttering in the fence. She felt like she was puffing up a little. She worked good going one way, but when we turned around and they asked for a lope, she refused to take her lead. I cued her four times, and she knew darned well what I was asking, but deliberately took the wrong lead. Finally, I "got" it and quit asking. She was mad, and she let me know it. I am sure people in the grandstand wondered how I could make the eliminations when I couldn't even get my lead…

Meanwhile, back at the t-shirt concession, we found we didn't have time to sell, so we turned the project over to the kids. There was Lisa, Carolyn, and two Patten boys, and I told them I would pay them a commission on their sales… Get out of the way! They swarmed the grounds like locusts—even breaking up kissing couples—to hawk their wares. They sold every shirt, and Lisa even sold the grubby one she was wearing. They all made a little money, and we financed our trip. Mule riders are generous, too!

This trip was a bittersweet journey for Ray, as he got progressively worse that summer and passed away in September. So there was a very sad reason that Hemi became mine.

With Ray gone, I had too many irons in the fire. I was teaching high school Home Ec and Vo-Ag and was an FFA advisor, along

 **THE CALIFORNIA YEARS**

with being Scotts Valley 4-H livestock advisor. Lisa was in 4-H and Junior Horsemen, and I belonged to the Senior Horsemen. We had sheep and cattle and too many horses, and we had the family acreage leased—both the pasture/hay ground and the range land. I was grieving, stressed, and burdened by responsibilities. It was a really tough time. A lot of the years from 1977 until I moved to Montana are kind of hazy. I was putting one foot in front of the other and just coping with life then.

Hemi was a salvation for me. She just continued to trust me more and more and became a refuge for my soul. I stayed busy with the horse organizations. One parade really tested her. We were organizing a Hee-Haw Float for the Fourth of July. I think this was in 1978, and I was going to be Ida Lee Nagger, the one who had curlers in her hair and was always at the ironing board. Hemi was going to be tied on behind and wear a large flowered hat. This was a BIG test for her, as she was deathly afraid of having her ears hurt.

Janie and Hemi after the Hee-Haw Float, for Fourth of July. 1978. Hemi, wearing the flowered hat, and Janie, dressed as Ida Lee Nagger.

MAKIN' TRACKS

Note: I have had many mules since moving to Montana, and a major piece of advice is this—NEVER-EVER EAR A MULE DOWN! Someone had done that to Hemi, and she never got over it. For a year and a half, I had to unbuckle her headstall, slowly bring it up behind her ears, and then re-buckle it. She finally let her ears be handled while bridling, but until she died, you did not pet her ears!

You can see from the picture, that eventually I talked her into wearing the flowered hat, but she was not happy about it, and if a flower petal touched an ear, she would dodge her head. She drug Judy and me quite a ways before we got the hat tied on, and she advertised that it was a Hee-Haw Float, by braying continuously down the parade route. Boy, was she unhappy!

In probably 1980, the Senior Horsemen were going on a four-day pack trip into the Snow Mountain Wilderness Study Area, which is between Lake Pillsbury and Stonyford. It is now the Berryessa Snow Mountain National Monument area. It is beautiful, remote country. After school let out that year, I was fried and really needed to relax, so when the guys packed in the horse feed the week before the ride, I took Hemi and Drifty and my own supplies, went in, and stayed a week by myself. It was a vacation I needed! I rode every day, leading Drifty, and explored a lot of the area. By this time Hemi was no longer a "hemorrhoid" and was a real pleasure to ride. She was like riding a ballerina she was so light and agile on her feet. My Don Bentley saddle fit her well, and we got along fine with no crupper or britching. I almost hated to see everyone else show up a week later, as the beauty and solitude of the mountain were so restful and quiet.

Much of the time during this period, I saddled Hemi and lead Drifty—which is the reason Drifty never really got the training she deserved and never got past "well started."

That fall, Hemi took me into the Yolla Bolly Wilderness with friends. Again, Drifty packed the grub, and again, I had a wonderful, flawless trip aboard Hemi.

 THE CALIFORNIA YEARS

She was getting pretty well trained by the time we were ready to pull up stakes. She could run barrels and poles well enough to compete with the horses, and I was doing a little penning on her, as well as showing in pleasure and trail. She was good!

Hemi and Janie in Yolla Bolly Wilderness, leading Drifty. 1980.

 MAKIN' TRACKS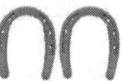

I entered her in some classes at the Lake County Fair. Their policy was that, to get premium checks, the animals exhibited must be stabled on the grounds for the run of the fair. This is so the spectators would have a lot of animals to see. Well, Hemi did not like the confinement of stalls and, as pointed out, could jump out at will—especially the old, low-doored fairground stalls. If I was there, she was okay, but I had to shut the top door and "jail" her up, to keep her in, if I left.

And wouldn't you know—she was just down the line from the purebred Arabians being shown. On her stall card was a place for her name and breeding, etc. Naturally, I put her "proper" name on the stall card, and on the *Breed* line, I wrote "Half-Assed Arabian." I thought it was funny, but I guess the neighbors didn't because my stall cards kept disappearing... Of course, I kept replacing them...

Hemi and Janie running barrels at Bull Ring Arena, Lakeport. 1980.

You will read more about moving to Montana in an upcoming chapter.

THE CALIFORNIA YEARS

Torepast aka Miss Torepast

Torepast was born in 1975. Her mother was Skip Past, and I don't remember who her sire was. She was a registered QH. She grew up to be a beautiful light red sorrel mare, with a star and strip on her face. She had a very nice disposition and was a pleasure to train—which I did, as she was mine from birth. It is too bad that if a horse just does what it's supposed to do and is a delight, then you don't have any "stories" to tell on them; you just have good memories.

Janie on Miss Torepast, up on family range land. Circa 1978.

 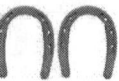

MAKIN' TRACKS

There was only one memorable episode I had with Torepast, and believe me, I learned something very important. She was two, and we were on the main ridge jeep road behind our range, so we'd ridden quite a ways. I was riding her with a snaffle and had a homemade running martingale on her. It was made out of ski rope and had two rings the reins ran through and a neck strap holding the ring straps. I learned the hard way to always use your saddle strings to secure the neck strap to your saddle. Otherwise, when your horse puts its head down to graze, the neck rope will fall forward and catch your horse right behind its ears, thus tying its head down and making it feel trapped. I have just described what happened to Torepast.

Of course, she panicked and started crow hopping. And hopping, and hopping, and hopping. She was easy to stay on—it was like riding a pogo stick—but I thought she'd never stop. When she did, I tied up her neck rope and have ALWAYS secured my martingale neck straps since then.

About 1980, Lisa had Sissy at a horse show at Lakeport, and someone wanted to buy her. When Lisa said her horse was not for sale, the lady asked if she had any other horses who might be. Lisa said to talk to me about Torepast. I really hadn't planned to sell her, but the buyer offered me a lot of money, and I took it. I had Hemi and Drifty, and I had Montana on my mind...

THE CALIFORNIA YEARS

Drifty aka Drift Past in CA

Skip Past's 1976 filly was a bay beauty named Drift Past. She was by Ken and Jewel Ware's stallion, a Driftwood-bred horse, and she had no white markings at all. As with all of Skip's foals, she had a good disposition, and we taught her to lead easily. However, she jumped right into a bad habit, as she pulled back hard from the first time she was tied and continued that behavior.

To get her to stop pulling back, we tried several things; we tied her to inner tubes, and we put a lariat around her girth and up through her halter. She didn't pull back every time she was tied — just on her own time frame. You had to always be aware that she might, and nothing we did changed that behavior. I hate that bad habit in a horse!

Drifty didn't get much attention for the first few years of her life. Ray was sick and then died, and I had Hemi and Torepast to ride. I started her and packed her some, but didn't really start riding her until I sold Torepast in 1980. Even then, I packed her more than rode her, as Hemi was such a pleasure to ride.

One incident of note happened one evening out in Grampa's pasture. Judy and Jerry went out in the horse/mule herd with a bucket of grain, expecting to catch one of them — we don't even remember which animal now. A huge fight broke out amongst the animals over the grain. Jerry was behind Drifty, and she caught his movement behind her in the dusk, thought she was under attack, and immediately lashed out with both hind legs. She caught him with both hoofs in the big muscles of his legs right above his knees and sent him flying. He hit writhing and moaning, and saying he thought his kneecap was torn off. He was lucky to "only" have been badly bruised.

None of us have ever taken grain into a herd again. I show it to them from outside the pen, leave it outside the fence, and expect my animals to be caught BEFORE they get a treat. This is a much safer way to do it. When Drifty saw it was Jerry she kicked, she seemed surprised at her target. When horses start vying for feed, they completely lose track of the humans in the "herd," and their kick packs a punch and can be lethal.

Judy, holding Drift Past, and riding Farmer. Maria Danforth, on mare Suzy. Picture taken in High Valley. June 1980.

Drifty packed loads through the Yolla Bollys and the Snow Mountain Reserve, and I rode her on some Horsemen rides, but when we moved to Montana, she was somewhere between "green broke" and "well started."

This is well behind my usual training goals. In my horse culture, the objective is to get a horse "straight up" in the bridle by the time they are five years old. You cannot show a horse that doesn't meet that criteria, so that created the goal. I want to ride my horse with one hand and have them light in the mouth with a good headset and responsive off my legs. The least cues I give to get the most response from my horse is my target. Ideally, a symbiosis occurs between horse and rider, and communication is subtle. Drifty never got there...

If you can't direct a horse with one hand, how do you open and close gates, throw a rope, or lead a pack string? People who are still riding a 15-year-old horse in a snaffle bit and needing two hands to direct him, should ask themselves that...

By 1981, a half-broke Drifty climbed into a trailer with Sissy, Hemi, and Suzy and began a new life adventure in Montana.

 THE CALIFORNIA YEARS

Chug aka Chug Past in CA

Chug was a 1977 filly out of Skip Past. She was a pretty, chunky bay with some white on her face, and she had a good personality. After Ray's death, I had too many horses and didn't have time for a young horse, so in 1979, I traded her to Sharon Kirkpatrick for the grey mare she had named Arctic Witch—Hemi's "twin." (She has her own story.)

Sharon hoped she would make a stock horse and sent her to Jack Adams for training. She had cow sense, but was too laid back and lazy to make a reined cow horse, so Sharon sold her to Nicky Littrell, and her story runs out.

The Witch aka Arctic Witch

Arctic Witch was a well-named mare! In 1976, Sharon Kirkpatrick bought this mare in the Sacramento Valley from a lady named Sally Semis. She was an iron-grey mare with a light grey face, about three years old, and pretty goosey. Buffer Wright had good luck training a brother to her, and Sharon was looking for a stock horse prospect. She had good conformation and was a registered Appendix QH, being half TB.

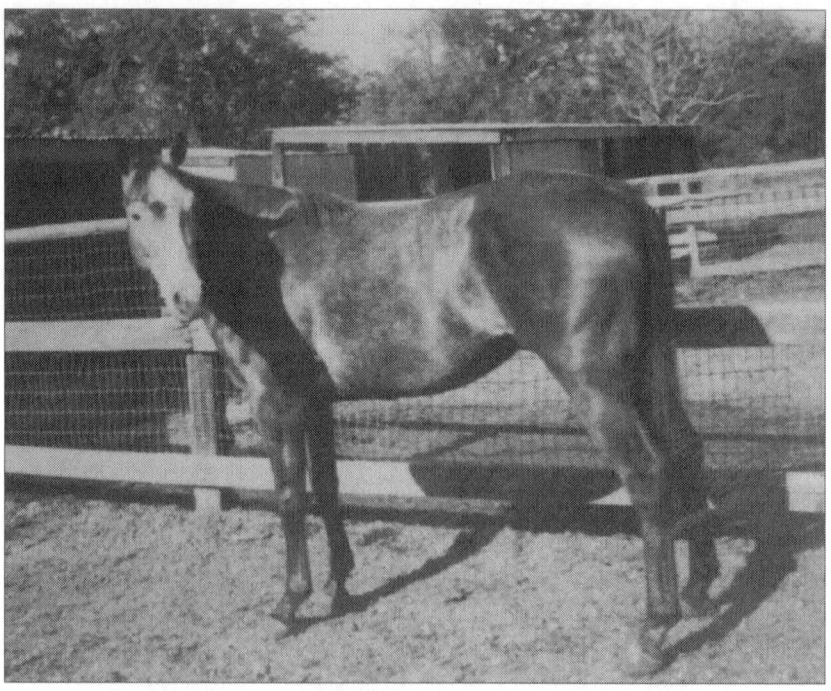

Arctic Witch, at Scotts Valley Training Stables. 1977.

Buffer started her and rode her quite a while, because Sharon wanted the "goose" out of her. She seemed to go good in the mountains, but she had bucking tendencies. Sharon took her when she thought the mare was safe and got bucked off big time—she said the mare could click the stirrups above your saddle with every jump.

 # THE CALIFORNIA YEARS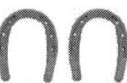

I had a nice filly named Chug Past about that time, out of Ray's good mare Skip Past, and Sharon liked the looks of her, so we traded. I was doing a lot of riding and thought I could pack the Witch and take her in the mountains and get her better broke.

That seemed to work, and I started riding her and was getting along good with her. BUT I stupidly let down my guard on a trail ride. I turned around in the saddle to talk to the person behind me and put my hand on the top of her rump. I have never been launched that fast or that high—ever. There was an explosion, and I was airborne! I did a half flip in the air and landed in the packed hard trail on the back of my neck! It stunned me, and it took me a bit to get my wits—and then my wits could see that she was bucking through a dense Manzanita patch with my good saddle...

Did I give up—no! Did I get back on—yes! Did I go to the doctor—no! Did I still want her—NO! I finished the ride, and when I got home, I called Dale Seibold, a horse trader in Williams, California, and asked him if he was interested in buying a pretty grey mare.

Anyway, Dale knew the whole story on her; knew me, Buffer, and Sharon; and traded me $600 worth of hay for her. I was glad, and my horses and mules were glad, because they ate on the Witch Son-of-a-Bitch all winter. My neck hurt for a year and a half.

I expected Dale to can her, but the last I heard of her, he sold her to a lady in the Sacramento Valley who just loved her and was riding her happily in a FLAT saddle. A tip of the hat to her; she's a better cowgirl than me!

Sharon's final words on her are, "Age probably changed her."

This could very well be. The mare had excellent foundation training, and she had lots of wet saddle blankets, but both Sharon and I had kids to raise, and sometimes it's best to just cut your losses rather than get crippled!

The Montana Years

 **MAKIN' TRACKS**

 THE MONTANA YEARS

Moving to Montana

I always had a fascination for and a desire to see Montana, Idaho, and Wyoming. I had Charles M. Russell's pictures on my bedroom walls, had read all of Will James' books, and just had a good feeling about that country.

I sold the little flock of sheep and the cattle we had and financed a trip to those states in 1978. My mother Edwyna and daughter Lisa came with me. We had a 1974 ¾-ton Ford with a big camper on the back, and that is what we traveled in. We saw some beautiful country, and I was developing a real need for a major life change as my personal losses and responsibilities were weighing heavily on me.

My two favorite places on the trip were Challis, Idaho, and the Bitterroot Valley in Montana. I made it a priority that, wherever we moved, there had to be an FFA program in their high school for Lisa. I started the Vo-Ag program at Kelseyville High School and was, and am, a strong believer in the FFA. Challis, Idaho, and Stevensville, Montana, both fit the bill.

Lisa was 11 years old, and I was a single parent, dealing with too many things to make a move at that time, but the seeds were planted, and a goal was formed. I decided I had to wait until Lisa got out of 8th grade, so she could start high school in a new place. I started liquidating, simplifying, and organizing, so that I could seriously consider it by 1981.

In June of 1981, right after school was out, a good friend Maria Danforth, her little sister Tina, and Lisa and I planned a trip. I wanted to re-visit Challis and Stevensville and seriously think of relocating to one of those places. Maria was single, 24, and ready for a change, also.

Molybdenum mining had begun around Challis since 1978, and the area was filled with mobile homes full of miners; Challis lost its appeal.

The Stevensville area and Bitterroot Valley, meanwhile, remained as beautiful and inviting as ever. We stayed in Victor

MAKIN' TRACKS

with good friends Sandy and Betsy Brooks—Betsy had been Lisa's first grade reading teacher. We had been friends since I was in 4-H and had visited her Konocti QH Ranch in Kelseyville. Anyway, we spent a week visiting and looking around at the job opportunities (kind of slim).

One night, Maria and I stepped out to see the Bitterroot social life and went to the Longbranch Saloon in Victor. Bob Wire and the Halfast Band were playing. Bob had on a cap that said, "Show Me Your t___s." Hmmm, that was different!

They actually were a good band. There was lots of dancing going on, and we were having a good time. Maria met a tall, good-looking cowboy type, Jeff Freeman, who was working as a guide/outfitter. Sparks flew!

By the time we left to go back to California, we were both ready to make the commitment to move. We quit our jobs—she worked at NAPA in Lakeport, and I taught at Kelseyville High School. Maria made arrangements to liquidate her property, and I drew out my investment in the California Teachers' Retirement Fund. My sister Judy, her boyfriend Dean, and her daughter Marta were going to live in my place while I tried out Montana.

The first part of August, we were ready to make our first "move trip." It was quite a caravan.

Maria was driving my ½-ton, cherry-red Chevy shortbox pickup. It had a homemade camper top on it, given to me by a neighbor. It was cab high and had a rack on top of it for a boat, so we put my 12-foot aluminum rowboat up there. Hooked on was an old, single-axle, one-horse trailer. It had been in Gessner Green's barn for nearly 40 years, and he gave it to me. It was a relic—open-topped with wooden sides, and it sported a very old, yellow and black California license plate. We completely loaded it with packed boxes.

I was driving the '74 Ford pickup. It had a flatbed and stock racks. We double decked it so it had packed boxes, hay, water buckets, and hoses on the upper deck, and the lower deck was full of Lisa's registered Hampshire sheep. I was pulling a matching green, Stidham four-horse trailer, with Sissy, Hemi, and Drifty in it, plus Maria's big mare Suzy. It was the "California Clampetts," off to Montana!

We stayed the first night at the fairgrounds in Winnemucca, fed and watered the sheep on the truck, and put the horses and mule in a corral for the night. We all slept in the camper shell of the ½-ton.

The next day, the Ford started making some racket from underneath. I got out and looked under there, but couldn't see anything wrong, so we kept going. About five miles north of Shoshone, Idaho, the racket under the truck became deafening, and then the driveline fell onto the road. I had just enough momentum to top a little rise and steer into a driveway to the left. We coasted part way down the hill towards a ranch with a number of outbuildings. Maria followed behind me. We got out and walked down to a shop, where we saw a guy's legs under a tractor. He heard us coming, backed out, and stood up. I can't imagine his shock in seeing our invasion and hearing that we were "stuck" in his driveway. Bad enough, the rag-tag outfit, but the vehicles were all plastered with California license plates! Poor man!

He was very congenial and offered to look and see what was wrong with the truck. He immediately said the U-joint on the drive train had broken. Bless him, he said, "I'll call the NAPA store in Shoshone, tell them what you need, and get them to stay open for you until you get there." Then he added, "I can fix that for you."

We couldn't believe our bad luck, followed by such good news! We drove to Shoshone, got the part, and went back to the ranch. He had me pull down on the flat by his shop. He crawled under the truck and, within a short time, had it fixed. He would take no money for his help and wished us well. We were back on the road well before dark. He was crawling back under his tractor when we left.

I don't even know that man's name, but will be forever grateful to him. I'm sure getting rid of us in a hurry might have been part of his motivation, but what he did for us was priceless. It shows why the Code of the West, which most ranchers live by,

 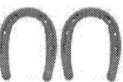

is really based on the Golden Rule and is what makes country people very special.

That night, because of our breakdown, we were driving after dark, and we could see we weren't going to make it to Challis. We were somewhere near Mackay, and I was really sleepy. That is a windy, narrow road, and I could not find a wide spot to pull off in. It had to be about 10 p.m., and we saw lights on in a ranch house. I pulled into their driveway and knocked on their door. Again, a rancher came to our aid and gave us permission to park in his barnyard for the night. We left the horses in the trailer. In the morning, there was frost on the ground, and our horses and mule were shivering, as they had California summer hair. We found out later that Mackay is 5,900 feet in elevation, so we picked cold country to stop in. We felt badly for our animals and draped our sleeping bags over them for warmth when we started down the road.

Posing under the Montana highway sign, in 1981.
L to R: Tina Danforth, Lisa, Maria Danforth, and Jane.

 **THE MONTANA YEARS**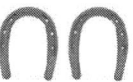

Fortunately, we made it to Victor, Montana, and the Brooks Ranch without further incident. We left the red pickup and trailer, the horses and mule, the sheep, and some packed boxes at Sandy and Betsy's. We had a back load of black Angus heifers to take to California from the Shearbrook Ranch in Stevensville.

Sandy and Betsy Brooks, Victor, Montana. They provided a place to stay, advice, and pasture for our animals, when we moved to Montana. Betsy also found us a place to rent. We count them as wonderful friends! 1979.

Jeff and Maria had been corresponding since their June meeting, and Jeff offered to help us drive the cattle to California. We were happy to take him up on it, because we were planning to drive straight through—about a 24-hour trip. Our planned route took Hwy 93 south to Wells, went west on I-80 to Reno, and then took Hwy 20 into Lake County. North of Wells, both Maria and I went to sleep, and Jeff was driving. He came to a stop, woke us up, and said, "We're in Ely, where do I go from here?" ELY? ELY? What happened to Wells?

That was an instant wake-up! We got out a map, got our bearings, saw an east-west road across Nevada—Hwy 50—and

 MAKIN' TRACKS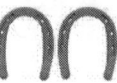

decided to take it rather than drive the 138 miles back up to Wells. If you look on the map, it is 319 miles from Ely to Reno, and the road is a roller coaster, up, down, up, down, around and around through desolate old mining country. It is named "The Loneliest Road" in Nevada for very good reasons. I can say I saw it once.

What a trip on those poor heifers. Up and down, back and forth, and it got HOT! They really needed water, but I couldn't do much about it. We were lucky to get gas.

We saw a motel/restaurant/bar alongside the road. There was a water hydrant with a hose attached outside. We stopped, and I went inside to see if I could squirt the cattle down and maybe help them cool off a little. There was one person inside—behind the bar. I introduced myself, told him of my situation, and asked if I could use some water on the cattle. He looked me in the eye and said one word, "NO." Of course I didn't expect that, and I just stood there speechless. He looked me straight on and repeated himself, in a little louder manner. No explanation at all. I stood there like a dummy for a little bit, thinking maybe he would say why, and then left. I'm still wondering WHY???

We made it back to Lake County and delivered the cattle, and they came through the trip fine. Hauling them gave us gas money, so it was worth the extra effort.

Maria and Jeff were at her house, madly packing away. I had everything pretty well packed up, had the truck backed up to the porch of my house—a double wide—and had loaded up some boxes, but had taken a break before loading furniture, because it was so hot and muggy. We were keeping an eye on a brush fire in Mendocino County to the west. It had been burning for a couple of days, but was looking really ominous and building a lot of smoke. Judy, Marta, and Dean were there, as they had moved a lot of their things in as I was moving out. Danny Patten was there, too, to help load the heavy stuff. We all decided to take a drive up on the range to check the fire. Holy Smoke—and unholy smoke, too! That fire was coming at us almost faster than we could drive, and we hauled *** as fast as we could back home.

 # THE MONTANA YEARS

We turned on hoses and sprinklers and set a backfire to the west of us as soon as we saw the fire get past our neighbors. The brush burned like we'd poured gasoline on it. It was burning away from the house, making a firebreak; then the wind changed, and a wall of flame at least a hundred feet high was coming right at us. Everyone ran as fast as they could to their vehicles. Judy, Dean, and Marta got to her truck first, and by the time she was driving out, flames were on both sides of her. Lisa and I were right behind her in the Ford. Danny had parked his rig over by the tack shed, and by the time he got to it, the oxygen had burned out of the air, and it wouldn't start. He ran and jumped in the back of my truck, and we all powered through the flames to get to the county road. It was a close call! The volunteer firemen and their trucks were down there on Hendricks Road. They were watching with field glasses and told me, "Your house is completely engulfed and burning!" My God!

We knew we had to get on down the road and try and save Grampa's big barn. A self-appointed pipsqueak from the local radio station told us we weren't allowed to drive down the road. As you can imagine, I was in no mood for THAT right then. I wanted to slug him in the nose so bad! Instead, my language was VERY unladylike, and I told him to get out of my way or I'd run over him! Good thing for him, HE GOT.

I have told some about this fire in Patchy's story. His grazing habits helped the firemen, and they saved the big barn and the nursery barn down the road.

The strange atmosphere of the firestorm moved the fire in weird ways, and it set fires a mile ahead of itself. It burned right up to the back of houses in Lakeport five miles away. It covered a good 35 miles, from a little east of Ukiah to Lakeport, and was started by some kids playing with matches.

The way my house burned down was really strange, too. I had quite an area of "defensible space" in the back yard—a big, well-watered lawn, with a dirt road on the other side. The flames from the fire never reached the house, but in our hurry to get out of there, we had left the back door open. The heat and atmospheric conditions created spontaneous combustion inside it, and it literally exploded into flame. Once a fire starts in a mobile home, it's a goner!

So, when I moved to Montana, I only THOUGHT I was a burned-out school teacher. I was REALLY BURNED OUT when I got here. Good thing for us that Maria had all her household goods. Judy and Dean were badly affected, too, as that fire cleaned us all out. What a mess!

After something like this happens, you find out if you had enough insurance... I didn't, and my loss was MUCH greater than my policy paid. Another sad lesson learned! But I collected what I could, put it in the bank, and LEFT CALIFORNIA for good!

Betsy, being such a good friend, had been watching the papers for us and had found a 2-story, 3-bedroom log house on 10 acres for us to rent. It was on Sunset Bench, which is on the east side of the Bitterroot Valley, about five miles from Stevensville. It was a Montana dream home, with big picture windows giving us a panoramic view of the Bitterroot Mountains. It was far enough off the road for privacy, was fenced, and had an established garden and a good eight acres of irrigated pasture for our animals. Plus, we had Gene Magini for a landlord and neighbor. He and his wife Mary were wonderful old time ranchers and the nicest people in the world!

A day or two before we got there, a Ravalli County Electric Co-Op lineman, Ric Brown, was up our power pole and was about to cut off the power to our "new" house—for nonpayment by the previous tenants. Gene knew from talking to Betsy that we were on our way, but he had never met us. He told Ric, "People are on their way with all their household goods, and they will need their power when they get here. If they don't pay, I WILL!"

Ric checked with the company, and his boss said, "If Gene Magini says leave the power on, LEAVE IT ON!"

Boy, were we lucky! We were also lucky that Gene and Mary allowed Jeff to also be part of our group, as he and Maria were now "an item." I'm sure they thought we were a band of Hippies!

 # THE MONTANA YEARS

We got to Montana in time to get Lisa enrolled in school and in the FFA, so she was able to jump right in and show her sheep at the Ravalli County Fair, which is always Labor Day weekend. She was able to make friends that way, even before school started.

Jeff had a job with Spence Trogden's 4T Outfitters and was busy packing in camps, etc., right away. Maria couldn't get a job at the local NAPA, which was disappointing, and I was overqualified to get a teaching job, as money is always tight in small schools, and they could hire two kids right out of college for what they would have to pay me.

Suzy, Maria Danforth Freeman's mare, with her mule colt, Slim.

When September rolled around, we saw a wanted ad in the newspaper, where Swanson Ranch needed apple pickers. We knew, if we could pick pears and walnuts in California, we could darn sure pick apples in Montana—and we did. Charlie Swanson's grandfather had planted the original orchard in 1910, and those old trees were gargantuan. It was a little scary reaching out off the top of 12-foot ladders to pick some of those trees, but we did it.

MAKIN' TRACKS

After that, the young orchard planted by Charlie was a piece of cake to pick. After the apples were picked, we sorted them. Then they needed cider makers. Then Lois Swanson needed house cleaning. Then Charlie needed pipe picked up. Then there was plowing to be done. Maria hadn't driven tractor much, so I got the plowing job.

I have driven tractors since I was 12 years old, but never a NICE tractor—always old, open air tractors. Charlie's big Ford with the cab was a revelation! It had a four-bottom plow with a hydraulic turn-over and AMENITIES! The wind would blow, and I never felt it. It got cold, and I turned on the heater. It started to sleet, and I turned on the windshield wipers—and I listened to the radio! I called Dad and told him what a REAL tractor was like to drive!

When Charlie needed help in the spring with pruning, he called and asked if I could help him—but he could only pay $3 an hour and lunch. His wife Julie is a very good cook, so I went to pruning. One day, a spring blizzard blew in, and it was snowing so hard you couldn't see the tops of the trees. I said to Charlie, "Now I see why you don't have migrant farm labor up here—you can get college graduates to work for half of what they get!"

Maria got a job in the Mighty Nice Bakery in Stevensville, and I helped the Brooks feed cattle, calve, and lamb. About March, Sandy and I went to the Shearbrook Ranch annual bull sale. I had just joined the local saddle club, and they were serving lunch there.

Well now, doesn't the Universe work in mysterious ways? There was a very good-looking man there who I had not seen. A neighbor, Paul O'Leary, said, "Have you two neighbors met yet?"

When we said we hadn't, he introduced me to Eric Lambert, who had been working in Baker, Montana, and was now home—in the house directly east of, and adjacent to, my place. Wow! My next-door neighbor—single, good looking, and right next door! Thanks, Paul!

As you can guess, we began dating... Right about when I thought I was going to starve out of Montana, Eric found two jobs—one for Archie Remoir as an equipment operator on a

THE MONTANA YEARS

transmission power line Eric was building, and the other for me to milk Archie's cows, since he was going to be running a crane.

The cow milking job was great. I milked at 6 a.m. and 6 p.m., and the rest of the day was mine. There was a pasture for my horses and mule and a small house with all utilities paid. Lisa became best friends with Archie's daughter Lisa, and the two Lisas were peas in a pod and hell on wheels!

I milked cows until the next fall and then took a one year, Vo-Ag teaching job at Big Sky High School in Missoula, filling in for Mike Cavey, who took a sabbatical.

Looking back on all this, I'm amazed that Maria and I had the nerve to just pull up stakes like that. She says, "I knew we could do it!"

I'm sure glad she was right. I guess it shows that you need to follow your instincts, because that is a higher power, giving directions. When those directions seem clear and strong, take the trail, and trust yourself!

I'm darned glad I grew up on a ranch, because it sure wasn't my education that fed Lisa and I here; it was ranch experience and the strong work ethic that comes with that, which enabled me to make it in Montana.

We also knew enough to keep our mouths shut when we got here. We knew no one cared how they did it in California. We all made a pact to show up, observe how they did it in Montana, and quietly copy that. It worked.

Note: That spring, Jeff and Maria got married. They moved on, had two children Callie and Chance, and eventually started their own outfitting business in Clinton, Montana. Maria's mare Suzy became the proud dam of two mule foals, Slim and Salty.

 MAKIN' TRACKS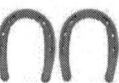

Sissy aka Famed Miss Fancy in MT

The fall of 1981 began the start of Sissy's exploration of Sunset Bench. We lived west of the Big Ditch right-of-way. The right-of-way road runs along the levee of the Big Ditch from Lake Como to north of Stevensville and was built for irrigation in 1910. Some parts of it belong to the land owners; some parts, to the ditch company, so one needs to check on ownership and get permission to use it. Being newcomers, not only did we not know this, but we didn't do any checking on it either. We just rode up Pine Hollow, went down the ditch, and kept going. We were actually trespassing on Eric's land, but didn't know it—and he was working in Baker, Montana, so he didn't know it, either.

Where the ditch meets South Sunset Bench, we met neighbors who have become life-long friends—Tony and Lynette Coller and their daughter Elaine. They owned a large ranch, about a mile south. Lynette was a 4-H leader, and Collers had cattle and raised Quarter Horses. Elaine was about five and raced around on her pony Chrissie.

That winter, Sissy began her high school rodeo career. Clark and Bobbi Kinney, Robin Hood, and the owners of The Pony Palace organized a school for the kids. I took Lisa and Sissy and three other Sunset Bench girls and their horses down there on Saturdays, and they practiced all winter. Sissy had been roped from, so she knew the game and how to rate cattle. Lisa had a lot to learn about roping, but had good teachers and was a good student.

The first year, Lisa and Sissy competed in the District Rodeo Finals in Dillon.

Here are Lisa's memories of that event:

On Friday, it was beautiful weather, and all the goes were fast. Then, on Friday night, it started to rain. It rained so hard the water ran off my hat, like a river. The arena was so muddy that Sissy was covered. I had to take a hose to my tack and to her, just to see what

THE MONTANA YEARS

color it was. She never slowed down, and we ran/slid the barrels, poles, breakaway roping, and goat tying. There are pictures somewhere of us turning the last pole, and the mud is so thick on her belly you can't even see my cinches. I made State that year, in goat tying and breakaway roping.

Lisa, running barrels on Sissy at Hamilton, Montana. 1982.

Back to Jane:

My memory of that rodeo is that every raincoat and poncho in Dillon was bought out, and half of the people in the grandstands were wearing black garbage bags to stay dry. The arena was SO muddy that one of the goat tie-ers got off, got her feet stuck in the mud, and fell on top of the goat, breaking its leg. The kids that drew up on Friday definitely had the best of the deal!

The next spring, Sissy carried Lisa to success in breakaway roping, barrel racing, and goat tying. She qualified again for the State Championships, and in 1983, she won fourth in the state in goat tying and won a set of spurs. After that, Lisa's interests turned elsewhere, and she quit rodeoing.

Lisa breakaway roping on Sissy, at Hamilton, Montana. Phil & T Photography. 1983.

That spring, Sissy was bred to Collers' good bay stud, Dingleberry, and got in foal. In the spring of 1984, Sissy gave us quite the experience. The article I wrote about it was titled,

"Twins — Boon or Boondoggle?"
Eric went to check Sissy about one in the morning on April 14, came in, and got me out of bed. The mare was down, in labor, and only one foal foot was apparent. I got behind her, reached in, found the other front foot, checked for the nose, and all appeared normal. The foal, a filly, slipped out. She was small,

 # THE MONTANA YEARS

and thin—very surprising, as Sissy's first foal had been robust. We waited for the cord to break, and then iodined her. Eric said, "You don't suppose she's carrying twins, do you?"

In answer, Sissy started straining, and two more feet appeared. The first foal's placenta was coming at the same time, so I helped pull the second foal—a colt. Sissy was very tired and lay still for a good five minutes. We iodined the second foal and started toweling them off—it was only 28 degrees. The filly was pretty thin and weak and was having trouble getting to her feet. They were both feeling cold—especially the little one. The inside of her mouth was so cold she couldn't suck. We didn't have a proper place prepared, so we strawed down the stock trailer and got mother and foals in it, and I got a sleeping bag and crawled in, too.

I got the colt under part of the sleeping bag and covered him with straw, and he warmed up and went to sleep. The filly I put inside my goose down jacket, next to me, and then wrapped the sleeping bag around us. She also finally warmed up and went to sleep.

We milked the mare, put the colostrum in a bottle, and got a cup or so in each of them. The next morning, it had warmed up, and we put them all in the corral. I called Lynette, and she came over and helped me, as Eric had to go to work. We gave each of them a selenium-vitamin shot, and between us, we were able to get them to suckle the mare. Sissy was an amazing mother through all of this.

It was a 70-degree day, and the foals gained strength and nursed on their own. They were both rather down on their pasterns, especially the filly. In a few days, their legs were better, but they had opposite "foal problems." The filly was scouring, and the colt needed an enema. Double trouble!

When they were four days old, we weighed them. The filly weighed 39 pounds, and the colt was 59 pounds. They were pretty small. The weather was set to turn, and our barn wasn't built then, so Lynette said to bring them to her place and put

them in a stall, which we did. By the fifth day, the filly's legs gave out on her and became terribly crooked.

Dr. Pruyne suggested putting casts on her legs until they could develop enough to support her. How to get her there? It is 35 miles to Missoula, and Lynette had the answer—put her in her Mom's motor home. The filly rode in style.

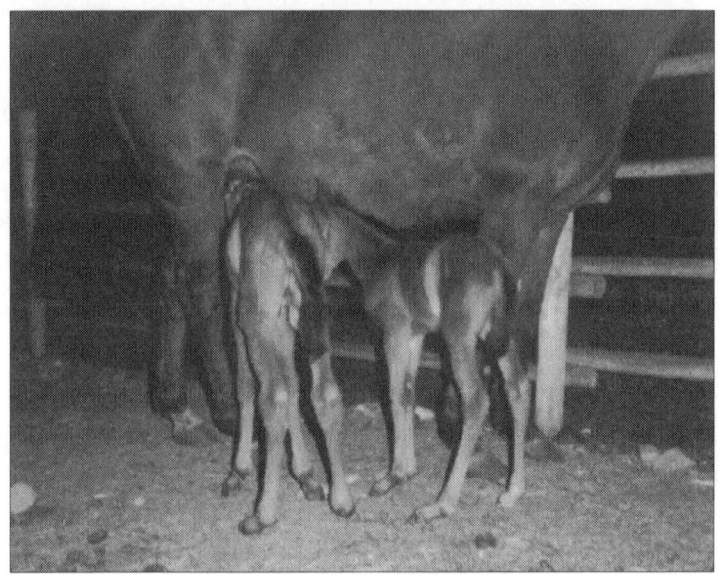

Sissy's twin foals, in 1984

When we got home, we had more challenges. Dr. Pruyne sent us home with Foal-lac, because he was afraid the mare wouldn't have enough milk. The filly was hungry, but she was mad—at us, at her new legs, and at the bottle we were forcing on her. She would not drink. We got her propped up, and she nursed her mother like crazy. She could not get up and down by herself and would only nurse her mother, so Lynette and I took turns babysitting her. I slept with her. She nursed, piddled, and laid down with her head on my pillow, and in a couple of hours, we repeated—all night. She was to have her casts on for 10 days. Between Lynette, me, Eric, and Lisa, we babysat them 'round the clock. We even tried to get a nurse mare into the

THE MONTANA YEARS

program, which did not work out well. I wrote a day by day, blow by blow account of all of this. It makes you tired, reading it.

The culmination of it all was, through super human effort, we got the filly's front legs straightened—only to have her hocks deteriorate because of the strain on them, and we had to put her down. It was just heartbreaking for everyone involved.

The old-time horsemen would have knocked her in the head right off the bat. Looking back, that would have been the thing to do, I guess. New-time horsemen get their mares checked for twins at 13 to 18 days of gestation, and if there are twins present, one can be "pinched off," and this problem eliminated.

The answer, to the title of my article, is definitely: "Boondoggle."

Sissy's colt grew up to be a very nice little gelding, and Lisa sold him to a good home.

Lisa leading Korri Schoening on Sissy.
Fort Owen Inn Arena. 1987.

MAKIN' TRACKS

I rode Sissy for 10 days in the Bob Marshall Wilderness in 1986, and she was a delight. She was always just a solid mare to ride. She was not what you would term overly friendly—she had started life as a cowboy's horse and was "all business." But she was there for you in everything you asked of her, and you could count on her.

*On a pack trip into the Bob Marshall Wilderness, 1989.
L to R: Hemi, Baron (behind), Janie on Sissy, and Drifty. Bob Marshall sign on far left. This was July 7, 1989, and that is snow on the ground. This is the Pyramid Pass Trail, and there was 6" on top of the pass.*

In 1988, I asked her to have a mule for me by breeding her to a jack. The spring of '89, she presented me with a cute buckskin molly mule that I named Hot Flash. Flash has her own story.

Sissy was more or less retired after that and had to be put down in 1992.

THE MONTANA YEARS

Hemi aka Ms. Hemorrhoid in MT

We arrived in Montana in late August of 1981, and the property we rented had 10 fenced acres of pasture. We went around it, cleaned up some old wire, and made it safe for our four head—Hemi, Drifty, Sissy, and Suzy. There was no barn on the property, and I was a little concerned for them in the coming winter. Sandy Brooks, who had ranched for years in the Stanley Basin where it is REALLY cold, said not to worry about it—just make sure they had plenty of hay. The property had big pine trees and a ravine they could use as a wind break.

Mother Nature takes care of her critters, and they all grew much denser winter hair than when they lived in California.

The next spring, I joined St. Mary's Saddle Club and started going out with Eric. I rode Hemi with Eric and Baron quite a bit. Eric had a two-horse trailer with a ramp on the back and two Dutch-type doors up above the ramp. That summer, we pulled into the driveway here and unloaded Baron. That was when I was milking cows up at Remoirs, and that was where we were going to take Hemi. Eric had a standard size, straight load, two-horse trailer, with a divider in it, so it was fairly narrow. It was, however, seven feet tall. As Eric led Baron away, Hemi had a fit and a huge burst of scrambling, and all of a sudden, she leaped out of the back of the horse trailer and landed on her head in the gravel. We were shocked.

Fortunately, she wasn't seriously injured; she just had some skinned-up places. We never dreamed she could turn around in that small space, let alone leap out. She was always tied in the trailer after that. It was one of those "you'd-have-to-see-it-to-believe-it" sort of moments.

We put both her and Baron back in the trailer and took her home first. By that time and until she died, she was absolutely in love with Baron and did not want to leave him. On pack trips, you could turn her loose as long as Baron was tied and have no fear of her leaving him.

MAKIN' TRACKS

The first year or two that Eric and I rode together, he wanted nothing to do with Hemi. He had never been around mules, and he didn't really appreciate some of her quirks. Then he rode her... She was a Cadillac! I had trouble keeping him off her. As the chestnut brood mare began popping out mule babies for me to train, Eric rode her more and more.

He rode her through two trips into the Bob Marshal Wilderness. One was an eight-day trip, and one was a 12-day trip. Baron packed the grub both times.

He got to feeling really comfortable riding her and decided he'd take her alone and go hunting in the foothills up above us. I told him I did not think that was a good idea, as she hated to go by herself. She spooked at her own shadow when you rode her out alone.

He took her anyway and got about four miles from the truck when she jumped out from under him, left him in the snow in the road, and beat feet for home—with his rifle in the scabbard. She had a mechanical hackamore bit on and roper reins, which were still up, so she could make good time. He got up, tracked her cross country for a few miles, and finally caught up with her—she had run up against a cross fence and was stymied. If that hadn't happened, she might have come clear home to Baron.

Eric caught her, got back on, and rode her right back to, and past, where she dumped him. He looked up, and on the ridge in a white pickup sat Ross McIntyre and Bob McElhaney. They had watched the whole episode and were more than happy to give Eric the "horse laugh" over getting dumped off his ass on his ass!

In 1984, we heard about Montana Mule Days, which was going to be held in Condon, Montana, for the second time. I wanted to see how Hemi would stack up against the Montana mules, so we loaded her and Baron and went up there. At that time, it was a one-day show.

I entered her in 10 classes and pretty much cleaned up. One class that about ate my lunch, though, was the packing class. They had not expected any women to enter, and the load consisted of four, 50-pound blocks of salt. This meant mantying two blocks for each side and a dead lift of 100 pounds for each side. I weighed

 **THE MONTANA YEARS**

about 130 pounds then, but was in good shape. The deal was that you started with a saddle horse and a bare pack mule. Time started, and you saddled the mule, then mantied your loads, and packed the mule, and when you were on the horse, leading the mule, time stopped.

Hurry-Scurry Race, Montana Mule Days, Condon, Montana. 1984.

    I was thinking so hard about how I was going to get the salt on Hemi, that I forgot to check her cinch. I got the salt up, loaded, and tied, with some great effort. She was standing with her feet braced and leaning to hold the load. Before I could get the other 100 pounds of salt lifted, the pack saddle gave up the ghost and

MAKIN' TRACKS

slipped around on her side, and there was no hope of packing her without starting over. Since Baron was there, she sidled up to him for comfort.

The committee made an executive decision and decided I could have help in re-doing my load. I tightened my cinch, had Jim Stromberg help me lift the salt, which I tied on both sides, and completed the class. I didn't win, but I did "get 'er done." Hemi won High Point Mule for the day, and we won a silver belt buckle—which I still have.

We made going to Montana Mule Days an annual event for the next 15 years and were on the committee putting it on for that long, too.

The next year, 1985, Hemi won the Grand Champion Saddle Mule in the halter class and her share of ribbons. She was an all-around mule. Through the years I have won in pole bending, barrel race, keyhole race, trail, pleasure, and equitation (both Western and English), cattle penning, flag races, ribbon races, musical sacks, boot races, and packing contests.

They have a rather unique class called the dress-undress, which I have also won on Hemi. You must take off a complete suit of clothes, including boots, while mounted and moving. What you wear underneath is your choice. Some chose bikinis to the spectators' delight. If you drop an item of clothing, you cannot get off to pick it up. You then have to put all your clothing back on! That class is—to this day—a crowd pleaser.

Dress-Undress Class, Montana Mule Days, Condon, Montana. Janie, picking up lost article of clothing. 1985.

THE MONTANA YEARS

Another class of great renown is the costume class, and it has created some memorable moments. One time at Condon, I was "Lady Gawdawful," a take on Lady Godiva. I wore nude-colored long johns and was sidesaddle, with a horrible horsehair wig and a basketful of flowers. Other contestants included a clown, a nun, a prospector, and a World War II cavalry officer, leading a pack outfit and with a vintage gas mask on his saddle mule.

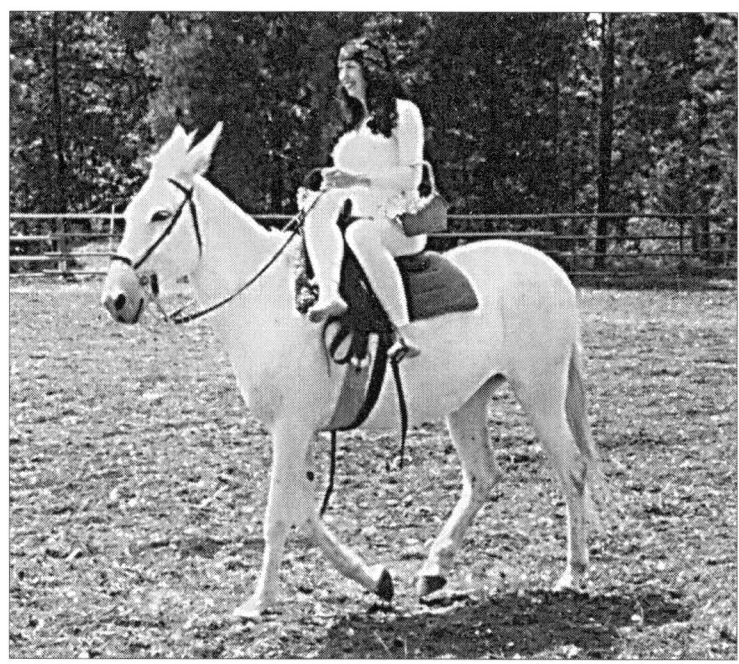

In Costume Class, dressed as Lady Gawdawful.
Montana Mule Days, Condon, Montana. 1984.

The prospector's donkey started losing his load. The pack slipped, and frying pans were clanging against the gold pans. As the donkey drug his handler past the clown, she lost control, and two mules were running—past the sidesaddle nun, who went down in a pouf of black and white. Three were headed for me, so I jumped, flowers flying! The only one left in control was Pete Samuelvich, the vintage cavalry guy, with all his vintage gear. He got the blue ribbon; the rest of us got the dirt...

MAKIN' TRACKS

Hemi and Jane, dressed as Dr. Quinn, Medicine Woman, for Costume Class. Montana Mule Days, Drummond, Montana. 1994.

Another time, Hemi and I were "Dr. Quinn, Medicine Woman," and I got a WWII equine hospital litter to rig up on her. I dressed up in old-fashioned clothing, and we put a blow-up doll on Hemi's litter, with the proclamation, "Drunk on her Ass." I carried a medicine bag, and Hemi had other signage. Hemi had come a looooong way to carry that litter—the handles on it were on both sides of her ears.

Another costume event I involved Hemi in was at the Winter Fair in Missoula. It was in early February, and they had some halter classes and a costume class. I put a Valentine's Day tablecloth on her, hearts, and a red halter, and advertised, "Delish-Ass Candy." I dressed all in red—a long red dress and red hat—and carried a big, heart candy box placard with "I'd Bust My Ass For You" on one side, and, "I'm Ass Over Teakettle For You" on the other.

We used to have a lot of fun at Mule Days and other mule events, and everyone then cared more for the FUN than for collecting ribbons.

THE MONTANA YEARS

Eric riding Hemi across the pack bridge at Big Prairie. Bob Marshall Wilderness. 1989.

Janie and Hemi, Costume Class for the Missoula Winter Expo. Missoula, Montana. 1991.

L to R: Ann Greer holding Drifter and Janie holding Hemi. Montana Mule Days, Drummond. Drifter was Hemi's full brother, and they aged the same and looked like twins. 1995.

Hemi & Janie Lambert receiving a high point award from Sandy Brooks. 1986.

THE MONTANA YEARS

*Janie Lambert, on Hemi, in sidesaddle outfit.
Winter Expo, Missoula, Montana. 1986.*

*Grandma Jane Lambert demonstrating to kids how she used to ride
Big Enough, backwards. Drummond, Montana. 1996.*

 MAKIN' TRACKS

Hemi posing in front of the Big Ditch on our property. 1996.

I took her over to Salmon, Idaho, one time to test her against those mules. She won everything, including High Point Mule. She was GOOD!

THE MONTANA YEARS

Dismounting, during musical sacks. Montana Mule Days. Condon, Montana. June 1988.

As time went on, Eric had Zack to ride, and I was training Zipper and Hot Flash. Our five grandkids took turns riding Hemi, and she took very good care of them. One year—it may have been 1996—we took all five grandchildren over to Mule Days in Drummond. We put up a wall tent and had a wood stove for them, because it was rather cool that year. All five—Korri, Kyle, and Kayla Schoening (Lisa's) and Josh and Erica Lambert (Dan's)—showed mules that year. It was a three-ring circus to keep track of them all and to keep track of who was riding what mule in what class. Eric's daughter Dawn was there to help, and Lisa also showed up. That was the last time we had all of them together, so it was memorable for all of us. By that time, Montana Mule Days was a three-day affair.

They all won multiple ribbons and had a wall of ribbons in their tent, displayed just like the "important" people on the show circuit.

 **MAKIN' TRACKS**

In 1996, Hemi was shown for the last time. Erica won the Showmanship with her and the youth barrel race and placed in everything else she entered. Hemi was developing a lump on her back, which later was diagnosed as cancer. She was put down here and buried in late fall of 1997. She was 24 years old.

For such a rocky start, Hemi and I did anything and everything together for 21 years. She taught me so much and gave me such unconditional love that I miss her still. I cried for six weeks after her passing and am crying now as I write this. I loved that mule with all my heart…

 THE MONTANA YEARS

Drifty aka Drift Past in MT

I was a little concerned with whether Drifty would grow enough hair for a Montana winter as she didn't seem to need much in California. But, as noted, Mother Nature takes care of that. From 1981 on, Drifty grew a double coat—a thick, darker undercoat, and bay, longer hair over the top. She shed in two stages, too. Interesting.

I rode her some that winter. I was taking Lisa to the Pony Palace to learn rodeo skills, and if I didn't have a trailer load of Sunset Bench horses, I took her and worked her. She was a nice horse. As an adult, she was about fifteen hands and had beautiful QH conformation and a really nice head. Except for her periodic pull backs, she had no "holes."

Janie riding Drifty on Bitterroot Stock Farm. The wind came up and filled the poncho, and Drifty ran away. Jane saved the beer. 1983.

MAKIN' TRACKS

In 1983, Eric and I went to a breakfast ride up on the Bitterroot Stock Farm, east of Corvallis. It is a beautiful, old, historic ranch, once owned by Marcus Daly, Butte's Copper King.

Anyway, it was drizzling rain, so I wore a red poncho. It was just one of THOSE mornings, so we decided to have a red beer to start the day. Eric asked me to hold his, while he was doing something. A gust of wind came up and blew that poncho up like a balloon. Of course, that spooked Drifty, and she took off. Ever try and ride a runaway horse with a beer in each hand and a poncho across your face? I have! It's pretty exciting!

Fortunately, Baron had been used as an out-rider horse on the track, and he and Eric saved the day. I still had both beers, as my priorities were obviously much different *then* than they would be *today*...

About 1985, a couple of friends from California—Charlie Wood and Roy Boynton—came up to visit, and we took them fishing, southwest of Hamilton, up Roaring Lion Creek. The fishing used to be good there, but it is a rocky, rocky trail. The rocks turned into boulders up where the fishing was good. We were coming out, after catching our limits, and Drifty got her hind foot caught, down in some of those big rocks. In trying to get free, her weight shifted, and she lurched sideways, towards the creek. Her foot popped free, and she kind of launched off the trail. Charlie, who was riding her, was thrown off balance and falling off, at the same time. All we saw was Drifty fall on Charlie, as they went out of sight in the bushes. Then, there was a big splash, and Drifty was in the creek. We heard Charlie yelling for help! He was wedged into a sandy pit and couldn't move. Drifty's weight had wedged him in, and then she rolled off into the creek. This was a stroke of luck for Charlie, as he was not hurt at all. He was happy, as he had a Montana adventure story to tell!

When we got Drifty out of the creek, we discovered she had cut her hind leg on the outside of her cannon bone on the right-hand side, and it was cut across the top and down the back side, so that a big flap of skin was hanging down. It needed stitching to heal properly.

 # THE MONTANA YEARS

L to R: Baron, Eric, Drifty, Hemi, and Zeke.
Up above Peterson Lake, after Drifty's wreck.
If you look closely, you can see the hematoma on her butt. 1985.

By the time we got back to Hamilton, it was about 5 p.m. on a Sunday night—not a prime time to find a veterinarian. After a number of calls, one answered. He was a very good vet, but was known for drinking a lot of whiskey then. He said to bring her over, so we did. His practice was at his house.

He came reeling over when we unloaded her and said, "Well, THAT'S a cut, all right."

I said, "I was hoping you could sew her up."

"Well, now, if you want her sewed up, I can sew 'er up…"

He numbed her leg, and I got under her and held it up for him, and he stitched her back together—beautifully. He put a wrap on her and said, "How soon do you want to use her?"

I said, "As soon as she heals would be fine."

He gave her a shot of long-lasting penicillin and then was administering some straw-colored liquid. When I asked what it was, he said, "Bute! You can ride her tomorrow!"

MAKIN' TRACKS

When her leg healed, you could not find a scar... But I did NOT ride her "tomorrow"!

In 1987, when Zeke was a two-year-old, we had a light pack on him, and he was tied on behind Drifty. Drifty had a load. She had Ralide pack boxes, loaded 75 pounds to the side, and she had a top pack with a couple of sleeping bags, which was lashed down with a diamond hitch. We were headed to Holloway Lake, which is up Sweeney Creek, in the Bitterroot Mountains. Most Bitterroot trails go up the bottom of the canyon. Sweeney Creek trail is different. You switchback up the mountain with your rig, and the trailhead starts at about 7,000 feet.

The Bitterroot Mountains are steep—there is no other way to describe them. This trail is very picturesque, and the view to the east is awesome, as you look across the valley and over to the Sapphire Mountains. This is a decent trail, but it travels on some side hills as vertical as a cow's face. On one such side hill, there was some slab rock with a little moisture on it. Young Zeke did not like it, scrambled around, fell down, and pulled Drifty off balance, and she fell down and off the trail. I was behind them, jumped off, and got Zeke loose from her. If she could have held still for a minute, we might have got her head uphill enough to save her from rolling down the mountain... Instead, away she went! She rolled like a fat sausage around and around, down through some alder brush, then turned, and the last we saw of her, she was going end for end, down a rocky chute, and out of sight, the terrible crashing just going on and on. We were sick!

We tied up our stock, and Eric took his .357 out of the saddlebags. We didn't see how she could come out of that without a broken leg or internal injuries. I was crying, and Eric was steeling himself. We had bad footing going down to check on her. She had gone down the hill about 200 yards, and when we got to her, she was sitting at the bottom of a rock chute on her butt, just like a dog. She was dazed, in shock, and not moving. The brush was ironed flat up above her. The last 20 feet had been a sheer drop off, and she had landed on her rear end in the rocks. My stomach turned over at the thoughts of what was to come.

THE MONTANA YEARS

I got to her first and talked to her and stroked her neck. When some light came back in her eyes, I asked her to stand up—which she did, with all four legs intact! We took her pack off and looked her all over, and except for some minor abrasions, the only big injury she had was a very large hematoma on her buttock where she had hit. She had lost the ax off the top pack up in the alders, and Eric retrieved it.

I started leading her slowly, in a zig-zag, up the mountain, and she finally made it back up with the other animals. Eric was heave-ho-ing the pack boxes back up, and I went down to help him. When we looked inside to see what might have broken, we were amazed. All was well. The only casualty was the cork popping out of the Almaden wine bottle, and only a cup or so of wine had spilled—right onto the toilet paper. We had Chardonnay "wet ones."

We put my saddle on Drifty and put her pack on Hemi, and I walked and led Drifty to the first camping spot we found—above Peterson Lake. She was so lucky to not have been more seriously hurt. Zeke, and the heavy pack, caused her to roll down the hill, but those tough boxes and the top pack must have also cushioned her as she went. The rocks burnished the "Ralide" right off the boxes, but the boxes were a life-saver for Drifty.

We used lighter breakaways to lead our young mules with after that.

Off and on, I both rode and packed Drifty. She was a pack horse on two trips through the Bob Marshal—in 1986 and in 1989. She worked hard and risked her life for us.

At that time, we had no place to dry dock our animals. All we had were lush permanent pastures. Trying to keep the weight off Drifty became a problem, and I was afraid she was going to founder as she gained weight easily. I had colts to ride, property to care for, and not enough time in the day for everything. Eric was working out of town.

We had some friends who lived in Condon—Carrielee and Tom Parker. Carrielee really liked Drifty and wanted to buy her. Tom was a packer in the "Bob," so he had jobs for her, and the

 **MAKIN' TRACKS**

grass in Condon lacks power. I figured she'd be going to a good home and sold her to Carrielee in 1989, after we finished our pack trip. Carrielee took her on the Montana Centennial Cattle Drive that summer.

Then, Carrielee left Tom and Condon, and took Drifty who knows where. That was NOT the deal I wanted for Drifty...

 THE MONTANA YEARS

Baron

Baron was foaled in 1972, west of Stevensville, up Kootenai Creek. He was born into an Appaloosa herd, but had no Appy characteristics—no white sclera in his eyes and no "coloring." He was a solid bay colt, with just a little white on his forehead. The breeders sold him as a weanling, as he didn't fit their program. The guy who bought him gave him to his daughter, and she started riding him as a long yearling. Eric and Paula were still married at that time. Eric first saw him at a gymkhana when he was barely two and said the girl was running him unmercifully for that age.

One morning, at a café in downtown Stevensville, the girl's father offered to sell him to Eric, as they were moving. Eric thought he would be a good horse for his son, Dan, and Dan thought so, too, and sold his ten-speed bike for $60 to chip in on Baron's purchase price of $150. Dan, in 1974, was 10 years old, and he had to wash dishes for a year to pay back his debt on the horse.

Dan had a lot of fun riding Baron and continued to gymkhana with him some, went with Eric on elk hunting trips every fall, and when he got a little older, did some roping on him at the Fort Owen Arena in Stevensville. The whole family—Eric, Paula, and kids, Dan and Dawn—were members of the St. Mary's Saddle Club, which was basically a trail riding outfit.

In 1978, on a four-day camping trip to Elk Lake, which is behind Lake Como, a bat began dive-bombing the riders. It was swooping around in broad daylight and acting strangely, so everyone figured it might be rabid. They trotted down the trail to get away from it and then stopped to wait for Steve Anderson, who was leading the pack string. Dan and several others had dismounted. The bat had taken refuge under the Cheyenne roll on Dan's saddle, and when Dan went to remount Baron, he grabbed it while getting on. It bit him in the finger and then flew off. Everyone then headed back to the trailhead, except Steve Anderson's son Bill, who stayed, sitting on a log waiting for his dad. The bat came out of nowhere and flew at Bill, who picked up a stick and knocked it from the air, killing it. He put it in a baggie, and he and Steve arrived at the trailhead with it.

Eric, Paula, and the kids loaded up and headed to the local hospital with the bat to have it tested for rabies; then they went out to dinner. When they got home, a sheriff's deputy was waiting for them with the news that the bat WAS rabid and that Dan needed to get to the hospital immediately.

This bat bite made national news, as the serum had to be flown from Florida to Montana. Dan had to undergo 21 shots in his abdomen to ward off rabies, but suffered no other ill effects. This is not so much a horse story, as a human-interest story, but Baron was definitely involved.

In my life, I have encountered a number of rabid animals—skunks, foxes, deer, and bats. Some areas are more apt to harbor the disease, and some years are worse than others for it to show up. My grandfather and his brother Clyde also had to have this shot treatment—they were tubing a sick steer that had rabies. Anytime a nocturnal animal is out in the daytime and not acting right—beware! Also, be aware that our domestic animals can be bitten and get it, too. It can be a death sentence to be diagnosed with it.

Dan enrolled in a Monte Foreman clinic one time and rode Baron. Monte had the students work on their sliding stops. The cue was to say Whoa and drop your rein hand down to touch the top of the neck right in front of the saddle. Dan says Baron got really good at it.

After that, Dawn and Kristen Baker were galloping their horses bareback in the powdery dirt alongside the railroad tracks that were behind their house on Pine Street in Stevensville. The dirt was just like flour from being driven on. Inadvertently, Dawn let her rein hand down and bumped Baron's withers, and he sat down into a beautiful, sliding stop. Unfortunately for Dawn, she kept going and landed in a giant pouf of powdery dust and was completely hidden from view. When the air cleared, she was sitting in front of Baron, with the reins still in her hand, but completely unrecognizable. Kristen had hysterics...

 # THE MONTANA YEARS

In the late '70s, Paula took Baron to the racetrack to pony the Thoroughbred racehorses she was training. He came home muscled up and in shape from galloping all summer and well used to leading high-strung youngsters and keeping them in line.

By 1980, Dan had turned his interests to girls and cars and sold Baron to his dad, so Baron became Eric's horse.

Paula and Eric split the sheets, and she went to the track to continue to train Thoroughbreds, and Eric went to Baker, Montana, to build power lines. He has been in the power line trade since 1962.

When Eric and I met at the Shearbrook Ranch Sale, it was still winter. That spring, the Saddle Club was having a Breakfast Ride. It was on the morning of the beginning of Daylight Savings Time in 1982. I had Hemi in the trailer and was approaching Eric's driveway as he was pulling out. He was headed to town because he thought he had an hour more than he actually did. He had Baron in the trailer and told me to follow him, as I was a little unsure of where the ride started.

We rode together some on the ride, and Eric asked me out to dinner. It was the start of a double love affair. Hemi fell hard for Baron, and Eric and I have been together ever since!

Baron had a split personality. He could be the nicest horse to ride—head down, with a nice flat-footed walk, or he could use the most bone-rattling, prancy jog that would jar your teeth all day. It was his call.

Through the years, Baron was probably packed as much as he was ridden. Eric says Baron has packed out more elk than any other horse in Ravalli County, and I think he is probably right. Eric has been an elk hunter since the 1950s and has hunted with many other very serious elk hunters (many in the immediate family), so the total number of elk Baron packed totals MANY more than what Eric himself has killed.

One packing story for Baron happened on an icy, bear grass-covered, incredibly steep hillside. Eric shot a big cow. Where he shot her would have been an easy pack, but when she went down,

 MAKIN' TRACKS

she slid a hundred yards down the hill into some dense timber. Snow-covered bear grass creates a toboggan run.

Anyway, we went and got the animals. Eric had Hemi, I was on Drifty, and we had Decker pack saddles on Baron and Zack— Zack was a long two-year-old. Baron was shod, and Zack was not. We tied up on top and led/slid Baron down to the quartered cow. There was a little level hump behind a tree for Baron to stand on while we loaded the hindquarters on him. Eric turned him a little to start up the mountain, causing Baron's feet to slip on the ice and snow, and the weight of the elk took him down. The tree he had been tied to kept him from going on down the mountain. Baron tried several times to get up, but had no footing. He got mad! He knew the meat had him pinned down, and he turned his head and began trying to bite it off, and I mean seriously bite it off!

We untied the hind quarters and pulled it away from him, and he was able to stand up. Without the elk, he was able to climb out of there. We brought Zack down, put the meat on him, and sent him up the hill. Zack was like Hemi on his feet—a ballet dancer. He went up and stood by Baron with a "piece-o'-cake" look on his face.

L to R: Erica Lambert and Kayla Schoening riding Baron backwards. 1988.

THE MONTANA YEARS

Eric, dressed as Santa Claus, riding Hemi, and Baron packing presents. On Sunset Bench. Bitterroot Mountains in background. 1986.

Eric Lambert on Baron, deep snow on Eastman Ridge. Sapphire Mountains. 1985.

 MAKIN' TRACKS

Dawn Lambert on Baron, in front of crabapple tree. 1985.

One time, on a pack trip into the Bob Marshal Wilderness—maybe 1986—Eric rode Hemi, I rode Sissy, and we packed Baron and Drifty. We turned the animals out to graze with their hobbles on. We heard a commotion and found poor Baron, dazed. He had jumped over a log into the creek bottom. There was a cut bank about three feet high under the log, and when he hit, he stood himself on his forehead in the rocks. He was lucky he didn't kill himself—shades of "Baby"—because his forehead filled with little air bubbles. It felt like bubble wrap under his skin, so we think he must have fractured some sinus cavities. He sure didn't feel good for a few days, and we laid over to let him recover.

Coming out of there, right before we started down the steep, windy Holland Lake trail, Baron's pack suddenly turned on him. The cinch had loosened with travel. The pack turned towards the downhill side, and it already was a steep drop off. Being a wise horse, he turned himself around immediately and put the tipped pack to the uphill. We got him righted and re-packed and everything tightened well before going on. We felt thankful that the load slipped where it did, because not too much farther on, you

were looking down your stirrup a thousand feet to Holland Lake, and the trail is not overly wide... This trail requires uphill traffic in the morning and downhill traffic in the afternoon, because there is no room to pass on it.

Baron would do anything we needed of him. Everyone in the family has ridden him one time or another. I made a commercial for Stevensville's Western Days one time. The old horse had a pretty good handle on him, and I was supposed to run right at the camera, stop, and gallop off towards Stevensville. I really blasted him towards the camera and director and then set him down hard—one of his Monte Foreman slides—and they were showered with dirt. The lady director about swallowed her teeth. The footage came out good, and we have a commercial video of Baron "in action."

Eric's daughter Dawn rode him in her role as NILE Queen in Billings, back in 1983. When I told my mother that Dawn was "Queen of the NILE," she said, "Doesn't she need a barge for that, rather than a horse?"

The NILE—short for the Northern International Livestock Exposition—is a very large event: horse show, rodeo, and livestock exhibition. It was a grueling contest and prestigious to win. Baron performed flawlessly in the Grand Entry and in his queen runs. He and Dawn looked fantastic!

When our grandkids came along, he became a babysitter to them. Especially Kayla and Erica loved to ride him. They rode double and were double trouble, as they rode two facing ahead; one facing ahead, one backwards; and one time two backwards! Baron didn't care.

One time the Saddle Club was out here, and a local farrier was going to talk to the group about shoeing. Baron was the demo horse. The farrier and his friend had been nipping a little and got brazen with their demonstration. They presented "speed shoeing." One of them picked up and held a front foot and was working on it, while the other one had the diagonal rear foot picked up. Baron just quietly balanced himself and put up with it.

 MAKIN' TRACKS

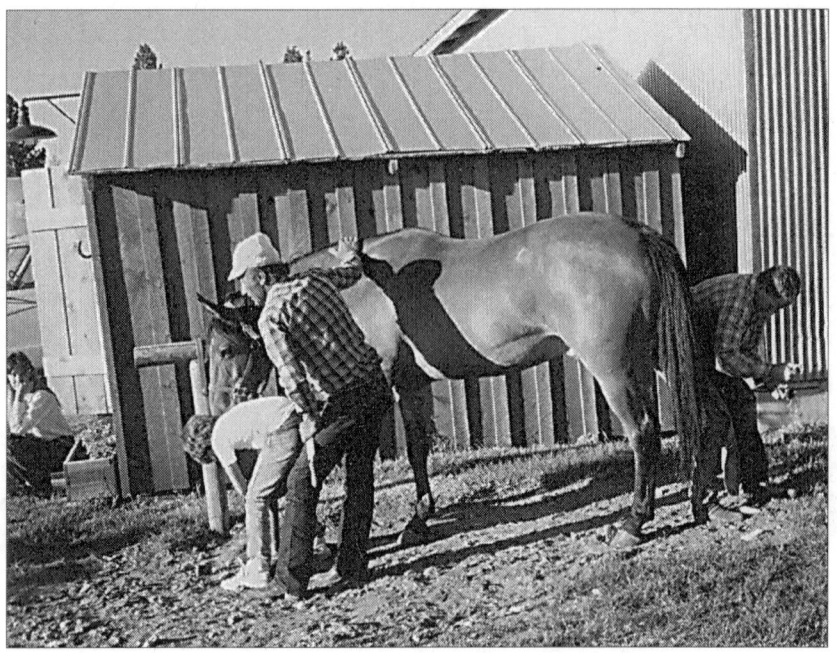

Unknown people demonstrating speed shoeing on Baron, in front of old tack shed. 1988.

The summer Baron was 26, he took his big last trip to the mountains. Kayla rode him, her brother Kyle rode his paint mare, Eric rode Zack, and I rode Hot Flash. We traveled up into and through Skalkaho Basin and met up with some friends who had ridden up from the Willow Creek Trail. We led them through to the old vermiculite cabin, and we had a barbecue and party and spent the night. Kyle and Kayla had their horizons widened by playing dice with the adults—and winning! That was a long trip, but Baron seemed to enjoy himself every step of the way.

He was taken out of retirement one last time that fall. Eric went hunting up on the Calf Creek Game Range and shot a cow, gutted it, quartered it, and walked back to the truck. He came home, got Zack and Gypsy, and went back up there to pack it out. His hunting partner, Tom Alsaker, met him at the trailhead with his horse, Buck, and mule, Red. It was dark by the time they headed up the mountain to get the cow.

THE MONTANA YEARS

They got the quarters loaded up—the hindquarters in meat bags on Gypsy, and the front quarters tied on Red. On the way out, Eric noticed Red's load shifting, and he hollered at Tom to "Hold up!"

Eric stepped off Zack, looped his reins over the top of a dead tree which was leaning over, and started to adjust Red's load. Gypsy walked up alongside Zack, and he turned his head to look at her, snapping off about six feet of the dead tree. He took off, dragging the tree with Gypsy behind him. Gypsy and Zack disappeared into the dark. They were all about three miles from the trucks and trailers.

Baron, being packed with elk hindquarter.
L to R: Tom Alsaker, Dan Lambert, and Eric Lambert.
Sapphire Mountains. 1992.

Eric and Tom had flashlights and tracked them until they ran out of snow; then they lost their tracks. They rode back to the rigs, unloaded Red, and tied him to the trailer. They led Buck away from Red, so that he would bray, in the hopes that it would call in Zack and Gypsy. After an hour, Eric decided to come home, get Baron and Zipper, then come back, and look some more. Tom stayed a couple more hours, with Red doing his part to call them, and finally gave up and headed back to Missoula about midnight.

Eric came home about eleven, loaded up some more tack, and ate a very late meal, and then we pulled the four-horse trailer into the pasture about one a.m. Baron and Zipper came running—they thought their friends were home. When Eric opened the tailgate, they both jumped right in the trailer. We haltered them inside the trailer, tied them up, and headed back to Calf Creek, which is a 40-minute drive from home.

We were at the trailhead before daylight, and as hunters arrived, we asked them to look for our animals and to be aware they were up there. We were worried sick about them—especially Gypsy, who had some age on her and was packed with half of a large cow. We could just picture her pinned down in the snow...

At daylight, I got on Zipper and rode toward the north. Eric, on Baron, headed south. In about an hour, we had good news. Asa Yerian had come up there hunting, found them, and tied them up. The good news reached Eric. When he reached them, he got the weight off Gypsy immediately. I got the news through some hunters and rode over. (No cell phones then.) We put the meat bags on Zipper, she carried the meat to the trailer, and I led Gypsy. Zack was chipper as he could be, since he just had a saddle on— but he about walked poor old Gypsy's legs off all night. In the daylight, we saw their tracks EVERYWHERE! Zack had roper reins and did go back to where the trailer was at some point, because we found a piece of his rein there the next morning. At home, Gypsy took long rests for a few days.

That was Baron's last big adventure, and he voluntarily loaded himself to get there!

As he aged, Baron developed Crohn's Disease and grew excessively long winter hair. One year, after a blizzard, he was covered in snow and ice and had long icicles hanging from his hair. I used his picture on our Christmas card, with the caption, "Who needs jingle bells?"

 THE MONTANA YEARS

In 2004, at age 32, Baron was put to sleep underneath the crabapple tree. He had a sudden colic attack caused by an internal tumor. What a horse he was!

Baron, after a blizzard.
Christmas card picture, "Who needs jingle bells?" 2002.

 MAKIN' TRACKS

Buddy

Back in 1983, I went to the Missoula horse sale and bought a chestnut brood mare and a well-broke, good-looking palomino gelding. Both purchases were impulse buys, because I wasn't looking to buy ANY horse that day. I don't even remember why I was there with a trailer.

Anyway, the gelding came into the ring; he had a handle on him, and I liked his looks. He went fairly cheap, and I bought him. I knew Dawn was in the hunt for the queen title in Billings, and I thought he might work there.

Queen of the NILE, Dawn Lambert on Buddy.
In NILE kick-off Parade, Billings, Montana. 1983.

 ## THE MONTANA YEARS

We got him home, and he was a nice horse. Good to handle, saddle, and ride. He could really stop and turn—for a week. Then he came up lame. He had been sold up in Kalispell and had been consigned by the Flathead Lake Lodge. I called the owner up there, and he gave me the bad news on the horse. He was a good horse, they had used him a lot, but he had been diagnosed with navicular disease, so they had sold him. An unscrupulous horse trader had bought him, done a "quick nerve" treatment on him, and resold him in Missoula. After hearing this, I looked closely at his front legs, and you could see where he had puncture marks on both pasterns. The nerves were "nicked" enough to numb his feet, so he became temporarily sound. I was a SUCKER!

Well, what to do? We all liked him, and he was a fun horse to ride, so we had the veterinarian nerve him for real, and we rode him all summer. That fall, we took him over to Billings for Dawn to ride, along with Baron, in the NILE festivities. I tried to find a buyer for him over there, without any luck.

When we came home, I talked to Sandy Brooks about him. I hated to send him to the killers, as he was a nice horse, but with numb feet, he wasn't a good candidate to ride in the mountains. Sandy, an old packer, had a soft spot for him, too, and offered to buy him. Sandy had some years on him and had a couple of other old "pensioner" horses, which he just rode around the ranch. So, Buddy spent his last days eating grass over at Sandy's, with some other nice old horses.

Horse Traders! Buyers, Beware! I don't seem to learn very fast...

 MAKIN' TRACKS

Chestnut Brood Mare

I went to the Missoula horse sale in 1983 and bought a "three-in-one package" — a nice looking liver chestnut mare with a husky colt at her side and bred back to a QH stud in Canada. The announcer said all her papers were in order and that she was a permanent registered AQHA mare. I liked the looks of her, and the price was right, so I bought her and brought them home.

I am ashamed to say that I do not remember her name. I did not take the time to even get to know her—she was just a fixture and a baby producer. That is the sad state of affairs for most brood mares, and they never get very trusting, because the only time you handle them is when you want to DO something to them—trim feet, give shots, worm, or breed. No wonder they seem nervous when you halter them. Anyway, here she was only called "the brood mare."

Brood Mare in front of our barn, with Zack by her side. 1986.

This whole deal had a steep learning curve, in that the paperwork was in order for the mare and her colt, who we named Joker, but there was only the name of the man who had bred her in Lethbridge, Canada, and no indication of a breeder's certificate. It took months of sleuthing and phone calls to finally get that for

THE MONTANA YEARS

the unborn filly, and I think there was some shady dealing in the transaction and some feuding. Also, when you looked closely at the mare's markings on the registration papers, they did NOT QUITE match...

We ended up with two nice, registered AQHA horses from her, but their breeding may have been mysterious. Her following offspring were all mules, so registration papers were not in the mix. This mare delivered Joker in 1983, Fantabar in 1984, Zeke in 1985, Zack in 1986, and Zipper in 1989.

One funny story in conjunction with this mare happened in a summer in the '80s. My husband Eric was working out of town, so I got the job of putting up the hay. This mare had scratched the cornea in her eye, and Dr. Swartz had prescribed two medications for her—one to dilate her eye and an antibiotic. I made a mask for her to wear over her eye, because the dilation made her eye sun sensitive.

Well, wouldn't you know it—while raking hay, a hay fiber scratched my right eyeball, and it was irritated and watering. I figured, if the antibiotic ointment was good for the mare, it would be good for me, so I used it for a couple of days. Then one morning when I got up and looked in the mirror, my right eye looked like the Black Hole of Calcutta! Yikes! I realized I had put the dilation cream in instead of the antibiotic. Now, I was worried about the consequences of it, so I called Dr. Swartz, who laughed, and then told me to call Dr. Goicoechia, the local optometrist, for his advice. When I told Dr. G., he also laughed, and said, "Little bitty eye like that, might stay dilated for a week! Wear sun glasses."

The two doctors then conferred and had a good laugh over it. Dr. G. reminds me of it every year, when I go in for a check-up.

Out in the hay field, in the bright August sun, even sun glasses wouldn't cut the glare. I finally cut some dark construction paper to fit between the eye and glasses to completely black it out. It is not easy to rake straight rows when you are only using one eye. Always read the label!

When we decided we had enough mules, we sold the mare to a guy who wanted to raise his own... And he did.

 MAKIN' TRACKS

Joker

In 1983, when I bought his mother at the horse sale, Joker was at her side. He was a good looking, stout, dark sorrel colt with a star on his forehead. He was nice to handle and was easy to halter break. When he was a two-year-old, we had Floyd Stockert start him and put 30 days on him. Floyd said he crowhopped a little, but came along good.

I rode him for a couple of years, and he turned into a good horse. He got big—both tall and heavy muscled.

Joker, looking over the fence. 1984.

When he was a three-year-old, Dawn rode him on a Saddle Club trail ride into the Selway Wilderness. We rode out of Wilderness Gateway, and that Idaho country there is steep. We were on a trail on a really sheer hillside. It was camouflaged by large ferns, which were growing right next to the trail, and you didn't notice the big drop off. There was a muddy spot there, and

THE MONTANA YEARS

Joker, being inexperienced at that time, walked on the outside of it and stepped off the trail. It was such a fast drop that, with that first step, Joker was suddenly four feet below the trail, and Dawn was dead level with the trail and surrounded by ferns. I was behind her and yelled for her to get off. She leaned out and scrambled to the trail. Joker's next try put him another four feet down the mountain, then another four feet, etc., until he was enmeshed in a brush pile a good 30 feet down the hill.

L to R: Joker, Baron, Jane Lambert, and Hemi. South Bitterroot Mountains, above Fish Lake, at the Chain of Lakes. 1985.

We sort of fell off the hill to get to him and got him loose from the brush. He ended up in the bottom of a ravine, and we were able to lead him up the bottom, where it climbed and interceded with the trail. He had a rather severe injury to his right hock where a stick had stabbed him.

I gave Dawn whichever animal I was riding and told her I'd take him back to the trailer. She was living in Billings then and didn't have the chance to ride much.

It was three miles or so to walk, which in those days was an easy stroll for me. HOWEVER, I was wearing my new Tony Lama

 MAKIN' TRACKS

Buckaroo boots, with high, underslung heels and high tops. Real old time cowboy boots, and I loved the looks of them! I found out really fast why the old-time cowboys never walked when they could ride. Wearing "high heels" in steep country is not good. By the time Joker and I got back to camp, I was limping far worse than he was—I should have ridden him, judging from the blisters...

Anyway, he healed up fine from the accident.

Joker was a nice horse, but he had foot problems—he outgrew his feet. He had round feet, with flat soles and shelly hoof walls. As he kept growing, we just couldn't seem to keep shoes on him, and he had sore feet issues.

We had quite a few animals then. We didn't have a dry-dock place, and being on irrigated pasture didn't help his feet out. I made a decision which I have regretted ever since: I took him to the horse sale and sent him through the ring loose. It was partly a financial decision, as canner prices were very high right then.

I left him off there, and he was confused and hung his head over the corral. He called out to me as I left—a really plaintiff whinny which I heard as, "Don't leave me here!"

This makes my heart heavy to write this. Joker deserved better. I wish I had tried harder with his shoeing. I wish I'd tried harder to find him a different home. I wish I had done lots of things differently here...

Horses are so trusting. Every time we catch one, they trust us to take care of them. They don't know where they are going, or what we are going to ask them to do, but if we have done our job as a communicator to them, they trust that we will take care of them. Joker was a trusted and trusting partner to me, and I let him down.

 THE MONTANA YEARS

Fantabar

The chestnut brood mare produced a nice sorrel filly with a white blaze on her face in 1984, and we named her Fantabar. It had been a rigamarole to get her breeder's certificate out of Canada, but we did, and "Fannie" had AQHA papers.

Dawn Lambert on Fantabar, Billings. 1985.

We gave the mare to Dawn for a birthday present in 1985. She took her to Billings, where she was living at the time. She started Fannie over there and rode her some—as work would allow. When the job petered out, and Dawn was hauling her back "home,"

 MAKIN' TRACKS

Fannie got scared of the big trucks passing her and bruised her stifle badly while trying to climb the trailer walls to escape. We treated her for quite a while, as she was badly swollen with a big "rug-burn" type of injury. Dr. Swartz told us to put olive oil on the injury to keep it soft. He said olive oil would do a good job of penetrating and softening, and he was right.

She healed up fine, and Dawn sold her, as she was "in transition" right then and looking for a job.

We lost track of her for a few years, and then she showed back up in the neighborhood, in an interesting way.

Way back when Dawn was a teenager, she had a black mare named "Lucky Lady." When she outgrew her, Dawn sold her to a neighbor, Nevie Alford, who lived below us. Nevie had her for years and enjoyed her.

One day, a grown-up and married Nevie called to say that she had another one of Dawn's horses—she had purchased the grown-up and now well-trained Fantabar. She lived about a mile above us, so Fantabar came back to her old neighborhood and raised several foals for Nevie.

 THE MONTANA YEARS

Zeke

The first mule we named Zeke was out of the chestnut brood mare, by a standard jack named Blue Zebulon. He was foaled in the spring of 1985 and was sorrel with no white markings. That same spring, Drifty delivered a molly mule named Jazz, so Zeke and Jazz grew up together here.

Eric Lambert showing Zeke at halter.
Montana Mule Days, Condon, Montana. June 1988.

 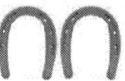

MAKIN' TRACKS

Zeke was a nice mule. He was cooperative and took to training well. We showed all our mule colts as yearlings at Montana Mule Days, and it helped train them. They got hauled and were exposed to wagons, riders, and lots of activity. They also learned to be tied for a few days running. It really helped to bomb-proof them.

Zeke and Jazz were small mules, but we led them with pack saddles when they were two. Zeke is the one that pulled Drifty off the trail.

L – R: Eric Lambert on Hemi, Baron, Jazzie Genie, Jane Lambert on Zeke, and Jerry Stamm on April, leading Clark, right before the horse fly incident. Picture taken on the pack bridge, at the west end of Lake Como, Bitterroot Mountains. 1988.

When Zeke was three, I showed him at Mule Days, and he did very well. He was an ambitious little guy and was fun to ride. He could really walk out.

That summer, we took a pack trip up behind Lake Como, and I rode Zeke. He was in the lead on the south trail and really picking them up and putting them down—*makin' tracks*—as they say. The horse flies had been bad and were biting both man and beast—big,

THE MONTANA YEARS

black, hungry ones. A large one landed on Zeke's forehead, right between his eyes. He never missed a beat, hardly paused at all, turned his head to the left, reached up with his left hind foot, and swiped it off his face. He straightened up, kept his walking rhythm, and trucked on down the trail. I was astounded and asked Eric, "Did you SEE that?"

He said, "If I HADN'T seen it, I wouldn't have believed he could do that..."

I replied, "I always knew these mules could kick my boot heels off—but now I know they could kick my earrings off!"

Many times, I have had mules reach up with a hind foot and scratch themselves behind an ear, while I was mounted on them. I have never had a horse do that. Mules are a lot more flexible than horses, as proven by Hemi, turning around in the two-horse trailer!

We made the decision that fall to sell both Jazz and Zeke, because they only grew to be about 13:2 hands, and we needed taller animals. We had Zack as a two-year-old by then, and he was already taller than the three-year-olds.

We sold both of them to a sheepherder from Wilsall, Montana. He wanted them to pack salt to his sheep, and their size was perfect for him, as he was about 5'6" and 130 pounds. We had good reports from him, and he had them for years.

 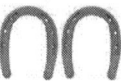

MAKIN' TRACKS

Jazz aka Jazzie Genie

Jazzie Genie was born in 1985, close to the same time that Zeke showed up. Her mother was Drifty, and her father was Blue Zebulon, making Jazz and Zeke half-siblings. She was a pretty little mule—a bay just like her mother. She was easy to halter break and handle. She, like Zeke, went to Montana Mule Days in 1986, 1987, and 1988—the first two years to be shown in halter classes and the third for both halter and performance. Mule Days at that time was in Condon, Montana.

Jane Lambert, teaching Jazzy Genie to lead. 1985.

 # THE MONTANA YEARS

Jazz was a different mule than Zeke. She tended to be lazy and a little resentful, if asked to do much. She was rather mutton withered, and she didn't care to get in a hurry with her walking. She had an odd eye, too—not like her mother's at all. It wasn't a kind eye; it had a recessed look to it—kind of a window into her personality, I guess.

I rode Jazz some, but didn't really like her. She was not very cooperative, and you had to work pretty hard to get anything out of her. Like Zeke, she only got to be about 13:2 hands tall.

She went to pack salt for sheep in Wilsall with Zeke. A good job for her...

Do you want to raise mules? This is a tip from an old mule man, who years ago told me that, in selecting a jack for your mare, the looks of the jack were immaterial—as they were ALL homely. He said a jack's offspring was the proof of his worth as a sire. He said any "jack man" who wouldn't show you his colts was hiding something.

If you want to have an idea of the mule you will get from a jack, look at his colts—the ones out of the type of mare you HAVE. If you have a Quarter Horse mare, it won't show you much to look at colts out of a Tennessee Walking horse...

 MAKIN' TRACKS

Zack

Zack was born in 1986. His mother was the chestnut brood mare, and his father was Timberjack, owned by Jim and Marilyn Stromberg. He was a real cutie. He was sociable—until Eric decided to halter break him... He resisted, he reared, and he resisted some more. Then he got mad, fell down, and went on strike—he just laid flat out. Eric got down on the ground with him, talked to him, scratched him, and made amends. After a few lessons, he was okay with being led.

Zack's first haltering. He got mad and flattened himself—on strike. Eric Lambert, standing over him. 1986.

When Zack was a yearling, I started sacking him out. Standard operating procedure with mules is to put the sack on the end of a long stick. This seems to work well at the start because, if any kicking occurs, the "operator" is out of reach.

THE MONTANA YEARS

Jane Lambert, sacking out Zack. 1987.

We always handled our mule foals a lot, and they were gentle. We showed them at Mule Days from the time they were yearlings on, and we always had to body clip them WITH the grain of their hair, especially in their yearling year, as they were very slow to shed. After that, usually they just retained long hair on their bellies, so the clipping was easy. With the sacking and the clipping, they got used to a lot—even before they got to the show.

That fall Zack was led with a little light pack; the next year, as a two-year-old, he packed groceries on some summer trips and helped pack out five elk during hunting season.

I started riding him as a three-year-old. This was in 1989, and at that time, Eric was working away from home. I was working afternoons at the local feed store and was doing the irrigating here. Luckily, we had access to ride on the very large McIntyre Ranch, about 10 minutes up the road. I got up early, set dams and moved pipes, and then loaded up Zack. I could get in a couple hours of riding, before moving dams again and going to work. The Ross, Jean, and Rod McIntyre Ranch helped me to train three mules— Zack, Zipper, and Hot Flash.

 MAKIN' TRACKS

Zack was a character, and he had his own sense of humor. From the time I first noticed, as a two- or three-year old, he would lay in wait to whip you across the face with his tail. At first it seemed coincidental, but it was a regular occurrence and timed perfectly. He always seemed nonchalant, but if you watched him, he was SO pleased when he whacked someone! I got so I would grab his tail as I walked behind him—and if I didn't, I would get a stinging reminder.

Jane Lambert showing Zack at Montana Mule Days. Condon, Montana. 1989.

Zack was shown at Montana Mule Days for 11 years in many different events. He became very well trained and won many ribbons. One year, Lisa entered him in the Ride-a-Buck class. Everyone comes in bareback and is given a dollar bill. All entrants put the dollar under their inner thigh, and the ride begins. As different gaits are called for, and as dollar bills fall, the class becomes smaller. The last one to keep their dollar bill wins. Lisa is a good rider, as she has ridden since she could walk, and Zack was SMOOTH. It was a good combination. She won it hands down, even jumping barrels, before it was over.

Zack could out walk almost anybody—he could keep up with gaited horses. Every one of his gaits was comfortable to ride. When he grew up, he looked like a Quarter Horse with long ears, and he moved much more like a horse than most mules. Some mules seem to get more donkey traits—like Jazz—and others are like Zack. The hybrid combinations that make up mules are interesting, and even full brothers and sisters can be very different.

THE MONTANA YEARS

Zack could run, too. He flattened out and grabbed ground—he did not scamper. We had a *very* inconsiderate neighbor with a *very* poorly trained poodle some years ago. I was riding up the Big Ditch right-of-way, coming home from Coller's, when this neighbor came through a gate with his dog. Zack was not afraid of dogs as he had been around them his whole life, BUT, in this case, an apparition flew at him! This 80-pound poodle had on a bulky dog coat with silver and maroon flying fringes, and it came hurtling full blast, straight at Zack! BAM! Zack was going the other way and hitting on all eight cylinders! I had been leading a horse—and her rope jerked loose, and she was left in the dust.

I have ridden some pretty good reined horses in my life, but I have never had an animal turn that hard, and accelerate that fast—ever. Thank God for past experience and good muscle memory, because I have no idea how I stayed with him. Thank God and U-Haul—that rotten neighbor is gone, too!

Jane Lambert on Zack. Hunting season. Sapphire Mountains. 1990.

 MAKIN' TRACKS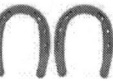

Zack had a lot of miles and experience on him when I got invited to move some cattle up on the Bitterroot Stock Farm. Charlie Yerian was cowboying up there and asked Terry Frost and me to help. Miles and experience Zack had, but not around cattle. We did fine, just driving a kind of lazy bunch up the draw, but when we got on top, we picked up some others, and one was a bunch-quitter. Zack was fast and had a good rein, so I took out after her. I started hollering and waving an arm at her, trying to turn her back. Zack started bunching up under me, and the more hollering and waving, the worse he was, until he just stampeded off across the hill. When I got him stopped, he was all fired up... And it finally dawned on me—he did not know I was yelling at the *cow*. In his whole life, the only time I raised my voice was when I was yelling at *him*. He didn't know why I was yelling at him, and he thought he was in trouble. Dumb human...

Through the years, we had sheep, and the neighbors had both sheep and goats. Zack did not like either of those critters. Some mules will go after small animals with a vengeance. Our dogs learned early on to stay away from the mule pasture. We've seen our mules run fox off, too. Zack did a tap dance on some neighbor's sheep that snuck in with him one time. I don't know if they lived or not. By the time we got over there, the sheep had staggered back through the fence. We have found dead lambs that got on the wrong side of the fence. Mules can be handy with their feet.

The funniest thing he did was grab the other neighbor's goats when they came to visit. It didn't start out funny, as we were trying to save the goats' lives, and it was a three-ring circus in the pasture, with at least three mules trying to stomp goats to death. Zack wasn't stomping—he was chomping, picking them up in the middle of the back, and tossing them around, like rag dolls. After we finally got them separated and the goats back home, Zack was making horrible faces. He spent the next hour or so, making faces, and wallowing his tongue around—trying to get the goat taste out of his mouth.

Zack was always pretty level-headed. Both Eric and I have had grouse fly up from right underneath him with no reaction. One time, over in the sagebrush at Coller's, we were looking for

THE MONTANA YEARS

Bitterroot flowers, and a newborn fawn jumped up right under his belly. It floundered in a bush, making a very startling cry for its mother. It scared me a whole lot more than Zack, as he just looked at it as it ran off.

Another time, up Calf Creek, Eric rode over the top of a flock of baby turkeys with no consequences. The mother hen was far more upset than Zack.

When Zack was five, he became Eric's mule. The only thing he packed besides Eric was meat during hunting season. We have several sets of meat bags that drape over a riding saddle, and sometimes our saddle animals got to become pack animals that way.

Zack was stout and strong, but he was only about 14:3 hands tall. He was a dark chestnut as an adult and had more heart and try than is hardly believable. Eric weighs over 200 pounds, and he rides with a custom-made saddle, britching, and breast collar, so Zack had a load for his size. Zack could power up the steep mountain above camp through a foot of snow while packing Eric and all his gear. He knew where the trail was, even when it was drifted clear over and completely unapparent. He busted through drifts that were chest high at times. If the going got tough, Zack got determined. He was a hell of a mule!

One time we were packed into and camped in Skalkaho Basin over a Labor Day weekend. There used to be a lot of elk in that Basin—until the wolves ran them out—grrr. Anyway, Eric was up, making coffee and banging around. Zack, hoping it was a grain bucket rattling, gave out his best bray—a nice long one. Very shortly, it was answered—by a bull elk. Another bray—another bugle. Eric looked over his shoulder, and a six-point bull elk walked out into the clearing. He was surprised to only see Eric as an adversary and soon disappeared.

When Eric became Line Superintendent for Ravalli County Electric Co-Op in 1992, we were able to do a lot more riding in the spring and summer, and when we weren't haying, we spent a lot of time clearing trail, hunting for shed horns, and scouting for game. We loved riding in the Sapphire Mountains, due east of Corvallis. Eric hunted there for 50 years. Zack and Eric covered a lot of territory there.

 MAKIN' TRACKS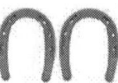

*Eric Lambert, riding Zack and leading Zipper.
Lake in Skalkaho Basin, Sapphire Mountains. 1999.*

One really nice thing about Zack was that he had the self-confidence to take off and ride by himself. Most mules like company and are nervous on solo rides. The years of my riding alone up on McIntyre's paid off. All colts must learn to trust their riders and to trust that we will bring them home. This seems to be an even harder lesson for mules, as they are very social animals, and many do not ever reach this point, like Hemi.

Zack became Baron's "right hand man" through the years, and they were great pasture buddies. Baron was "boss hoss" and made no bones about it, but he allowed Zack to stand right beside him to eat. After Baron was put down, Zack's grief was very evident, and he moped around for a long time. He actually became a loner after that and kept himself aloof from the herd.

Zack's agility was legendary with us, and he could thread through downfall like a dancer. One time, Eric had him up the East Fork of the Bitterroot, helping pack in a hunting camp, and a pack horse got loose and crowded by, above Eric and Zack.

 THE MONTANA YEARS

L to R: Dan Lambert on Spice Girl, Josh Lambert on Zipper, and Eric Lambert on Zack. Picture taken below hunting camp. Sapphire Mountains. November 2000.

Eric Lambert on Zack, coming off the hill above camp. 2000.

 MAKIN' TRACKS

It knocked them down a near vertical, 20-foot drop off. Zack turned and slid, bracing himself, and the slide took him right into some downfall, running his front legs underneath it. Eric says he somehow gathered himself back out and jumped the whole pile of logs, down into the creek, saving them from a "pile" of their own.

Zack, in hunting camp, after a blizzard from the north. I used this picture on our Christmas card that year with the caption, "Tropical Montana, My Ass!" 1999.

About 2008, Zack started having digestive issues and colicked a few times, even needing to be hospitalized. In September of 2010, we were in Pendleton, Oregon, at the Round-Up, and got a call from our animal sitter and from our vet Dick Richardson, advising us that Zack was suffering with severe colic and needed to be put down. What a horrible, horrible shock!

Eric was just sick with grief. And it was just that much worse because we were not there for him. We will be forever grateful for our neighbors Dar and Vince and Dr. Dick for handling all his arrangements, including burying him for us. Zack was 24 years old and was one-of-a kind! We still miss him.

THE MONTANA YEARS

Zipper

Zipper was a full sister to Zack. We had in mind a team of mules, but that didn't pan out. Zipper was a sorrel and had a different personality and mindset from Zack. She did not move the same, and she was not as ambitious.

Jane Lambert greeting Zipper. She was cute and friendly. 1989.

She was a darling foal, and she was always nice to handle and train. She won blue ribbons in halter as a youngster and was very pretty as an adult. As with all our mules, she packed light loads as a long yearling and heavier loads and meat as a two-year-old. She and Hot Flash were born the same spring of 1989 and grew up together. This had both its advantages and disadvantages. At times, I rode Zack and led Zipper. After the youngsters were going well, I would ride one and lead one. I could actually bring along three mules this way, using them two at a time. However, Zipper and Hot Flash never got the solo time Zack had, and they weren't particularly brave to ride on their own; they both liked company.

 MAKIN' TRACKS

Kim Jacobs of Powell, Wyoming, had the best method for riding mule colts I ever heard of. His wife would take Kim and his mule somewhere and drop them off and then go and meet them later for pick up at a designated spot. Kim's mules never knew where they were or how long they were going to be gone. They learned to totally rely on him for directions and learned to trust that their ride would show up to take them home. They never got "barn sour" because they never knew where the barn was!

A memorable moment I had on Zipper was up above hunting camp one black morning. I think she would have been about five years old. At that time, I was riding an Australian saddle, which was lucky! We always got up to go hunting at "O-Dark-Thirty," because we had to be over the top of the mountain before daylight. This morning was more than dark—it was absolutely BLACK. Eric was in front on Zack and leading a pack animal. I was in the middle, and Tom Alsaker was on Buck, right behind me. Tom's mule Red was following.

Here in Montana, you are required to wear at least 400 square inches of hunter orange for safety. For safety for our animals, we hung orange flagging tape on their tack, and when we tied up, we put orange saddle covers on them.

When we turned the camp lanterns off, it was pitch black. Eric headed Zack up the trail, and we all fell in behind. It is a strange sensation to ride totally by feel, because you cannot see. (No flashlights—the elk could see us coming!) We got about 200 yards above camp, where there is a clear-cut, and a little breeze was blowing. All of a sudden, Zipper grabbed her tail and stampeded, crowhopping off into outer space! Crash, thrash, crash, *leaping lizards*! It was black as the ace of spades! I knew the clear-cut was full of stumps, small trees, and underbrush and had a big fall-off at the edge... All of a sudden, she quit. All was quiet for a few seconds. Eric's voice came out of the dark, "Are ya on? Or are ya off?"

My reply was, "I'm on! Where the hell ARE you? Keep talking, so I know..."

THE MONTANA YEARS

We got back in line, and Zipper was goosey as could be. Whenever we would stop, she would insist on turning clear around to face Buck. When some rays of daylight filtered down, I could see what had her upset. The flagging on her crupper had worked down, and the breeze had blown it under her tail—and she was convinced that BUCK DID IT! All the way up the mountain, she literally kept an eye—or two—on him.

I have never had a bucking spree in the dark before, or since, thankfully, and I am sure glad I was riding like the *Man from Snowy River*, because that form-fitter Aussie saddle kept me right in the middle, even when I didn't know where the middle was!

Zipper was a nice mule. She was about 15 hands tall and probably was asked to pack more than be ridden. Eric had Zack, and Hot Flash was mine, so I spent more time riding her than Zip.

One time, we got suckered into a packing job that turned ugly. We were camped down in Skalkaho Basin over Labor Day weekend. It was during archery season, and two guys came walking into our camp. The first guy said he was good friends with Kevin Frost and that he had shot a bull and needed someone to pack it out for him.

We had permission to use the road up through the Frost Ranch to get to our hunting camp, and we wanted to stay on good terms, so we thought we would help out Kevin's "friend."

First off, the bull was shot down in a hell-hole and even getting to it was a trial. Then, when we got to it, the meat was not only boned out, but it was still warm. There was a lot of meat, as it came from a big bull. They had wrapped it in cheesecloth, and it was like trying to pack congealed jello. We had not expected any of that. We showed up with two Decker pack saddles and ropes. We quarter our elk, leaving the hide on and the bones IN, so you have something to tie TO. That was what we had expected.

What a blubbery, rubbery mess! We'd tie it on and go a ways, and it would ooze out of the ropes. The meat hit the ground a number of times before we tied it in a way to stay. Then we missed the trail up the rock cliff, which is the fastest way out of the Basin but tricky to find because of all the other game trails. Eric and Zack

MAKIN' TRACKS

had led Gypsy quite far up the mountain when the game trail they were on petered out. I was down below with Zipper, who had the hind quarters on her. She turned to the downhill, put her head down to eat, and the load somersaulted her. She was pinned down, with her head down the hill. I got her ropes untied, the meat slithered off, and she stood up.

Meanwhile, up the hill, Eric had his own trauma. Gypsy's load turned, and she got it to the uphill side, but she was braced with all she had and was in danger of rolling down the hill. I climbed up as fast as I could and helped to brace Gypsy, while Eric got the load off. The breast collar was cutting across her neck so hard it had her dented in. When the meat came free, it rolled a ways, and then we carried it the rest of the way down and put it on a large flat rock. We hoisted Zipper's load up there, too, then rode back to camp, and had a couple of stiff drinks.

The hunters had packed their head, horns, and cape back up to their truck. They came back down to see where we were. We were bushed, and our mules were lucky not to have gotten hurt. We weren't too happy.

Eric told them that their meat had about killed our mules and that we were done for the day. We would pack the meat out in the morning, and for them to be up above the old vermiculite cabin at 11:00 am. It was a two-hour pack to get there. Let me say here that, at that time, we and our animals were in good shape. We had to be, as that is rough, unforgiving country.

The meat was easier to handle that morning. It had stiffened up overnight, and we wisely brought the Ralide boxes and panniers to put it in. We went around by Fool Hen Lake, instead of trying the rock cliff again, and when we got there with the meat, the hunter "generously" gave Eric 50 bucks.

When we saw Kevin Frost later, he didn't even know the guy, let alone was his "friend." Well, "friend," that meat was the dirtiest, grittiest, grungiest stuff we ever dealt with, and if justice was served, it tasted just as bad as it looked when it was served to you...

THE MONTANA YEARS

Jane and Eric Lambert in front of old vermiculite miner's cabin. 2001.

One spring day, Dawn and I were riding up on the Calf Creek Game Range. She was on Baron, and I was on Zipper. We heard a noise up the ravine and saw my Border Collie, Tess, herding a calf elk right toward us. I hollered, "That'll do," to Tess, and she dropped down in the grass.

Baron looking at calf elk, which was confused and trying to nurse Zipper on the Calf Creek Game Range, Hamilton, Montana.

MAKIN' TRACKS

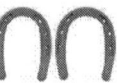

The calf was a new one, and it was very confused. It decided that Zipper was its mother and ran right over and tried to nurse her. This flustered Zipper, and she started whirling in circles to get away from the calf. Dawn and I could see cow elk up on the ridge and figured one of them was the calf's mother. The calf was bleating and zeroed in on Zipper... What a dilemma!

This is a reserve where elk are protected in the spring to allow them to calve in peace, and it is well named. We have all seen elk calves up there, but this was the first "up close and personal" encounter—which put Zipper in a dither...

Dawn and I both had cameras, and we got some nice pictures of the whole incident, while wondering what to do. Finally, the calf moved off away from us, and we rode away fast, so the cow could come and retrieve her calf.

When the grandkids came along, they started riding Zipper and meshed well with her. They rode her on trail rides, and they showed her at Montana Mule Days and won many ribbons in the youth classes. The last time she went to the show was in 1998, and Kyle was the only grandkid with us. He wanted to try and win High Point Youth and win a silver buckle. He had been practicing and got along very well with her. He entered in a lot of different classes over the three-day show and was winning, but Zipper was getting really tired of it all by Sunday afternoon. She went on strike and wouldn't leave the horse trailer. Kyle was upset and crying and mad at her. I told him, "She's done. Let's unsaddle her, tie her up, and feed her. She's not liking this anymore."

"But Grandma, if I don't get enough points, then I won't win the buckle."

I told him, "Well, that's the breaks. We can't wreck a good mule by asking too much of her when she's tired and cranky. She's worked a whole lot for you already, and you either have enough points by now, or you don't. She's done."

Kyle and Zipper won the High Point Youth buckle for 1998. She had *done enough*!

THE MONTANA YEARS

Kyle Schoening, showing Zipper at Montana Mule Days, Drummond, Montana. They won High Point Youth and a silver buckle. 1998.

Hemi taught me that you don't push a good mule too far. The first time she let me know was by dragging her feet to the pleasure finals in Bishop, California. Several other times through the years, she would get tired of the "show" game and start being reluctant to head to the arena. I always listened to her and quit. It is just not worth it to push an animal into something they are not enjoying anymore for a two-dollar ribbon. Dawn once had Zack quit on her during a Play Day, and we told her the same thing, "Get off. He's done."

Zipper, Eric Lambert, and Zack. Early hunting season. Sapphire Mountains, up above the vermiculite miner's cabin. 2001.

 MAKIN' TRACKS

Eric on Zack, leading Zipper on the rock cliff trail above Skalkaho Basin. This a challenging, uphill climb, and the trail is hard to find. September 1996.

With the kind of riding we were doing, we needed happy mules underneath us. We were in rough, rugged country. Our lives depended on our mules, and having them as willing partners for the whole rest of the year, was far more important to us than ribbons from a show.

As Zipper got older, she began displaying behavior problems going downhill. We had her feet x-rayed, and she was found to have developed navicular disease. We retired her, and when she got really lame in 2002, we put her down and buried her near Hemi.

 THE MONTANA YEARS

Hot Flash

I was 45 years old in 1989 when Hot Flash was born. Since I figured her for my "menopausal" mule, I named her that. What do you expect from a person born on April Fool's Day? If you guessed irreverent, you are right. Eric and I got married on Halloween, too. We observe major holidays...

Flasher's mother was Sissy, and her sire was Timberjack. She was a large foal, and her legs were rather crooked at birth, so she stayed in a small area for the first 10 days, and she straightened up.

Sissy and newborn Hot Flash with Jane Lambert. 1989.

This is a selenium deficient area, so we fed a good prenatal supplement, developed for western Montana and sold by our veterinarian. We also always gave foals and lambs a selenium shot right after birth. We figured that Flasher's long legs just didn't have quite enough room inside her mother. She was soon fine.

She was a pretty buckskin color when she was little, but became a bay in adulthood. She took after her maternal grandmother and grew to 16 hands tall. Her height and mutton withers made her hard to get on, and she was "stump broke" to

stand next to anything—anything—which would give me a chance to get on *fast*.

I had a custom mule saddle made for her, which fit all three of the QH-cross mules we had. Once a person rides a good custom made saddle, it spoils you for factory made ones...

I started and rode Flash exclusively, and she was easy to train. The year of packing we gave our mule colts made all of them easy to train. They learned to stay on the trail, not bump into trees, carry weight, and cross creeks all before they had a rider. The mule show got them used to crowds, buggies, noise, and being tied. Having a bit in their mouth and getting directions from a rider was an easy transition for them.

I have trained many young animals—dogs, colts, mules, and kids. If you can get any and all of them into adulthood without self-destructing, you are doing well. They all need direction, discipline, consistency, and patience. Lisa will tell you I had more patience with my animals than her... And it's true!

Jane Lambert on Hot Flash and Eric Lambert on Zack. Typical hunting day picture. Taken in "The Hole," Sapphire Mountains. 2000.

THE MONTANA YEARS

When it comes to training horses and mules, there are some differences. Horses are more forgiving. They will take a lot more from us than will mules. Horses will withstand more repetition in their training and usually are less challenging. Mules are really smart and catch on much faster at times, but actually take longer to train, because they get bored very easily and will resent it if you start cramming a lesson down their throats. A horse will let you go in circles for hours and just put up with you. A mule will get really tired of that in 10 minutes and want to GO somewhere… Horses are tolerant; mules get defensive. I have heard it said, "Mules MUST be trained the way horses SHOULD be trained."

In all cases, as a human leader, you must make your training signals clear and consistent and your disciplinary actions fair and firm. You must be the "boss mare," but your objective should be to forge a willing partnership.

Jane Lambert on Hot Flash, getting ready to show English. Montana Mule Days, Drummond, Montana. 1998.

 MAKIN' TRACKS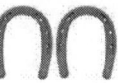

And Flash was willing. She did everything asked of her. She was good minded and kind, and I have only good memories of riding her. No wrecks, no runaways, just lots of good, solid miles in rough country, and non-eventful rides into and out of hunting camp. She was a good partner. She also won her share of ribbons both for me and the grandkids. I showed her in performance classes, English and Western, but not speed events.

1998 was the last time we went to Montana Mule Days. Our colts were all trained, the grandkids lost interest, and we didn't need any more ribbons. We concentrated on being in the mountains with our well-trained animals and did that for as long as we could. I thank Montana Mule Days for giving me the incentive to put the formal training on our mules. No one wants to BE an ass, ON an ass, in public, and *that* was my motivation... My reward was riding well-trained, safe animals for many years.

Hot Flash was another of our animals that outgrew her infrastructure—like Joker. As she got older, coming down hill became painful for her, and she developed arthritis in her knees and was retired early. We always figured arthritis would cause her demise, but in January of 2004, she developed colic. We discovered her in agony one Sunday morning. The snow was all disturbed where she had thrashed around during the night, and she was suffering.

Eric had his left arm in a cast from his wreck that fall, but he walked out to where she was and put her out of her misery. He said she never even blinked. He shot her, as previously described in Patchy's story.

We buried her near where she fell, and eerily, all her pasture buddies stood vigil on her grave for at least three days. We ALL mourned her passing.

 THE MONTANA YEARS

Brandy

Back in the spring of 1989, I saw an ad in the paper for a half-Thoroughbred, half-Welsh horse. I was a sort of a "jump-the-gun" grandma, looking for a horse for Lisa's children. The oldest was only four at the time, so perhaps I WAS over-excited about the idea!

Anyway, the horse was in Hamilton and was owned by a little boy, who had been involved with Pony Club down there. I can't remember the reason they gave for selling her, but it was because she was too much horse for him and had become VERY barn sour—which we found out later.

Brandy was a beauty. She was a dark bay with a blaze face and was about 13:2 hands tall. She was built like a miniature Thoroughbred, and she was very athletic. She was good to handle and load, was easy to catch, and had a good handle on her. Both Lisa and I rode her, and she tried us pretty hard in the barn-sour department. That behavior did not pay off for her, and after a few "discussions," she got over it. By the time the kids were old enough to really ride her, Lisa and I had made sure she was a safe kids' horse.

L to R: Zack, Baron, Eric Lambert on Hemi, Drifty, held by Jane Lambert on Brandy. At trailhead to Pyramid Pass. Bob Marshall Wilderness. 1989.

 MAKIN' TRACKS

I rode her in late July on a 12-day pack trip into the Bob Marshall Wilderness. She was a pleasure to ride and as tough as they come. The more I rode her, the better she was. Getting her out of an arena and on the trail was really good for her attitude.

L to R: Kayla Schoening on Baron, Korri Schoening on Hemi, and Kyle Schoening on Brandy. Kyle's 9th birthday ride. McIntyre Ranch, foothills of the Sapphire Mountains, east of Stevensville, Montana. June 1995.

We amused well-known outfitter Smoke Elser on that trip. He was not our outfitter—we had none. He rode into Big Prairie with another party and then came over to inspect our loads. Zack had partially pulled a shoe on a tree root, and we stopped at the Ranger Station in Big Prairie for some help. One of the rangers was a farrier, and he reset the shoe. Our animals were all tied at the hitching rack when Smoke pulled in with a string. We saw him inspect our loads carefully. Zack had a sawbuck saddle with panniers and a top pack, tied with a diamond hitch. Baron had on Ralide boxes strapped to a Decker, with a top pack buckled on the boxes. Drifty had a Decker with mantied loads and an ax on one side and a saw on the other. We had a style for EVERYBODY!

I had a real shock a few years after we owned Brandy. I was grooming her, and under her thick, black mane was a BRAND! There was no mention of a brand on her bill of sale or brand inspection papers. She had come from a Kalispell equestrian center, to Hamilton, to us. The brand was barely visible, even with

THE MONTANA YEARS

her summer coat, but clearly was a dot, bar, dot—like a division symbol, on her left neck. I just felt sick. In Montana, for a bill of sale to be valid, it must show a horse's brand and location on the paperwork. No brand was shown on her paperwork, so legally, we did not own her—the guy who owned her brand owned her.

The only thing to do was call the brand inspector about it—he was a friend, Boone Jones. Boone looked it up and found the man's name who owned the brand—he lived in Polson, Montana. I got his address and wrote him a letter about Brandy and about buying her for my grandchildren, etc., and tried to "persuade" him by enclosing a picture of all three of them on Brandy.

He was very nice about the whole thing. He called me, and we had a long visit. He was really mad at his ex-wife over it. She got Brandy in the divorce and was supposed to keep her for HIS kids. The "ex" had sold Brandy to the outfit in Kalispell—without the proper brand papers. He had every right to come and get his horse.

Anyway, he said her name had been Stoney and that she was the most sure-footed horse on ice he had ever seen. He sent me the proper paperwork for her and said, if we ever wanted to sell her, to let him know. Whew! We dodged a bullet there! Thank you, thank you!

L to R: Steve Morton, Lisa riding sidesaddle on Brandy, and Marilyn Stromberg on Miss Kitty. Creamery Picnic Parade, Stevensville. 1989.

 MAKIN' TRACKS

Brandy was a whale of a little horse. She had been jumped in Pony Club events, and she loved it. The kids jumped her over logs every chance they got. She was tough and sure footed and loved going in the mountains.

Kayla Schoening riding Brandy, getting ready to show in Stevensville. 1995.

From first introduction, Brandy did not like mules. She was handy with her hind feet in keeping them away from her. She never did warm up to them, kept her distance, and made them keep theirs, too.

In September of 1989, Eric took Brandy as a pack horse 21 miles into the Bitterroot Mountains behind Lake Como. They packed Jerry Stamm's hunting camp into Bell Lake. The string packed half a ton of hay, a tent, camp equipment, and some groceries, plus sleeping bags for the riders involved. They had about 15 pack animals on this trip. Eric rode Hemi and packed Baron, Zack, and Brandy. The riders stayed overnight and rode out the next day. Brandy's place in line was behind Zack, as she didn't want him behind HER.

 # THE MONTANA YEARS

She also packed meat the first few years we had her. Packing grandkids was easy duty after all this…

Lisa rode Brandy off and on, and these are her stories:

One day, I decided to ride Brandy right after we first got her to tune her up a little. I was in the field on Mickey Morton's place in the Three Mile Area. I started out, loping some simple circles and trying to get her to take her leads. She would not do anything I asked. I spent over three hours that day, trying to get her to do what I wanted. I remember being sweaty and frustrated, but impressed with her will. She was the most stubborn, hard-headed horse I had ever ridden. Not mean, or vengeful, just stubborn. I was more stubborn than her, and we both tested each other. In the end, we came to greatly respect each other. She knew what was expected of her when the kids rode her and what my expectations were when I was on her.

Ed Cummings decided one winter that it was a good idea to calve 300 head of Black Angus cows on the hill way above the calving barn. I was working for Ed, so I took Brandy over there. I bundled up in thermals and insulated coveralls, hung saddle bags and other bags to hold ear tags and medicines on my saddle, and spent the day on Brandy, calving, tagging, and recording calves. There were always several over-protective cows. One cow would see me coming from several yards away and would come after me. She finally settled down enough for me to get close to her calf. I stepped off Brandy, grabbed the calf, and started to ear tag it when the cow came for me. I was in a bad spot, with nowhere to go. Brandy came over and took on the cow, staying between the cow and the calf, until I could get it worked. She did that a couple of times that winter. Without a doubt, she saved me from great harm!

There was also a cow that got down in the creek, fell through the ice, and went into labor. I was on Brandy, and I roped the cow, and we tried to pull her out of the water, but couldn't. So then, I left Brandy with the cow tied to the saddle horn, and I got down in the creek, which was about waist-deep, and delivered the calf under water. I got it up and on the bank, breathing. The cow was more helpful then, and Brandy got her pulled out, too. I took the rope off the cow, threw the calf across my saddle, and got the cow and calf to the barn, where we all warmed up. Both the cow and calf survived.

She loved working cows, and she was the perfect size to maneuver in and out of the herd and to get on and off. She was not always big enough to pull one out of trouble, but she sure tried!

I did some team penning on Brandy down at the Fort Owen Arena in Stevensville. One time, she started doing an excited, bounce thing—not a rear up, just a bounce. Then it escalated, and she got higher in the air and started rearing. Steve Morton was a partner that day, and before our next go, I picked up a stick about a foot long and a couple of inches around and carried it into the arena.

I had the job of covering "the hole," and as the cattle came around, I was watching my team mates and the cattle. I felt Brandy start to come up, so I took my stick and rapped her on the head right between the ears. She went to her knees. It was the weirdest feeling ever. All the spectators did a big AHHH, and I started grabbing leather, because I wasn't sure what was going on. I pulled up on the reins, she stood up, shook her head, and helped pen the cattle, and our time was fast! We all got a good laugh out of it, as everyone said both Brandy and I had priceless looks on our faces! Brandy never reared again, either.

Lisa's kids weren't riding Brandy much after a while, so we loaned her to Erica, Dan's daughter, over in Idaho. Erica rode her for several years and won a lot of ribbons and a Year End High Point award. When she outgrew Brandy, we brought her back to Montana.

Since the grandkids had outgrown her and were off in other directions, we found a perfect new owner for her, Ashley Dewey. Brandy and Ashley were a good fit, and Ashley won six blue ribbons on Brandy at that fall's Ravalli County Fair. Tragedy struck that winter when Brandy got her hoof caught in a root wad, turned upside down, and suffocated before they found her. She is buried on Sunset Bench.

THE MONTANA YEARS

Gypsy

Ray and Sue Lyons raised Gypsy. Her father was Montana Jack, and her mother was a paint mare named Redwing. Gypsy was born up the West Fork of the Bitterroot, about 1976. She was a chestnut and white pinto mule and was very nicely marked. She was a little over 15 hands tall and was stockily built with a large barrel and a big spring of rib. She was drafty looking and had a very mellow personality.

Sue remembers that, even as a foal, Gypsy loved to have her butt and ears scratched—and always did as an adult, too. She was a "people" mule.

Hank Meyers broke Gypsy to drive, and she was going well. Then Ray had a runaway with her and ended up in the barrow pit alongside a dirt road. This was on the way to their house, and the homemade cart was "the worse for wear." Sue pulled it home, and Ray led Gypsy. That's about how it always goes—the man drug his ass home, and the wife pulled the load… (Oops, THAT'LL get me in trouble!)

Asa Yerian, driving Gypsy, pulling in firewood for hunting camp. This is the clear-cut above camp where Zipper took off bucking in the dark. 1993.

 MAKIN' TRACKS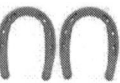

Gypsy carrying the WWII litter for the Costume Class at Montana Mule Days, Drummond. Her signage says "Pack 'em in, Pack 'em out." Eric Lambert on Zack is leading her. Circa 1995.

Gypsy, packed with the front quarters and horns of a bull elk, Eric Lambert, and Zack carrying meat bags with the elk hind quarters. Below hunting camp tent. 1998.

THE MONTANA YEARS

Packer's Scramble, Montana Mule Days, Drummond. L to R: Zipper, Dawn Lambert, Zack, Gypsy, and Eric Lambert, mantying loads. Eric was in charge of this class for years. It took a truck to bring all the items to pack for the class. 1996.

Lyons primarily used Gypsy as a pack mule, and she made many trips into the Bob Marshall Wilderness. One time, when she was packing in the Scapegoat Wilderness, a dingy mare, who was tied behind her, jerked her off a 30' cliff. She pedaled down and stayed on all fours. Sue said the big problem was getting her yarded back up to the trail. She came out of it with only a small cut on her shoulder. Another lesson in making a breakaway that will BREAK!

Ray and Sue sold her to David Stenerson, and he logged with her for a couple of years, and we bought her from him in 1995.

She was a really nice mule, just as honest and kind as she could be. We drove her, pulling logs into camp, and that really made headway with our hunting camp wood. Dawn entered her in the log pull at Mule Days and drove her to a cart, and she won ribbons in both classes. She had a completely uneducated mouth and barely plow reined, both in driving and riding. She was level headed, though, and never tried to run off.

The grandkids rode her quite a bit, and on the trail, she was perfect—she would stay in line and follow along, just like in a pack string. They rode her in parades, too. If you had her in the arena and were trying to go through obstacles, there was no power steering—it was all "Arm-Strong." In performance events, she did best in things like the *Ugly Hat Contest, Lead Your Ass to Water,* and *Costume Class.*

 MAKIN' TRACKS

Where she really shone for us was packing. She would pack anything we put on her and do it willingly and quietly. She did not have to be led; she followed along in her place. If her pack shifted, she stopped. After it was re-balanced, she started up again. She was very wise. Eric says the only thing wrong with her was that we didn't get her sooner.

L to R: Hot Flash and Kyle Schoening, Gypsy and Kayla Schoening, Zipper and Erica Lambert, Zack and Korri Schoening, unknown, and Hemi and Josh Lambert. Mule Days, Drummond, Montana, when we had all five grandchildren there. 1996.

Creamery Picnic Parade, Stevensville, Montana. R to L: Kyle Schoening on Hot Flash, Kayla Schoening on Hemi, Korri Schoening on Gypsy, Lisa on Zack, and Jane on Zipper. 1996.

She worked for us for years and then came down with arthritis and had to be put down—around 2001.

 THE MONTANA YEARS

White Mules

*Eric and Jane Lambert in the wagon.
White mules were borrowed from Larry Worth.
Eric spent one whole winter rebuilding this spring wagon.
It had belonged to Carl Swanson's parents and had been stored in
Charlie Swanson's barn since the turn of the century.
The wheels and running gear were protected by chopped hay;
the rest was shot. This is its debut, in the Creamery Picnic Parade.
It is now owned by Jim Swanson,
and so is back in the Swanson family. 1989.*

 MAKIN' TRACKS

Spice Girl

In 1998, Lisa, Eric, and I went up Sweeney Creek to look at a two-year-old QH filly that was for sale. This turned into another one of *THOSE DEALS*. The Sweeney Creek man had bought a mare from a man because of a feud. A QH stud went across the fence and bred the neighbor's mare. The stud man wanted a fee— the mare man wanted damages. It got ugly, and the mare went to Sweeney Creek.

The sorrel mare we looked at was the product of the wayward stud. Purebred, but not a whisper of a chance for papers... Lisa and I were looking for a project and decided to buy her together— for $200 each.

The only thing the old guy had done with her was throw her hay. She was just barely halter broke and had never been in a horse trailer. We finally bribed her into the four-horse with some grain and got her home.

She was a very pretty, bright sorrel with a nice head and blazed face. She knew nothing, but had a good disposition and learned fast. In fact, knowing nothing was good, because she had no bad habits to undo. She was here, and Lisa was working, so I did the pre-training on her. I sacked her out, taught her to pick up her feet, and saddled her.

Then, one evening, I went out to check the animals and discovered that Spice had a severe barbed wire cut across her right buttock—it was a good eight inches long and gaping. I called a local veterinarian and made arrangements to bring her in on an after-hours call. Spice was not happy in the stocks, and when the numbing shots started, she started kicking. The vet kept whacking her, and she kicked harder. Good training, for kicking...

When it was said and done, she had rubber drain tubes inserted between the stitches, as the cut had been fairly deep. I was pretty concerned, what with the kicking spree!

After she healed, and the stitches needed to come out, I decided to try and de-sensitize her, as I did not want to get kicked.

THE MONTANA YEARS

I tied her up to the hitch rail, then tied up her right hind foot, and started running a flag all over her. After a couple of times of this, she was very quiet and calm and showed no signs of kicking. She let me take out her stitches and tubes with no resistance.

Not too long after that, I took her up to Superior to have Alta Boyes get her started under saddle. I didn't think to tell Alta about the vet "incident." She called to ask me why I thought the mare was kicking at the driving lines… That was easy to figure out… Alta did a lot more bomb proofing on her, and she was always fine after that. Every action has a reaction with a horse, and they have lots of memory…

A good learning curve for Spice, and for grandkids Kyle and Kayla, occurred one late fall/winter day. There was a good foot of snow on the ground, and the kids and I went out to catch Spice. Normally, she was not hard to catch, but this day, she decided to run. She was in a fairly good-sized pasture, and she was really giving us some action. Finally, I stationed Kyle and Kayla where they could shorten her running room by turning her back with snowballs. That was working, but she wasn't wearing down very fast. Grandma was getting a lot "wore" though, trying to run in the snow with knee boots on.

Finally, Kayla said, "How long do we have to do this, Grandma?"

And I answered, "Until midnight, if that's what it takes…"

I'm glad Spice gave it up not long after that, because I know I'd have never made midnight… But I found out a long time ago that giving up and letting a horse get away with that behavior is a sure-fire way to train them to be hard to catch. Spice learned and never pulled that stunt again.

I grew very fond of this little horse—and bought Lisa out. She and I spent a week in the mountains when she was four, just Spice, our dogs, Katie (black Lab) and Tess (Border Collie), and me.

One day, I rode down to the old vermiculite miner's cabin to give Spice a drink. The dogs had been there many times, as it was Asa Yerian's hunting shack, and we had also camped there. As I approached the cabin, the door cracked open, and the dogs ran over and let themselves in. Then the door opened, and a really, spooky-looking guy came out, with another of the same caliber behind him. I was glad my .357 was strapped on my horn in plain view. I called the dogs, apologized for their "welcome," watered my horse, and rode on up the hill.

Spice Girl up on Horse Ridge, above the vermiculite cabin, shortly before encountering the weirdos there. Glad for the .357 on my old Bentley saddle.

That cabin had been a party house off and on for many years and once was a fugitive's haven—a stupid fugitive, who had written a life-threatening note on the wall of the cabin against his parole officer, who was also Asa's hunting partner's son. The dummy paid for that!

That afternoon, the two ratty-looking guys left in their pickup, which had a distinctively shaped cab on it, and I was relieved. My tent was pitched below the cabin a mile or so and up on the hill, above the road. A few nights later, around midnight, I heard the roar of an engine, going like hell and being gunned. As a pickup passed below me, I could tell by its cab that it was the weirdos. When they saw that my tent was still there, they turned around in

 THE MONTANA YEARS

the wide spot up the road and roared back off the mountain. I don't know who they were or what their business was up there, but I am glad the dogs flushed them out of the cabin, so they could see the big pistol on my saddle—I love the Second Amendment!

Katie and Tess sitting in front of the old miner's cabin. Good dogs!

The old vermiculite miner's cabin. Built 1932.
Torn down by U.S. Forest Service in 2008 for no good reason.

 MAKIN' TRACKS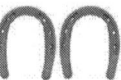

The rest of my time on the mountain was very enjoyable, as was the next year, riding this horse. She came along fast and was neck reining pretty well. I looked forward to riding her for years to come.

This is an aside from Spice, but at this time in her life, in 2000, a major event happened to the Bitterroot Valley and to Eric and I.

Eric was Line Superintendent for the Ravalli Electric Cooperative and was going down to turn the power back on to some residences in the south valley near Medicine Hot Springs. They had been threatened by fire, but were no longer in danger. This was on Sunday, August 6, about 2 p.m., and he asked me if I "wanted to take a drive."

Wall of flame coming at us, right before we drove north on Hwy 93, towards Sula Ranger Station. 2000.

 # THE MONTANA YEARS

After turning on their power, we went on down to Sula, where the fire camp was situated. Eric had gotten a call from them, saying another power line was threatened. As Eric was preparing to shut off the line, the whole complexion of the fire, which was burning on the west side of Highway 93, changed. The wind picked up, and became erratic and turbulent. Eric was barely able to snare the shut off ring with his hot stick. Suddenly, we were faced with a solid wall of flame, 200 feet high, coming east and straight at us. Lawn chairs, boxes, garbage, and cans were whirling in the air. The meadow, a half mile east of the approaching flames, suddenly burst into flame behind the waiting firefighters.

Eric made it back to the truck just as the green grass in front of the pickup spontaneously ignited. The firefighters in the camp were fighting for their lives as we powered up Highway 93 to the north. Eric stopped to talk to the incident commander at the Sula Ranger Station, who said the fire had turned deadly and that firestorm conditions were escalating. He said this type of fire was what they trained for, but hoped never to see.

Highway 93 had become unsafe, and we were directed to the Sula Community Clubhouse. As we approached it on a back road, a huge smoke cloud was on the horizon, and it was black as coal; it covered the whole area of the Vogt Ranch. Then a huge roar commenced, and Sula Peak burst into flame and was completely engulfed within two minutes. When the black smoke cleared, the flashing red lights of the local firefighters showed they had saved the ranch buildings.

Then the same eerie phenomena that I saw in 1981 in California occurred—spontaneous combustion, out in the irrigated hayfields. One by one, the big, round bales left out in the field ignited and started burning. No flames were near them, just the right atmospheric conditions. As dusk settled, I counted 20 of them, their fiery halos lighting the otherwise blackened horizon. When we visited that area a few days later, only blackened fire rings remained in the green fields. They were the only evidence of the whole hay crop.

 MAKIN' TRACKS

Because of my experience in 1981, I knew *exactly* when the fire became a firestorm, and I hope I *never* get that life lesson again.

In 2001, when Spice was five, a firestorm of an entirely different kind happened. She came up very lame. The diagnosis was severe arthritis and bone decomposition in both front feet—a death sentence. I was just sick over it.

This takes us back up to the first paragraph and the fateful words: *"one of those deals."* In the midst of those fighting human beings, the horses had been forgotten. The pregnant mare was sold into a west side canyon, which was very mineral deficient, and she was not given any pre-natal vitamin/mineral supplements. The filly was foaled into that environment, and no thought was given to feed HER any vitamins/minerals. The result was my beautiful, kind, trainable mare BROKE down, because the human beings in her life LET her down, and I had to PUT her down. That was another heart-breaking tear-jerker. It is just never easy to say good-by to a trusted companion. Necessary, at times, but NEVER easy!

 THE MONTANA YEARS

Idaho Adventure 2002

This chapter is a little different. It is not about one of my animals, but is nonetheless a horse adventure story that I originally wrote for *Idaho Magazine*, and it appeared in the May 2003 issue. It was titled "By Prop, Hoof, and Tread." This is an edited version.

When the phone rang, late in the evening of November 14, 2002, it gave me a start. It was Lynette Coller, asking me if I would be interested in flying into the Selway Wilderness with her and husband Tony. The mission was to rescue four horses, which were left stranded and at the mercy of the wolves and winter. They would have a sure death, if not ridden out. Of course, I said *yes*—it was an adventure!

Background: L to R: Emil's plane and Jack's plane.
L to R: Jane Lambert on Roman, Lynette Coller on Buddy,
Tony Coller on Blue and holding Stubby. Ready to ride to Paradise!

Lynette's cousin, Jack Vallance, a renowned back country pilot, had been contacted by Dr. Iacono, who owned the 154-acre, Running Creek Ranch, a privately-owned property surrounded by 1.6 million acres of Selway Wilderness. There are only four "grandfathered" private parcels within this wilderness area.

Unforeseen circumstances had forced Dr. Iacono to fly off and leave his horses. Usually, the outfitter from the North Star took the

MAKIN' TRACKS

horses out, but that year he left early, and the doctor and his wife Grace still wanted to ride. Then the barn and tack shed burned up at Running Creek, so there was nothing there to ride *with*. On the heels of that misfortune came word that Dr. Iacono's mother was terminally ill and that he needed to get to her bedside, ASAP. So the Iaconos flew out, leaving the four horses unattended in a large pasture.

On the phone, Lynette said we were going to fly in at the soonest possible opportunity, perhaps even the next morning, as the wolves had gotten very bad in there, and it had been a week since the doctor left. The morning of November 15 dawned perfectly for flying. We loaded our tack and drove to Hamilton Airport. Lynette's dad Zach Bugli was driving their pickup and pulling their trailer, as he was going to drive on into Paradise, Idaho. We would meet him and load the horses, after riding them out.

At the airport, experienced pilots Emil Schrader and Jack Vallance awaited us. We loaded the tack in Emil's plane and loaded ourselves with Jack. Emil took off first. Jack had airplane "virgins" with him, and we were all a little nervous. Jack had flown into this area at least 200 times through the years, so he knew what he was doing. We all hoped our Dramamine was working...

Our take-off was perfect, and we started our trip over the Bitterroot Mountains, going south and west, about 50 air miles, to Running Creek. The mountains were mantled with bright, new snow, and the view below was breathtaking. The Bitterroot Range is 10,000+ feet in elevation and is rough, jagged, glaciated country. It is very rugged and forbidding, with few places to land a plane. When we passed over the top to the Idaho side, there was a sea of fog below. Jack said, if the ranch was fogged in, we'd have to abort the trip.

It was clear, however, and as we made a pass over the runway, we saw Emil land with our tack. The ranch sits in a bowl, not far from the Selway River, and to get to the landing strip requires about four tight, spiraling circles down, before lining up with the little landing strip. It was pretty quiet in the plane as we watched our wing tips graze past the canyon walls... Then, with a swoosh, we were on the ground. Phew!

 **THE MONTANA YEARS**

We got out, and the horses came running—they were glad for company. We lit on the ground at 10:35 a.m. and were ready to ride by 11:00 a.m. Tony chose "Blue," a Percheron/QH cross, who had the fastest walk. He led "Stubby," a Bashkir Curley we dubbed "the dinosaur" because of his looks. Lynette chose "Buddy," a pretty black and white paint, and I rode "Roman," a blaze-faced bay, named after his own nose. I brought up the drag.

It was eight miles to Paradise. *That* sounded like the opportunity of a lifetime! We crossed the pack bridge over the Selway River, and in looking down, we could see the river's edges were already bordered in ice. It freezes solid in winter, and Jack Frost was closing in.

We all remarked about what good-natured horses these were, and we were glad, because the trail along the Selway climbed high above the river, and was fairly narrow. At times, we were looking down our stirrups a loooong ways...

Lynette Coller on Buddy and leading Stubby, going around the blind turn, high above the Selway River. In the river below were the bones of five pack mules, so a good name for it is Dead Mule Curve.

 MAKIN' TRACKS

One treacherous switchback, between "Bad Luck" and "Waldo Bar" is high, steep, and on a blind corner. I found out later that one time Bud Ruark came around the turn and met a bear on the other side. His big, paint horse made a catty, 180-degree about-face and saved Bud from a horrible wreck. Bud forever after that got off his horse and walked around that part of the trail. This was with good reason, as the bones of five pack mules lay in the river below. They were whiplashed off the edge, and all went off together. It is a dangerous curve. We were fortunate to only meet a few hunters, and those at a good place to pass.

Tony and Lynette Coller riding across the pack bridge over the Selway.

As for weather, we were very lucky, too. It was 40 degrees, sunny, with no wind and a bare trail. The sunlight filtered in and out of the canyon, and we took off and put on our sunglasses and gloves, as needed. We couldn't decide which was the better time, the flight or the ride. Both were beautiful and fun to experience.

 # THE MONTANA YEARS

When we stopped for lunch, Stubby proved himself a skilled beggar and especially relished Tony's licorice. The trail from there on was much more user-friendly, being wider, flatter, and closer to the river. In the spring, that country is full of rattlesnakes, and I have had friends tell me of killing six snakes on the eight miles into North Star, which is adjacent to Running Creek. Sure glad it was November!

By 2 p.m., we had reached the trailhead. Not quite *Paradise*, but close... We could hardly wait...

Zach had picked up a traveling partner, Bill Harris. We unsaddled and loaded the horses, and Lynette and I fixed ourselves a nest in the back of the pickup. Not room for five in the cab, so we readied ourselves and our cameras for *Paradise*. After about five miles, we knocked on the cab, and asked when we going to get there... Silence. Then, "Well, it was back down the road, five miles..." They didn't pull in. Disappointment! We STILL have not been to *Paradise*...

We got serious with piling saddle pads to sit on and gathering a sleeping bag around us. You just don't realize how sore your butt bones can get until you jounce over gravel roads for 45 miles in a stiff-springed pickup bed.

Getting back home *wasn't* paradise. We had to go over the 6,588-foot Nez Perce Pass, and the roads became snow-packed and icy. We stayed warm—except for my feet. Lynette had smartly worn pacs, but I had worn cowboy boots. There was only about six inches of snow on the road, which was better than the two feet they sometimes had by that time of year. It was, in fact, usually closed by then. It was pretty icy on the Montana side, but the horses rode well, and we made it.

We were very happy to get to the West Fork Road, where Bill Harris' rig was, and the pavement began. Lynette and I got to get into the warm cab! We were grateful for the last 60 miles of warm comfort, and I got my feet defrosted.

The horses were grateful for the nice corral and feeder full of hay at the Coller Ranch. Roman was clacking his teeth like

 MAKIN' TRACKS

castanets, looking at it, while his halter was removed. Those horses were hungry, and we got them out of there in just the nick of time.

The day we flew in there was the ONLY day we could have for the whole rest of the winter. Weather came in, the road was closed, and they would have perished. Dr. Iacono was very relieved to hear his horses were safe, and he made arrangements with Tony and Lynette to leave them at their ranch all winter.

Out of this story about prop, hoof, and tread, we all agreed that the prop and hoof part of the journey was by far the best of the whole Idaho Adventure!

 THE MONTANA YEARS

Zeke #2

We had lost both Zipper and Gypsy and needed a pack mule. In 2002, we heard that Kim Seeley had a two-year-old sorrel mule for sale. Kim was trying to breed black mules, and sorrel didn't fill the bill. He was out of a nice sorrel Quarter Horse mare and by a big, black jack named Colt 44. We went over to look at him, and he was kind of pathetic. He was undersized, looked under-nourished, and had a rather large hernia. He was technically two, but had been born the previous July, so he was really just a long yearling. Kim was more anxious to find him a good home than anything else, so she even offered to take him to the vet to get the hernia fixed—and paid for it. We named him Zeke, too. We liked the name and our other Zeke was sold by then.

Zeke made himself unpopular at the vet's. When they went to give him some Rompun prior to surgery, he reared in the stocks and struck Dr. Ward in the arm, nearly breaking it. Zeke was deathly afraid of shots!

When we got him home, we discovered the reason for his malnourishment—he had capped teeth. His front baby teeth were sitting on top of his permanent ones, and he couldn't graze and chew properly. Dr. Richardson tied him down most thoroughly to the hitching rail before working on him—he was not quite two, but already had a "rep."

Zeke took right off, grew, and filled out that summer. By the next year, he was big enough to take packing lessons and start carrying light loads.

He had a quirky personality. He loved to chew things up: ropes, his neighbor's halter, saddle strings, reins. He was always inquisitive and making mischief, like chewing the roof off the pump house! He opened gates, and he turned the lights on and off in the barn. He was a busy mule and worked to keep himself amused. One time, he took the halters off the animals on both sides of him in the horse trailer. He always got tied pretty short after that.

MAKIN' TRACKS

Zeke, being his usual, mischievous self, chewing up a rope. 2006.

*Zeke, posing in front of the blue spruce tree.
A very handsome mule. 2014.*

We had another colt, Cowboy, to train at the same time. His story is next. Cowboy and Zeke were inseparable pasture buddies. They were the same age, and both were high energy and playful. They staged mock wars all the time and would rear up at each other, flail with their front feet, and bite. They both looked moth-eaten from the bitten-off hair they created on each other—no blood, just hair. They used up a lot energy playing and were fun to watch.

THE MONTANA YEARS

Zeke was a real trial to Zack. He was always messing around while being led. He was pretty tough and didn't seem to get tired out, and he used his extra energy to be a royal pain—pushing up behind the lead animal, and trying to bite and chew on both beast and gear. He was a pest.

Zeke and Cowboy, playing in the pasture, 2003

During hunting season, when he was traipsing through heavy snow and packing meat, he toned down—but we were always careful how and where we tied him, so we didn't come back to chewed-up tack. He was a good pack mule, though, and packed out a six-point bull elk for Brad Yerian and a cow for Eric, as well as mantied loads in the summer months.

He grew into a 15:1 hand, stout, good-looking mule. We figured he had the genetics, as we had seen many Colt 44 progeny through the years, and they were nice mules. His mother was good-looking and well bred, too.

After Zack died in 2010, it just tore Eric's heart out, and we didn't go to the mountains very much. A friend, Rex Griffin, needed a pack mule for a trip into the Bob Marshall Wilderness. We offered Zeke to him. When he got back, he said the only thing

 MAKIN' TRACKS

wrong with him was that he didn't own Zeke's Bill of Sale! That trip really matured Zeke. He learned what a real JOB being a pack mule was. After that, he conserved his energy for packing his load, paid attention to where he was on the trail, and quit messing around. He grew up!

Eric Lambert and Tom Alsaker having a beer in front of hunting camp. Early in season. Sapphire Mountains, 8,000 feet. 1995.

With Zack's death in 2010, lots of things changed. By then, both Tom Alsaker and I were too stove up to handle that steep country, so Eric lost his hunting partners, as well as his good mule. The wolves had driven most of the game out, and the elk had moved to lower country. That was the first year that Eric did not set up a camp, and we have not set one up, since.

With no incentive to clear trails and with no saddle animals capable of handling that rugged country, we didn't have much of a job for Zeke any more. Eric reluctantly sold him to a good home here in the valley in 2014. He is doing a good job of packing for his new owner, and we are glad he is being used and has a job again.

 THE MONTANA YEARS

Cowboy

Cowboy was a Hancock bred QH, born in Cut Bank, Montana, in 2001. His only contact with humans was to be run in as a yearling, roped, thrown down, gelded, and branded. He didn't have much reason to trust us... And he didn't. The niece of the man who owned him brought some of her uncle's colts down to the Bitterroot to try and sell them so they didn't go to slaughter. Her uncle had found himself in a bind with too many horses and not enough time for them. Registration papers on the horses had gone by the wayside.

The niece had gotten Cowboy sort of halter broke, and that was about all. He was pretty rough looking in the early winter of 2003 when we went to look at him, but I saw potential for him and bought him for $675. Cowboy and Zeke became fast friends and were kindred spirits in the pasture. They had youthful enthusiasm and spent hours playing.

The spring of 2003, I started their training programs, sacking them out and saddling them up. They were both uneasy: Zeke because of his fear of shots, his hernia, and his tooth surgery, and Cowboy because of his other trauma. I spent a lot of time flagging them, using a long stick, and they calmed down. One day, I had them both wearing irrigation dams—that would have been a funny picture...but I don't have one.

It wasn't long before they were wearing pack saddles and carrying light loads. Cowboy was very leery of being handled on his right side, and I am sure it was because of his brand. He had been barbecued when he was branded. I am going to use a little space here to talk about branding horses.

Branding animals is a very valuable tool in identifying ownership. If a horse strays for any reason and is branded, that owner can be found and notified—like, if we had lost a horse in the Bob Marshall Wilderness.

That said, horses need different treatment for branding than do cattle. We have both hot-branded and freeze-branded our

 MAKIN' TRACKS

animals, and both ways can be done humanely. Horses have very thin skins and are much easier to mark than cattle. If hot branding, clip the area and immobilize the animal—in a chute, tie up a leg, use a twitch, or give Rompun—your choice. Apply a cold pack to the area to be branded, and hold it there for at least five minutes. Have the iron hot, and only leave it on the horse a *very* short time! About the time for the heat to penetrate the cold left by the pack is plenty. You don't want an ugly scar—just an identifying mark.

To freeze brand a horse, immobilize him, clip the area, put the iron into liquid nitrogen for 20 minutes or so, and apply the cold iron for 20 SECONDS.

In both instances, our experience is that the horse (or mule) hardly knows it has been branded. There were no strong reactions and no tail switching, and we got nice brands, too.

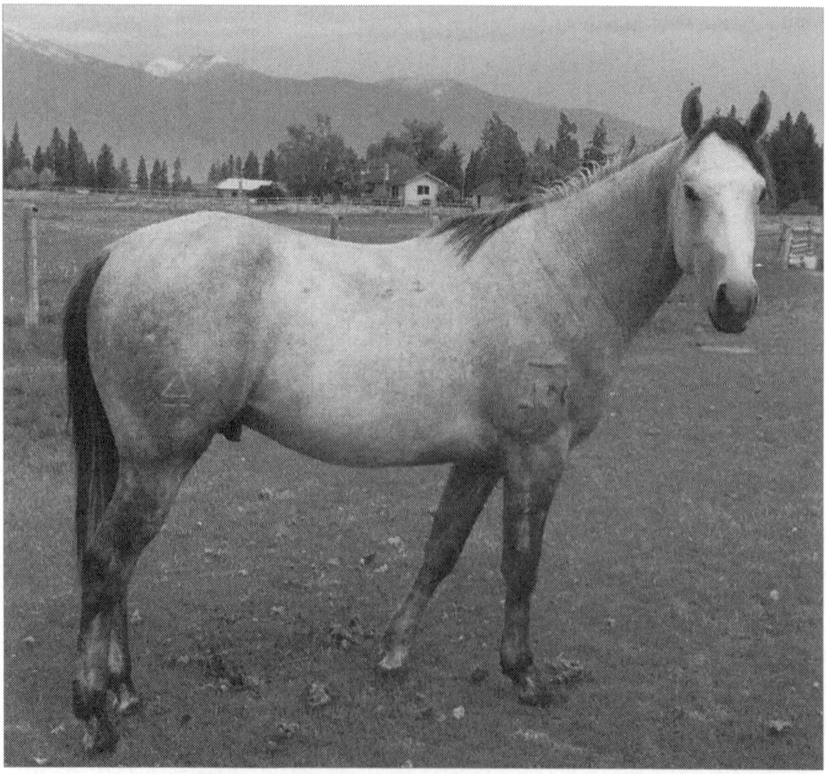

Cowboy. Notice his hot brand and our freeze brand Triangle Bar. 2005.

THE MONTANA YEARS

Cowboy's brand in this picture shows what a thoughtless branding he had. It is a Bar Backwards L N. It is burned very deeply in the Bar and the N, and the L and the N are not even the same size, which tells me he got scalded three times to get the brand. It is no wonder he was so afraid of people on his right side! A horse brand should be applied once and should not take up a large area. Get a nice iron for your horses and apply it wisely and humanely.

We also freeze branded Cowboy with our Triangle Bar brand, and it was a good thing we did, because his brand papers got lost. They were easy to replace, since he carried OUR brand. If he only carried the Cut Bank ranch brand, his ownership would have reverted back to them.

In 2004, when Kyle graduated from high school, I gave him the option of getting $700 for a graduation present or getting Cowboy. He wanted Cowboy. He was going to go to Wyo-Tech to study diesel mechanics, so we kept Cowboy while Kyle went to school. I continued to work with Cowboy until I felt he was safe. We packed him, but did not ride him.

Kyle started him and rode him sporadically for a few years. He sold him to his other grandfather Doug Schoening. Cowboy lived at Schoening's place for a number of years and then went to a home in Bozeman.

 MAKIN' TRACKS

Fooler

In April of 1998, Jim Stromberg called to tell me that I ought to come over to their place and see the little molly mule that had just been foaled. He knew that my old Hemi mule had been out of a registered Arabian mare—and this one was, too. Naturally, I had to go and see her. What a little cutie! I was scratching her and breathing baby mule breath, and then Jim said, "You know, she was born on April Fool's Day. Isn't that something?"

Something?! That's MY birthday! I was sandbagged—I had to have her! I bought her for $600 and made a deal to bring the newly named "Fooler" and her mother to my place until she was weaned, and then Jim would take the mare back. That way, I could halter break and socialize the foal myself.

The pasture I put them in was northwest of my house, so it was easy to keep tabs on them. The pasture was also very heavy with clover, and the clover caused problems. It gave the grey mare "scratches" on all four of her feet. Somehow, the action of the sun and the clover sets up a nasty dermatitis, right at the coronary band. It seems worse in the heels. It usually only affects white feet on horses, and it is hard to get rid of once it starts. I had to catch her daily, wash her feet well, and apply heavy layers of diaper rash cream all around her coronary bands to block the area from the sun. It is a painful skin condition, and I am glad the mare was cooperative.

Another offshoot of the clover was that it made the mare milk so heavily that Fooler was growing too fast and started to get epiphysitis in her knees. Mare and foal were moved to the corral away from the clover and healed up.

Fooler was a very pretty foal. When young, she was buckskin, but by the time she was a yearling, she was dark iron-grey. She was easy to halter break, and I spent quite a bit of time socializing her. She did not go to Mule Days, as had our other mule colts, and I think she could have benefitted from that, as she

THE MONTANA YEARS

had a high alert Arabian personality. I think the activity surrounding the show could have taken some of her edges off.

We packed her lightly as a two-year-old. When she was a three-year-old, I sent her to Superior, Montana, to Alta Boyes to put 60 days on her. Alta did a good job on her—as she always did—and I brought her home and started riding her. I should have thought this whole thing through, and remembered Hemi's early years a little clearer. I was a 33-year-old and riding most every day when I started riding Hemi; I was a 57-year-old grandmother when I started riding Fooler.

Fooler, held by Eric Lambert on Zack with Tess and Kate. Sky-lined in the Sapphire Mountains. 2001.

I had a few run-aways with Fooler. One time was straight at Coller's wheel line, and I began to wonder if she was going to jump it and where that would leave me, but she stopped. Half-Arab mules are a little scary—and scared, too.

I kept riding her, and she got continually more confident. We packed her every fall, and she packed out a few elk. In 2002, we had her in elk camp, and she colicked. It was early in the morning and it was cold, as it had been a cold fall—there was probably a

MAKIN' TRACKS

foot of snow at camp, which was 8,000 feet in elevation. We loaded her and Zack in the four-horse and went down the mountain to the veterinarian in Corvallis, Montana. He filled her full of oil and Banamine, and we headed back up the hill. It was so cold that the traction on the ice-covered road had been good, going down. HOWEVER, we did not take into consideration the sun hitting on a very steep, south-facing section of the road. We broke traction, and the truck and trailer started sliding backward off the road. Eric said, "We're going. The trailer is off the road, and we're going."

I am not a religious person. I believe in a higher power, but am not in anybody's religious box. But I had a prayer rise in my toenails, come clear to the top of my head, and spill out my mouth as, "Please, God!" It was a full-bodied expression and cry for help.

The big, heavy, four-horse Stidham trailer's back wheels on the driver's side went off the berm of the road at a 45-degree angle, and the axle settled, caught, and held us. WE STOPPED!

The back of the horse trailer was hanging over the bank, with about a four-foot drop off, and the trailer was tipped at an angle. Eric was able to untie the mules' halter ropes. Zack had been thrown to the floor, his legs under him, and he was caught in the angle between the wall and the floor and couldn't get his footing to get up. When I opened the swinging back door, Fooler, who was full of Banamine, bounced out like a jack rabbit, lit down the hill, and climbed back up to the road.

I managed to get in the trailer with Zack. He had cut his lip trying to get up, falling and hitting his mouth on the trailer floor. I had major adrenaline flowing and literally dragged Zack 180 degrees, so that he was headed out the back door. Between Eric and I, we yarded him out of the back of the trailer. He landed in a brush pile down the hill, got himself untangled, and made it back up to the roadway.

By this time, some other hunters had come along, blocked our wheels with rocks, and caught Fooler. I caught Zack. Except for his bloody lip, he seemed fine. I was shaking so badly I could hardly stand.

 **THE MONTANA YEARS**

Eric got chains on all four tires of the truck, and it pulled the empty trailer out of the bind and on up the hill. You can bet we chain up our vehicles MUCH sooner, rather than later, after that!

He had to go about a half mile before the road flattened out, and there was a place to re-load. I was sure wondering if either one of them would go back in the trailer, as harrowing as that wreck was. I petted and scratched on Zack and then asked him to go in — and he did, just like nothing had happened. Fooler bounced right in beside him, and we proceeded back up to camp. The next morning, Zack's ankles were pretty swollen from scrambling so hard to get up, but they went down in a few days. We were all *so lucky!*

A few nights later, I had one of the most realistic, clear dreams I have ever had, and I woke up with the *absolute* understanding that it had been Sandy Brooks, who had stopped that horse trailer! Sandy had passed over the Great Divide a number of years prior to that, but in this dream, HE WAS THERE! That was very spooky, but also very comforting, as there was no nicer man than Sandy, and if he truly is one of my Guardian Angels, I am in good hands. When I told this to Eric, I know he thought I was delusional and probably still does... But again, I say, the Universe works in mysterious ways.

The winter of 2002-'03 was really miserable at times, with very heavy inversion layers of freezing fog. The hoar frost covered everything, and it was just dreary and grey. After about a week of one of these spells, Lynette Coller called up and said she was just bummed out by the cold, dreary, fog. She asked if I wanted to ride up on McIntyre's and get above it, because she knew it was warmer and sunny up there. I was game, so we loaded the black Thoroughbred gelding she was riding and Fooler and drove up to the ranch. It was 17 degrees, and the fog was dense. Probably only ½ to ¾ of a mile up the hill, we rode right out of the fog into bright sunshine. It was blinding, but also mood brightening. It was 56 degrees up on the mountain, out of the fog. We rode for a couple of hours and really enjoyed ourselves. We were sitting out on a point, and Lynette said, "This must have been what Lake Missoula looked like, back when the whole valley was flooded."

 MAKIN' TRACKS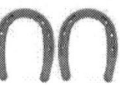

The solid fog bank below us filled the Bitterroot Valley, just like that glacial lake would have. Only Iron Cap rose above the fog line. We sat and took that concept in for a while. The view above the fog was memorable, and the sunshine, a welcome change. When it came time to ride back down, it was hard to go. The closer we got to the edge of the fog, the colder it got. Back at the trailer, it was the same frozen, 17-degree fog.

Fooler, packed with the front quarters of an elk. November 2003.

I rode Fooler quite a bit with Lynette and her black TB. Fooler could travel, and so could he. And as for traveling, I'll say this for my good friend, Lynette—she rides, she covers some country, and she *assumes* that you are still behind her—so you'd better be!

As a result, by the summer of 2003, Fooler was going pretty darned well. She seemed to have calmed down and was getting a good rein on her. She was responsive off my legs, and I was feeling confident with her.

Dawn, Laura Alsaker, and I signed up to go on a Maids of Montana Ride. It was an annual, all-women ride, and it was to be on Bannock Pass, which is in remote country. We took Dawn's black gelding, Zack, and Fooler. It was the longest trailer ride

 # THE MONTANA YEARS

Fooler had ever had, and a big part was on gravel roads. We went to Dillon, where the road turned to gravel and stays gravel through Grant and on to Bannock Pass.

Fooler was highly upset when we got there and very agitated. She had never been around that many strange horses, either. I had her in way over her head, but I gave myself credit for being rider enough to handle her.

I had a couple of spooking incidents with her the morning we started out, but she seemed okay after lunch. We had started down a long, sagebrush-covered slope and had stopped to enjoy the view and take a breather. I was sitting on her, relaxed, reins fairly loose, when something spooked her, and she whirled and made a jump downhill. I was caught off guard and was trying to get my reins gathered, when she made another jump down the hill, and I lost my right stirrup. I was still fumbling for a grip on the reins, headed down the hill, picking up speed, and she jumped a sage brush, which caused the loose stirrup to rise and then slam down on her ribs. THAT picked up the action! She accelerated a couple more gears, the hill got steeper, and she was jumping sagebrush as she went. I went off her right side and dove hard into the ground with my right shoulder, then bounced up, and did a body slam onto the ground, landing with my head downhill.

Wow! THAT was a hit! Everyone was yelling at me to lie still, but I really wanted my head uphill, so I kind of scrunched around and tried to get my bearings. I couldn't get my breath, and I was having major muscle spasms in my back and right shoulder. I was glad to have medical help on the mountain—a lady veterinarian from Worden, near Billings, Montana, was there. She acted as a First Responder and took a reading on me. Dawn came barreling down the mountain at a high lope to see if she could help. Fooler just bounded back up the hill to Zack.

After I lay there for a while, I sat up, then got up, and decided I'd be better off walking than riding. My veterinarian stayed with me the whole time, and I was *very* grateful for her help.

Another lady rode, hell-bent-for-election, back to the ranch to get help. The next time I saw her, *she* didn't look so good, either.

MAKIN' TRACKS

On her run, her binoculars hit her in the forehead and gave her two black eyes...

We slowly made our way down the mountain, and some guys from the ranch came and got us with a six-wheel-drive ATV, and we all crept slowly back to the ranch.

Boy, I was hurting! I have never had muscle spasms like that. I had torn muscles in my shoulder and between my ribs, and every breath sent them into spasms. I really didn't want to wreck Laura and Dawn's fun by going to the hospital, but they finally convinced me to go. I realized that, if I had internal injuries, it could go from bad to worse.

That was a grit-your-teeth drive to the Dillon Hospital, let me tell you. When I got there, I told the doctor, "I'll take some morphine, and I'll take it NOW, if you please." Thankfully, they gave me SOMETHING. Then they put me in an ambulance, and sent me to Butte at 90 mph. I was fuzzy by then, thankfully.

At Butte, they ran me through an MRI. Dawn and Laura called Eric and Tom, and they came over. The doctor came in, and said I had *tweaked* my liver, and I would have to take it easy for a while. He also said I should see an internist in Missoula.

They sent me home with some muscle relaxers and pain pills the next day. (It cost $10,000 for one day in the hospital. Next time you are shopping for a new "ride," consider that number against the purchase price. A safe horse or mule is worth a *lot* of money!)

Tom and Laura took Zack and Fooler home. Dawn stayed, rode the next day, and caught a ride home with someone else.

In a few days, I got an appointment to see Dr. Janczewski in Missoula. When she walked out to get me, she said, "So, you are the one who is lucky to be alive..."

Eric and I looked at each other, like, "WHAT?"

Dr. J. then said, "Haven't you seen the pictures of your liver?"

When we said, *no*, we hadn't, she showed them to us and explained what we were seeing. My liver had split from top to bottom. If the capsule around it had not held, I would have bled to death where I fell. The split in the liver was about 6" on the bottom and 2" on the top. She said a liver taking a concussion like that is

THE MONTANA YEARS

just like dropping a watermelon on the floor in the way it will split. She reiterated how lucky I was to be alive, but since the liver is the only organ which can regenerate itself, she thought, within a year, it should be completely healed. Boy, I felt beat up. I don't *ever* want to be that beat up again. Because of that feeling, I lost a whole lot of self-confidence as a rider, and I don't like to be challenged by a horse any more. I say I am in the "Dude Horse" phase of my life and plan to stay there!

That year, 2003, was a medically-challenging one for our family. My accident happened in July, and in August, Dawn had a serious accident with her black gelding. Then in November, Fooler struck again. Eric was leading her, and she was packing half an elk. He gave a tug on her halter rope, and she charged past him, knocking him down in a rock pile and breaking his wrist. He suffered horribly with the pain and ended up having two surgeries on his wrist. He hated her!

Fooler had to go. It wasn't so much about what she had done wrong, as about how badly HURT we both got. Eric gave me a deadline of April Fool's Day 2004 to get rid of her. He said he'd get rid of her if she was still here past that date.

I put the word out among mule people, and a man from Billings called and was interested in her. In March of 2004, we met him in Whitehall, he tried her out, and I sold her for $1,500. I told him the story of getting hurt on her and that I felt she was worth more than that with the training she had, but she needed to go.

He got along fine with her and brought her over here to Montana Mule Days a few years later. She had a $4,500 price tag on her, so she did turn out to be a good mule. She was another one like the Witch—age made a big difference.

Age makes a big difference with a rider also. I was older and slower in my reaction time. When I was younger, I would have had her gathered and doubled, and she never would have gotten in the second jump. My 57 years made me too old and too slow. I was in way over my head to ride her, and I put her into a situation that was way over her head, for pressure. She was the last colt I ever rode and the last colt I ever WANT to ride.

 **MAKIN' TRACKS**

Note: Chronologically, the next chapter should be titled "Reba," as she came to live with me in June of 2004 and is still with me. However, since she is my last horse, in a long line of horses and mules, I want her to have the last chapter in the book. Keep in mind, as you read the next few chapters, that Reba was here.

 THE MONTANA YEARS

Freya aka Brandy aka Sweetie

This mare has a longer name than she has a story. In 2013, we were horse short and needed a pack horse. My friend Kris Mackey and I were talking, and she said she'd like to find a home for a bay mare she had. It seems Kris' daughter, Heather, had bought this little bay mare—cheap—from a lady in Darby, Montana. After getting her home, "Brandy" was feeling her oats and dumped Heather off a few times, and Heather lost interest in her. Kris was tired of boarding and feeding her and offered her—free of charge—to me.

Well, the price was right, so I changed her name to Freya (Free-ah, get it?). We went to Darby and got her and brought her home. She seemed pretty gentle on the ground, and I tied her up to the hitching rail and walked into the tack room to get a brush. I never really left her sight, as I was just inside the door. On my straightening up and coming out, Freya pulled back hard enough to break the snap on the lead rope. I caught her and put another nylon strap halter on her with a nylon lead rope spliced on. I thought maybe I had done something to spook her.

Well, it wasn't long before she tried the new halter out for strength, and let me tell you, she gave it all she had. When she let up, she hadn't gotten away, but she pulled through the nylon strapping clear down to the next hole. In the next couple of days, she wrecked another couple of halters the same way, and I was done with her. After dealing with Becky, Honeycomb, and Drifty, I didn't even want to mess with THAT bad habit.

I called Vince Felty and asked him if he wanted a horse for a project—no charge. I told him her history and said I didn't have the inclination or the facilities to try and straighten her out. He came over and took a look at her and thought he might want to take her on—he was still training then and had good facilities to do it in. He took her home, worked her in the round pen, started her over, and when he tied her, he tied her high to a ring in the rafter of the barn, with a pulley contraption—which fouled up her

 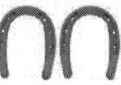

pull back routine and after a number of hissy fits, she more or less gave it up.

Anyway, he stuck with her, and he and Dar renamed her Sweetie. (Oh, the power of positive thinking!) Vince put quite a few miles on her and took her to cow camp one summer, where he put a lot more miles on her.

She is now a cowboy's horse in Ennis, Montana.

 THE MONTANA YEARS

Princess aka Baron's Fancy Princess

By 2006, Reba's feet were bad, and she couldn't travel in rough terrain. I needed a horse to go to the mountains. I saw an ad for a well-broke AQHA mare in Florence, Montana.

We went to look at her, and she was a very pretty, heavily-muscled grey mare. She was big, standing about 15:2 hands, and though I really wanted a shorter horse, I rode her anyway. She came from the Lone Star Ranch and was owned by Greg Ondrak. Greg and I rode around the ranch, and Baron's Fancy Princess was a nice, quiet horse with a good rein and was leg responsive. She had good, dark feet, had very nice conformation, and seemed good and sound. He said she'd done a lot of ranch work and that he roped off her. I ignored her height and bought her.

The first bad habit she displayed was being over-anxious in the horse trailer and pawing the walls with her front feet. Very noisy! Very irritating! She wasn't so bad if another horse was with her, but alone, she was a fright!

I rode her with the Happy Saddle Tramps, a ladies' riding group here in the valley, who ride every Wednesday. I got along good with her, and she fit in well with the group. I rode her quite a bit that summer and liked her—except for the noisy trailering.

That fall, Eric and I rode up above hunting camp. Even though Princess didn't have a lot of mountain experience, she handled her feet and the terrain quite well, and I was enjoying her. Then a very large buck mule deer appeared on a ridge above us. He was in the rut, as his neck was all swelled up. Zack and Princess both stopped, and we all watched the buck make his way across the hill. He was a dandy.

We started down the trail, which takes a big dive there, and all of a sudden, Princess was a psycho case. She tried to run off; she was shaking her head and kind of crowhopping down the hill. My first thought was that something was pinching her or making her uncomfortable. I got her stopped, got off, and checked all my

gear, which was difficult, as she was trying to run circles around me. Finally, Eric held her, and I unsaddled to make sure nothing was between her and the saddle pad, like pine needles.

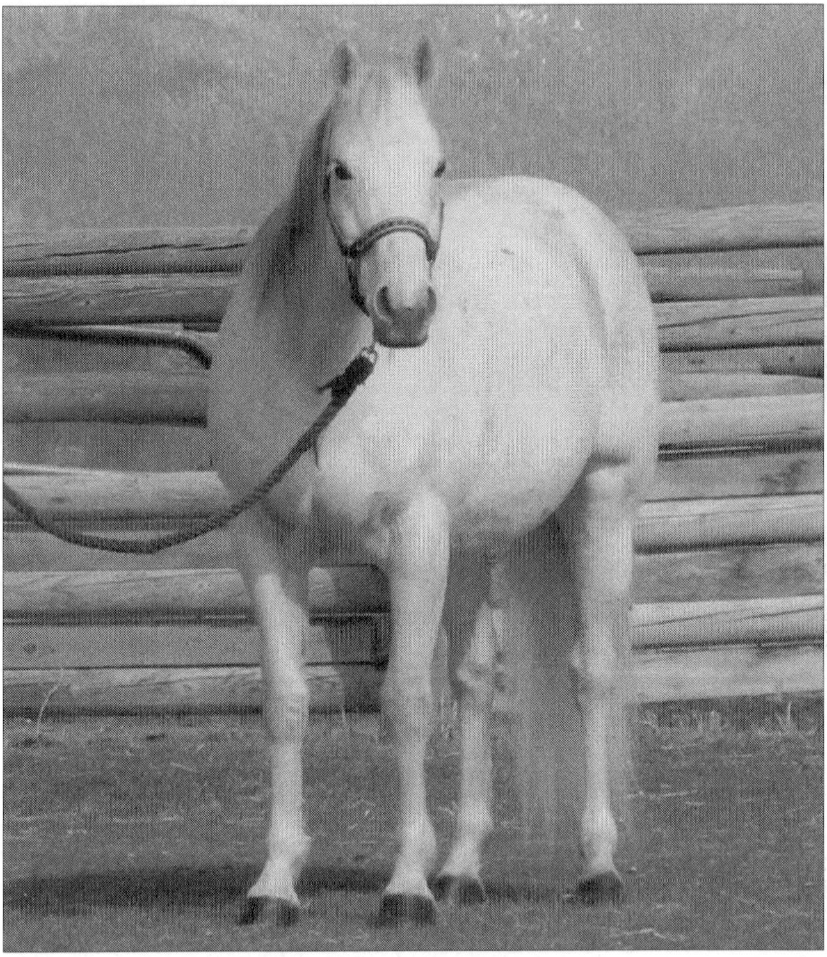

Princess, at the Coller Ranch. 2007.

All was fine with her gear, but she was going crazy. We finally figured that we had gotten downwind from the buck deer, and it was his odor that had her all fuzzed up. Actually, she was more than fuzzed up—she had turned hazardous to handle. She just would not calm down, and it was a struggle between the two of us to get the saddle back on her. She was blowing and snorting, her

eyes were bugging out, and her tail had a big kink in it. She had totally lost "whoa" from her vocabulary.

Since I had lost my desire to be challenged by a horse, I started leading her back down the mountain. It became too challenging to even lead her, so Eric took her rope. She was *so* nuts he couldn't hold her either, and she charged down the hill bucking and snorting as she went.

She went to camp and was waiting there for us. She was much calmer, and I unsaddled her and put her in the corral. The next morning, she had calmed completely down and was her old, quiet self.

I continued to ride her, and when hunting season came in October, we set up our camp and took her back up the mountain. She behaved herself and put up with being in a snowy corral, being saddled in the dark, and marching up the mountain in the dark.

Elaine Coller, tuning Princess up. 2007.

 MAKIN' TRACKS

One morning, when I went to get on her, her height proved too much of a challenge. I had her standing sideways to a steep place next to the road, was on one foot on the slick bank, and was putting my foot into the stirrup, when my foot on the bank slipped. (During hunting season, I *dressed*. Pac boots, long johns, wool pants, wool shirt, wool sweater, wool coat, and wool hat—I was about as insulated as a Polar bear and just as handy as a bear cub!)

When my foot slipped, I did a body slide right past Princess' front legs, past her, and down onto the road. To her credit, she never turned a hair, just put her head down to watch me go by.

So, Princess just had that ONE incident of whacky behavior. However, my confidence was too badly shaken to trust her after that, and the next spring, I advertised her for sale.

It was ironic. The very morning I decided to sell her, I went out to feed, and Princess walked up, gave me a stink eye, reached out, and BIT ME. I guess the feeling between us was mutual!

I got Elaine Coller to ride and market her for me. Elaine is a very good and fearless rider. She had a client who wanted to play broom polo and was looking for a horse. Elaine schooled Princess by whacking a Jolly Ball around her legs and underneath her at all speeds with a stable rake...

It worked, because in May of 2007, I sold her to a 14-year-old boy, who was a good hand and a broom polo player. This was a good fit, as her new owner gave her a job and rode the tail off her.

THE MONTANA YEARS

Skinny

Jane on Skinny, Asa Yerian's horse, and Tess, during hunting season. Horse Ridge, in the Sapphire Mountains. 2007.

Asa Yerian, on the trail down to Fool Hen Lake. Asa was 76 years old, still hunting elk and staying in the old miner's cabin to do it. 1999.

 MAKIN' TRACKS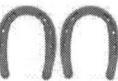

Hunting camp. Sapphire Mountains. October 1998.

Hunting camp, when moved off the hill and east 100 yards onto a flat area. Sapphire Mountains. 2005.

Eric at hunting camp, showing corrals.
Back L to R: Zack, Zipper, Skinny, Buck, and Red.
Front L to R: Katie and Tess. 2007.

 THE MONTANA YEARS

Sam aka Sam I Am

Sam was a grey QH gelding that I had known for a few years, as he was owned by one of our neighbors. After selling Princess in 2007, I was short a horse, so I had to borrow Asa Yerian's horse Skinny to ride during hunting season, as Reba's feet couldn't take the steep country.

Sam and Jane Lambert, on a Bitterroot Saddle Tramps ride. Argenta, Montana. Photo by Barb Garten. 2009.

When Sam came up for sale in 2008, I bought him. He was a 16-year-old, good-looking horse, about 15 hands tall, with good withers and a big hip. He was also a real dead-head. His previous owner was a very timid rider, and he sent him to trainers every spring to dampen him down so he could ride him. Eric, to this day, cannot understand why I paid so much for such a dead-headed horse. (Eric calls him a dud horse, not a dude horse.)

 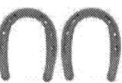

MAKIN' TRACKS

Of course, the answer is that I did not want to get hurt, and as previously stated, I did not want a problem horse, I just wanted a safe ride. That is what I paid for—the expectation of *not* going back to the hospital!

I stated that I was in my Dude Horse phase of life, and Sam was definitely THAT. He had a pretty good rein on him, but the slowest walk of any horse since old Buck. He was another one you had to hold a stick up against to see if he was moving. Spurs on him were *not* optional!

Jane Lambert on Sam, moving cattle out of the way, on Coller Ranch. They were filming a commercial that day and needed to film Clydesdale horses against the mountain backdrop with no cattle. 2009.

That said, I enjoyed him quite a lot in the three years I owned him. I rode many Wednesdays with the "Tramps" and was able to relax and enjoy myself and the camaraderie. Because of that, I rekindled old friendships and made new ones—chief among them getting to know Linda Habeck and enjoy her friendship. We have had lots of adventures since then.

By this time in life, I have nothing to prove in the horsemanship arena. I have been very lucky through the years to have ridden some damned fine horses in lots of different venues and have achieved all the goals I have set for myself with my animals. I knew what I was getting when I bought Sam, and I

THE MONTANA YEARS

appreciated him, because he met the expectations I had of him, and he provided me with the babysitting care I needed when I rode him. Different stages in life require different equines.

An interesting quirk this old horse had was sitting on his rump like a big dog. You'd look out in the pasture, and he'd be sitting up, surveying the country. He could remain in that position for long periods, too.

Sam, sitting like a dog, and Zeke #2, on the ground. 2009.

A not so interesting quirk was his trying to breed Reba. That behavior got so bad I had to separate them. Reba has a long, narrow scar on one hind leg caused by her kicking at him through the fence and peeling off a long strip of hide. I had Dr. Richardson come and look at the injury. I had saved the hide, in case it could be re-attached. He just laughed and told me to make a shoestring out of it. Instead, I used it on a hatband I made. When I am asked about the "exotic fur" on my hat, now I'm the one laughing...

Sam was also able to handle the rough country above hunting camp, so I got two years of hunting seasons on him before we lost Zack. Those two years of hunting were a real trial. Tom had quit coming, so it was just Eric and me to set up camp and take it down. That part was okay, but the hunting itself was something I really dreaded.

MAKIN' TRACKS

In the old days, we saddled up before daylight, rode an hour in the dark and tied up our animals, and then Eric and I went hunting. He went with his .30-06 and me, with my Canon. He had his route and ended by sitting on his favorite log from which he has a very high hunting success record. I also had my picture-taking route, and I would eventually make it to Eric's log. It was fun for both of us. But from probably 2007 on, the wolves were so bad that we did not feel right about leaving our tied-up animals unattended. I sat with them in the tie-up area with a .30-30 across my lap, while Eric went hunting. If you think I found this boring, you are right.

Our last trip, in 2009, put the frosting on the cake. It had rained a few days before we went up there, and then a cold front came in. We knew it was going to be cold, so Eric fixed me up a fire starter kit in the saddlebags. I had paper, kindling, slivered wood, fire starter cubes, and dry matches. Usually, that would have been more than enough to get a good fire started. It was zero degrees when Eric walked off to hunt.

The prior rain was a major issue. All the dry wood had a coating of ice on it, and it was damp underneath. I went through all my fire starter stuff, but no fire would start beyond the materials from the saddlebag, and they were soon burnt up. Sitting and stomping around weren't keeping me warm. I have arthritis, and my hands don't work well when they get cold. And they got so cold, I couldn't hold a Kleenex to blow my nose—or any other tissue, either!

I was just about to untie the animals and walk out with them when Eric showed back up. I had to have major help to get back on old Sam and could hardly hold my reins. That was my last elk hunting trip, and I am mighty glad of it!

In 2011, I found Sam a good home with a lady in similar circumstances to my own. She had gotten scared by the dingy horse she owned and was looking for a safe one. She rode Sam for two or three years and then gave him to another of our neighbor's kids. So, he is just down the road and back up on Sunset Bench. He's 25 now and still looks good.

 THE MONTANA YEARS

Reba

In March of 2004, I found a home for Fooler, so I was without an animal to ride and was keeping an eye out for one. Around May, I saw an ad for an eight-year-old QH mare, a three-year-old TB gelding, a two-horse trailer, some tack, and a ton of hay—total price, $1,600. Hmm. I called on the ad and then went to look at the horses.

The sorrel mare was tied up and saddled. I was in love at first glance—she was the Orren Mixer conformed AQHA horse I had been wanting since 1960. In my eyes, she was beautiful! I rode her around, and she was green as a gourd—just really didn't know much of anything—but she seemed gentle and cooperative. I picked up her feet, looked her all over, and liked what I saw. She was 14:2 hands tall and a really pretty red-gold sorrel. I hardly looked at the TB. I made the deal because I wanted the mare.

When I went to unsaddle her, I was astounded at how tight her cinch was—WAY too tight! Anyway, after that, I looked at the horse trailer—an old, Miley two-horse which was in such sad shape I wouldn't have hauled a Shetland pony in it. The hay was second-cutting alfalfa, and there was a ton and a half of it. The pile of tack wasn't anything to write home about, but replacement value would have been a couple hundred dollars. The TB was a dark brown and stood a good 15:2 hands. He looked sound. I knew I wouldn't keep him.

I went home and got my truck and trailer, and Eric brought a second pickup to take the Miley home. The horses loaded fine, and we got the hay, trailer, and tack. I got the paperwork on the horses, and the guy signed the title on the horse trailer. I did not pay enough attention to the paperwork, because I was so excited to own the newly-named Reba—named after the renowned, red-haired Reba McIntire.

A couple of days after getting these horses home, I decided to worm them. Reba offered no resistance to it at all. The TB was a real brat, and I ended up squirting the whole thing out the other side of his mouth onto the ground. Grrrr—I *knew* the horse was for sale then.

MAKIN' TRACKS

I left both of them tied to the hitch rail and drove down to the local feed store to get another wormer. At the counter, I was giving Jim Anderson the blow by blow of getting the horses and of having a three-year-old TB gelding for sale, when I asked if he knew anybody looking... And the guy right behind me says, "I'm interested in him. How much do you want, and can I come see him?"

I said, "$350. Follow me home, and you can look him over."

So he did. And he liked him. And he bought him. I gave him the wormer, so *he* could administer it. Happy Day! He went and got his trailer and hauled him off.

He was staying at Bill Snedigar's place. I called Marilyn Stromberg, a brand inspector, and asked her to meet me there, so I could transfer ownership of the horse. That unveiled the first snafu of the paperwork. The previous brand inspector had put both horses on one brand inspection paper—a no-no. Marilyn had to go through a bunch of rigamarole to get it figured out. It was lucky she knew both me and the other brand inspector and knew what to do. Keeping records of horse ownership straight in Montana is VERY important, and if you travel out of the county and get stopped by a brand inspector without proper papers, your horse will get impounded. Beware!

With the TB gone, I put the old Miley in the front pasture with a *For Sale* sign on it. In a few days, a guy stopped, looked at it, and paid me $300 for it. I gave him the signed title and away it went. So far, so good!

I had been catching Reba every day, brushing her, and getting to know her. When I had looked at the folder containing her breeding and information, I was really surprised to see that Reba and I *also* shared the same birthday—April Fool's Day. Eric said, "I hope that's not a bad omen." He was remembering Fooler...

Reba seemed like a pleasant horse. I had a set of shoes put on her and called Lynette to see if I could bring her over and work her in the round pen at her place. Lynette said, "Sure."

Well, that brought out a new, VERY unpleasant Reba. I started to work her off a longe line, and she pinned her ears and acted like she might "take" me. I had a whip and used it. Lynette suggested

THE MONTANA YEARS

just driving her with no line, so I took it off. Boy, that mare had an attitude! Ears flat back, evil looks, and biting action. She was nasty. I was asking myself, "Why did you buy a bitch like this?"

I worked her for a while, and then Lynette took her over, worked her over, and made some progress with her. Reba had a temper. She was a strong-minded eight-year-old, and she had obviously buffaloed some other humans badly. Reba had prior bad experiences in a round pen, and she had some dangerous ideas.

I brought her over again the next day. It was a repeat of the first day. Lynette said, "If she doesn't give this up in three days, you'd better get rid of her—she'll hurt somebody." Lynette is a lifelong horsewoman, and she had worked with older spoiled horses like Reba. I took what she said seriously.

On the third day, it was *Custer's Last Stand*, and it was Lynette vs. Reba! Reba was an alligator, and she was going to eat Lynette! She got the crap beaten out of her for trying that. Reba got initiated to a lariat war bridle and a bunch of welts, but she finally gave up the aggression and started paying attention. From that time on, she found out and figured out that the better she treated me, the better I treated her. We have had a great understanding and partnership for a long, long, time now. Reba is VERY smart, and she figured out how to cooperate in the nick of time!

After Reba had negotiated a better deal with human beings, I hired Elaine Coller to put 30 days on her. I hauled Reba over to Elaine's every day and stayed to watch her progress. The combination of Elaine being a talented horsewoman and Reba being very intelligent resulted in amazing progress for that little training time. Reba's turn-around in attitude was also amazing. Ultimately, she became as nice as she is pretty.

Training Reba mirrored training mules in some regard. Being smart, they caught on fast and did not regress. Once they "had" it, it stayed "had." Therefore, all the training had a forward progression to it, and she ended up being one of the easiest, fastest horses I have ever brought along.

 MAKIN' TRACKS

Jane Lambert on Reba, east of Sunset Bench, on the McIntyre Ranch. 2005.

One of her habits refers back to the way her previous owner cinched her saddle. To this day, she turns her head and gives me "the eye" when I go to tighten her cinch. In the beginning, she pinned her ears back and was mad about it. Now, it's just a "Please, not too tight" look. Like Hemi with her ears, Reba is protective of her girth. They don't forget.

Reba is a very thin-skinned sorrel. Everything needs to fit her right, or she galls easily. She also got ringworm one time in her girth area and still has some marks there from it. Harking clear back to the Big Enough days, I have always ridden with as loose a girth as I could get away with. It just makes no sense to over-cinch a horse and make it uncomfortable. We ride in steep country here, and I want my horses to be able to breathe properly if I'm asking them to work really hard.

A couple of months after the Miley horse trailer left, the second snafu surfaced in the paperwork of my "Reba deal." The original seller had signed the horse trailer title, but his signature had not been notarized, so the sale was not legal. When I bought it, the owner said he had just gone to work for Olson Trucking — our friends and neighbors up the road. I called Judy Olson to ask how to get in touch with the man. She said she'd like to know that, too, as he had abandoned one of their trucks and had disappeared... Oh, boy!

I contacted the Highway Patrol and found out the steps it would take for me to get legal title to the trailer. It took a lot of running around, time, and effort to do it. The middle man who had bought it from me came out really well on the deal. He made $100 in selling it to the third guy, and I was the "fall guy" for not providing clear title in the first place. Oh, these life lessons...

Back to Reba. I used to ride her a lot with the Saddle Tramps and in the country around here. Lynette's dad has some nice State ground leased, and it is a good place to ride. In fact, I followed Lynette on one of Reba's early rides up the bottom of that land. Willoughby Creek runs through there, and the trail crosses, and crosses, and crosses that creek. Reba was green as grass for trail manners and water crossings. Every time we came to the water, she made a steeplechase jump over it. Lynette said, "Just keep her coming. As long as she's not refusing, she's doing good!"

After about 30 jumps, we came to a wide, riffled area, and I talked Reba into getting her feet wet. Thank heavens! I was jumped out! She learned to quietly cross water after that, and now she likes to stop, sip, look around, sip some more, and have a leisurely drink. She doesn't mind wet feet, and she likes baths.

After I bought Reba, I went shopping for a different saddle. My old Bentley saddle fit her fine, but it weighs 48 pounds. At this age and stage, I could hardly get it on her. We went over to Bozeman Saddle Outlet in Belgrade, Montana. They advertise having 400 saddles in one place, and they do. Saddles are everywhere and stacked three high in some places. What a shopping experience! I'm glad Eric was there to help me sort through them, as lifting saddles around for two hours is a lot of work. It paid off, though, as I found exactly what I was looking for. I bought a 30-pound saddle made by Kellem from Gardiner, Montana. It has a 15" tree and a good, deep seat and cantle, and it was used enough to be broken in. The seat fit me, and the tree fit Reba, and I have enjoyed riding it for quite a while now.

MAKIN' TRACKS

While I am on the subject of tack, you may have noticed Reba's nice bridle on the book cover. The headstall is from Buckaroo Businesses in Billings, Montana. The reins are from Palm's Saddle Shop in Petaluma, California, and were purchased in the late 1960s. Her bit is a silver-overlaid, Santa Barbara cheek, Vogt bit with a copper-covered Salinas mouthpiece. I braided her neck rope. I love good tack and take good care of it. My life has depended on it at times.

In 2005, I toughened up my nerve and went on another Maids of Montana Ride. It was in the south part of the Bitterroot Valley, so it was in our neighborhood. Four of us went together—my daughter Dawn, Lisa Davis, Missy Lane, and me. Tad Lane and Eric went down and set up a wall tent for us to stay in so we had "style." The first day's ride was up a logging road, and it was rather miserable. It was all UP, and then it was all DOWN, and it was over 100 degrees and all in the sun. Not very exciting and hotter than hell! Lisa got sunstroke out of it. Her face was crimson, and she did not feel well at all. I decided to stay in camp with her the next day. Dawn was riding Zack, and when they left, Reba had a meltdown... She was all in a dither, whinnying non-stop, pacing, pawing, and *un-fit* to be tied. I was going to pull a gag on the "girls" that night and had brought along a set of horse goggles I had bought at a yard sale.

The goggles themselves were molded out of leather, and they had little peepholes cut in the very centers, so they really restricted vision. I put them on Reba to see if that would calm her. And it actually did. After a while, she settled down. When I took them off in an hour or so, she buddied up with Lisa's horse Dusty and forgot about Zack.

Later that night, I was able to demonstrate Reba's goggles in another capacity—as a heavy duty, brush-busting brassiere!

When the riders got back that afternoon, a funny incident occurred. It had been another very hot day, and one of the ladies decided she would wear bicycle shorts under her jeans so she wouldn't get chafed. She was in her tent, bent over, trying to peel the shorts off, when a friend rode up. The friend took one look in

THE MONTANA YEARS

the tent, covered up her horse's eye, and said in a loud voice, "Don't look, Cricket—you'll *colic!*"

Of course, she also had to share the story around the campfire that night. It still makes me laugh, and since then, I have used the line myself.

Even though the ride was not all that great, I was glad that I did return and ride again with some of the ladies who had seen Fooler and me pitch off the hill. It's always good to face your fears so you can move on. Like John Wayne said, "Courage is being scared and saddling up, anyway."

Then Reba got a bad shoeing. The farrier cut her feet way too short, and it set up an inflammation in her front feet with the same results as founder. She developed some changes to her coffin bones, and ever since, she has experienced pain coming down hills—especially anything very steep. She has flat, round hooves, which don't help her any either. The lucky part of this for her is that she couldn't go to hunting camp—the country is too steep for her feet. This meant that she stayed at home while all her pasture mates went. One year, she let herself out while we were gone. My neighbor found her on the lawn and put her back in. The next day, she was out again. She never went out on the road; she stayed on the lawn area around the house. She left a couple of piles on the patio where she had come up and looked through the sliding glass doors, awaiting carrots, I guess. The neighbor, Lisa Davis, finally found the opened gate and ran a chain around it.

Another time, Reba rolled next to the fence out by the road. She rolled into the woven wire, got tangled in it, got out of it, and ended up out on the road. Fortunately, she's "lawn broke" and brought herself into the yard and was grazing happily when I got home.

One spring evening, another Reba incident happened. Eric was cooking dinner, and I went out to do the chores. I went into the barn to get some hay and had to open a bale. Reba was standing outside the barn door and started messing with the latch with her lips. We have a door latch that you have to pick up the hasp, run the rod through the slot, and then the hasp falls back down. Not an easy feat to do with horse lips, but Reba locked me in! I heard the hasp rattle and pushed on the door—it was *locked*. I put the hay down and started trying to get her to UNLOCK the door. I talked to her and put hay up and down the crack in the door, waving it, in the lock area. She stayed right there, looking at me with one eye through the crack. She even talked to me a little—probably telling me to come out and feed her. No unlocking happened. I petted the barn cats, and I looked to find escape options and couldn't find any. Time went on. I thought Eric would notice that I was gone an *unusually long* time. I did have a hay hook, and I thought, if it got any later, maybe I could pry a board loose off the barn wall with it. Reba kept one eye on me the whole time, periodically asking to be fed. After about 45 minutes, I finally heard Eric calling my name and coming closer. FINALLY! I yelled, "I'm in here."

"Where?"

"I'm in the barn! Reba locked me in."

"What?"

"Reba locked me in. I'M IN THE BARN!"

"Huh! I wondered why you didn't come to dinner... How the hell did she do that?"

I don't know *how* she did it, but she did, and she *didn't* undo it. And I'm glad *he* finally found me when he did, and I'm glad *she's* never done it again!

I will say this for owning horses and mules through the years: I have made good friends with talented veterinarians. All horse owners need good vets! Although equines are large animals, they also seem to be fragile animals, and no one gets through a year without a vet bill of some kind. Once, an out-of-the-blue, huge sonic boom triggered the need for veterinary services here. It was obvious that Reba had been eating with her head below her manger when it happened, and when she threw her head up to get away from the noise, she hit the bottom of the manger and split her forehead open, cutting a gash across the muscling above her eye. She had also knocked herself rather silly from the concussion. Dr. Richardson came and sewed her up—and you can't even find the scar today.

THE MONTANA YEARS

A couple of weeks after that, we noticed that Zeke #2 had a fat cheek. Again, we called Dr. Richardson. Zeke had a split molar in his upper jaw. It had to have been caused by a very hard blow. In talking about it, we think the sonic boom caused him to whirl into one of the barn posts, slamming the side of his face and breaking his tooth. He had to have dental surgery. We had two vet bills from one BOOM!

When Reba couldn't go in steep country, I mostly rode her around the neighborhood or over at Larry Creek, where the trails are fairly easy. Tony Coller calls these little outings "Cupcake Rides." So, I guess for the last 10 years or so, I have been a cupcake rider.

At least my cupcake rides have been very enjoyable. Reba is light, responsive, and accommodating, and she is what you would call a well-trained horse. She has a nice headset and comfortable gaits. I have ridden her in a number of parades.

Jane Lambert, riding Reba and leading Eric's mule, Foxy. Advertising "Charlie Russell, The Cowboy Years" in the Western Days Parade, Stevensville, Montana. 2014.

Reba has been a big help in promoting an earlier book I wrote: *CHARLIE RUSSELL, The Cowboy Years.* For several years, we tied placards on Eric's mule Foxy, and Reba and I led Foxy in local

parades. Her pictures have been used to promote the book, and her picture is in the book. Thanks to Lynette, who took the photos, wrecking a good pair of cowboy boots wading through our irrigated hay field to do it.

In 2015, Reba "starred" in a PBS production of *Backroads of Montana*, titled "Russell Country." I talked about different places in north-central Montana, while catching, grooming, saddling, and riding Reba, and she performed perfectly. I was the one who was nervous and showed it.

Good friends. Janie and Reba.
Photo by Lynette Coller. September 2010.

Since 2010, I have had medical challenges that have interfered with my horseback riding. In February of that year, I had my left knee replaced. It takes a good three months to rehab a knee, but once I had it done, riding did not bother me at all. Then, I had my right knee replaced in 2012. I was able to ride that summer and fall. In February 2013, I had back fusion surgery and couldn't ride for six months. I rode at a low level from August through fall and was okay to ride in the spring of 2015. Then, my back gave out in June, and I had another fusion in August.

 # THE MONTANA YEARS

For someone who has had a life in the saddle, all this time out was hard, but I did learn that I do not need to ride my horse to still enjoy her. I spend a lot of time just watching her, being with her, grooming her, etc., and get a lot of pleasure from just being in her company. That was a wonderful lesson learned, because in the spring of 2016, I rode for an hour and a half, and my back hurt for a week and a half. That's NOT a good trade off, so I'm done.

Also, in the spring of 2016, Reba was diagnosed with ringbone, so she's done, too.

As Charlie Russell said, "Me and my old horse are both has-beens."

Better to be a has-been than a "never-was." At least I wore myself out having a really good time through the years and riding good horses and mules. I can ride happily off into the sunset with Reba, carrying the memories of all the other wonderful equines who came before her. I hope you have enjoyed their stories. I have enjoyed the memories and their telling.

Jane and Reba trotting in Lambert's hay field towards friend and photographer, Lynette Coller. Looking west with the Bitterroot Mountains in the background. September 2010.

 MAKIN' TRACKS

Janie and Reba. Photo by Lynette Coller. September 2010.

The Lambert Place from the air.
Top to Bottom: Lambert house, garage, shop, and barn.
Aerial Photograph by Mike Brierley.

 THE MONTANA YEARS

About the Author

Jane grew up in rural northern California and was attracted to horses at an early age. She and siblings Judy and Jerry started riding early and all grew up in the saddle. As a girl, you could describe Jane as "horse crazy," and now, in her golden years, you could still say the same.

Jane has taken many career paths—horse trainer, riding instructor, teacher, rancher, feed store manager, artist and writer—but always there were horses and horse-related activities. She counts herself lucky to have discovered her passion for those animals at an early age and had the ranch lifestyle to nurture the passion.

From California to Montana, Jane's life has included horses, with a number of mules thrown in for spice. Those stories have all been told. Currently, she and her husband Eric have about 30 acres to tend, irrigate, put up hay, and pasture out to cattle and sheep.

For the last 20 years or so, Jane has been a freelance writer, penning articles for *Western Horseman, American Cowboy, Rural Montana, Horse and Rider, Idaho Journal* and *Western Ag Reporter,* among others. Research for an article about the C.M. Russell Museum, led to further research and became a book, *Charlie Russell, The Cowboy Years.* This book received a bronze medal in the Will Rogers Medallion Award

 MAKIN' TRACKS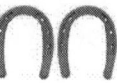

book contest. The Russell book led to opportunities with PBS, and Jane and Reba appeared in a PBS Special titled, "*Russell Country*" in 2015. In September 2017, a three-hour PBS documentary titled "*C.M. Russell and the American West*" will include Jane and Buddy.

In addition to writing, Jane dabbles in the arts: stained glass, leathercraft, painting, jewelry-making, sculpture, and beadwork. She also ties mohair cinches, braids tack items, and collects old horse gear and bits. She is an award-winning photographer and took many of the photos in the book.

Family motivation spurred the writing of this book, and Jane hopes her five grandchildren and five great grandchildren enjoy *makin' tracks* as they read it.

 THE MONTANA YEARS

About the Editor

A native Montanan, Nancy was raised on her family's ranch east of Billings, Montana. She and husband Scott home-schooled their children, Stephanie and Luke, who were awarded scholarships at Notre Dame and University of Oklahoma. Nancy attended Rocky Mountain College, earning her Bachelor of Science in Applied Management. After 20 years of working and plumb tired of town, she quit her job to live close to the land and focus on what she loves. A self-described jack-of-all-trades, she has been interested in almost everything that came her way. She edits, writes books and poetry; makes cowboy ceramic dishes; paints; sews, designs jewelry, and plays piano, flute and guitar. As writer, editor, co-editor, designer, typesetter, or illustrator, some of her projects include:

Jed, by Marilyn Linares, as told by Gerald W. Cook, 2017.
Finding Her Place, A Harper Anthony Novel, by Nancy Morrison, 2017.
This Land on Indian Creek, by Nancy Morrison et al., 2017.
Makin Fun with Family (working title), by James E. Walker, 2017.
Aubry Smith's Cowboy Art, by Aubry Smith, 2016.
Wolves At Your Door, by Earl Stahl, 2016.
Growing Up, Writing Down, Volumes I-III, by Al Anderson, 2016.
Displaced, A Harper Anthony Novel, by Nancy Morrison, 2015.
The Real Wolf, by Lyon & Graves, 2014.
Since the Days of the Buffalo, by Michael Bugenstein, 2013.
As I Saw It, A Biography of Pat Goggins, by Linda Grosskopf, 2013.
Charlie Russell: The Cowboy Years, by Jane Lambert, 2011.
The Weak Ones Turned Back, The Cowards Never Started: A Century of Ranching in Montana, by Linda Grosskopf, 2009.

Made in United States
Orlando, FL
28 December 2022